School inequality and the welfare state

John D. Owen

The Johns Hopkins University Press : Baltimore and London

The Johns Hopkins University Press, Baltimore, Maryland 21218
The Johns Hopkins University Press Ltd., London

Library of Congress Catalog Card Number 74-6834
ISBN 0-8018-1596-7

Library of Congress Cataloging in Publication data will be found on the last printed
page of this book.

Contents

Preface   vii

PART I

School inequality
in the United States

1. Introduction: the paradox of unequal schools in a welfare state   3

2. The distribution of educational resources in American cities:
   some new empirical evidence   14

3. Inequalities in the allocation of educational resources among
   cities and states   28

4. Economic and racial barriers to higher education in the
   United States   43

PART II

The welfare state demand
for a less unequal policy

5. The private demand for schooling: pressure for
   continuing inequality   59

6. The economic benefits of lower-class
   education in the welfare state   70

7. The political benefits of lower-class
   education in a welfare state democracy   102

8. Educational reform as a redistributive tool   113

PART III

Assessing the prospects
for change

9. Organized group opposition: the political
   economy of educational reform   119

10. Has schooling inequality been increasing?   135

11. Some suggestions for getting on with reform   149

   Appendixes   159

   Notes   185

   Index   211

Preface

This book developed out of my efforts to answer a number of questions on school inequality which I have been asking myself over the past several years. How extensive is school inequality (in the sense of a smaller than average investment in the education of poor children) in the United States today? Is it really in the long-term interest of the taxpayer and the employer to maintain school inequality in the social and economic milieu of the 1970s? Why has this practice persisted so long, and what are the prospects for a less unequal policy?

This set of questions obviously reflects a different perspective from that of a number of recent studies of educational policy. A good deal of this work (Christopher Jencks's *Inequality: A Reassessment of the Effect of Family and Schooling in America* is the most notable example) is instead concerned with whether an egalitarian schooling policy would eliminate poverty or economic inequality in the United States. When the issue of school inequality is approached in this fashion, the result must disappoint the reformer. The questions posed in the present work are somewhat less ambitious in the sense that I do not propose to argue that schooling reform could, by itself, end economic inequality. However, the interest-group analysis of the political economy of lower-class education offered here does, I believe, tend to provide answers which encourage rather than discourage those seeking reform.

In my efforts to investigate the political economy of school inequality over the past several years, I have received assistance from a number of individuals. I would like especially to thank James Coleman, John Holland, James MacPartland, and Edward McDill of the Johns Hopkins University Center for Social Organization of Schools; Gary Becker, Jacob Mincer, Melvin Reder, and Finis Welch of the National Bureau of Economic Research; Samuel Bowles, Herbert Gintis, Stephan Michelson, and others who have been associated with the Harvard University Center for Educational Policy Research; and Barbara Bergman, Robert Heilbroner, Henry Levin, Edward Nell, Mancur Olson, Francis Rourke, David Schwartzman, and Gordon Tullock. Alan Sorkin and Julian Stanley, of the Johns Hopkins University, read the completed manuscript and offered many helpful suggestions. Charles Pepper proved to be an unusually helpful and sympathetic editor.

I would also like to thank Hilmet Elifoglu and Kemal Bas for carrying out the calculation of, respectively, the indexes of racial segregation and discrimination in education and the measurement of the effect of education on welfare incidence. Part of my research on the materials presented here was subsidized by the College Scholarship Service and by the Johns Hopkins University Center for Social Organization of Schools.

PART I

School inequality
in the United States

1

Introduction: the paradox of unequal schools in a welfare state

THE COSTS OF UNEQUAL SCHOOLING

The American educational system is characterized by widespread inequality. Poor people and blacks have always received, and still receive, far less than their share of our educational resources. Despite the turmoil of the past two decades, the court decisions on school integration, and the education legislation of the sixties, there is considerable evidence (some of which will be presented in this book) of the persistence of this inequality. This bias is found both in the quality of schooling offered the poor (whether measured in dollars or by an index of physical inputs) and in the average number of years they complete. The result is a considerable difference between the amount of resources our society invests in the typical poor youth and its expenditure on children whose parents are average or above average in economic status.

This continuing resource inequality seems paradoxical, since the advantages today of affording equal educational opportunity to all Americans appear so obvious. Our society is badly divided by race and, perhaps less dramatically, by class. The social cost of this division includes such intangibles as the decline in the quality of life in our cities—characterized, as everyone knows, by rising crime rates, social disruption, and increasing racial tensions. Moreover, this division imposes a very high and rapidly rising fiscal burden on the state and retards our economic growth.

The fiscal consideration gives a new perspective on the question of schooling inequalities by offering that most conservative of political animals, the taxpayer, a solid financial interest in equalizing educational opportunities. In the present "welfare" state he bears the financial and economic costs of poverty to a much greater extent than he did even in the quite recent past. Welfare payments and other income maintenance subsidies to the poor; unemployment among the poor, especially the young poor, partly as a result of a rapidly increasing social minimum wage; and, possibly, a general erosion of work incentives among the poor as a result of these and other social changes now contribute to a heavy fiscal cost to the government and to a loss of potentially valuable labor services to the economy.

This economic and social change has its historical roots in the pioneering legislation of the New Deal period: the first federal welfare program (and, in fact, the Aid to Dependent Children program itself) and the Fair Labor Standards Act of 1938, the first effective federal minimum wage law. But only in the past nine years the dramatic rise in welfare payments has so increased the extent to which the costs of poverty are shared by the rest of society as to produce a qualitative transformation of the economics and politics of poverty in this country. Moreover, these changes are not apt to be reversed. Despite the very considerable public disenchantment with the present welfare programs, both major parties are committed to further reforms rather than to a return to pre-1965 practices.

This new structure of institutions for dealing with the poor—which will be dubbed the welfare state throughout this book—in turn leads to a qualitative change in the political economy of educational policy. For the first time, the argument for equality of educational opportunity can be put on a dollars-and-cents, self-interest basis for those who must pay the taxes it needs. For if the costs of poverty are increasingly borne by the taxpayer, the benefits of reducing poverty must similarly result in a reduction in his burden. Hence, insofar as lower-class education can contribute to this end, he will reap an indirect but very important benefit. Quantitative calculations (see chapter 6 below) indicate that his burden of poverty costs probably has already reached the point where extending lower-class education is to his financial advantage. Considering the preponderance of political power in the hands of the taxpayers as a group (which, after all, includes the employer class, the self-employed, and the great majority of employees who are above the poverty level) in comparison with the political resources at the disposal of the poor in determining educational policy (see chapter 9 below), this coming turnabout in the taxpayer's financial interest offers an important hope for future educational reform.

THE IDEOLOGY OF REFORM
THROUGH EDUCATION

Changing educational policy to bring it into line with the new political and economic realities would not require a sharp break with traditional American ideology. On the contrary, the American faith in the power of education to solve social problems and our eagerness to employ it as an instrument of social policy have long been regarded as outstanding national characteristics.

The American reaction to the Soviet success with Sputnik is a case in point. Sputnik was at least an important contributing cause of the ensuing school curriculum reforms, which increased the emphasis given to the teaching of mathematics and science, and of the establishment of federal scholarships and loans (through the National Defense Education Act of 1958) for college students. In the same period, the 1954 Supreme Court decision (*Brown* v. *Board of Education*) that school segregation is unconstitutional stands as another classic example of the national propensity to use educational policy to help resolve deep-seated social ills—in this case, racial segregation in American society.[1] In earlier periods, the American public school system was seen to be the key ingredient in the "melting pot" strategy of assimilating immigrants (a strategy that included special "Americanization" programs for adult immigrants[2]); in retaining and transmitting the virtues of a preindustrial society in the turmoil and poverty of the nineteenth-century city;[3] and in maintaining European religious and social mores on the frontier (as early as the seventeenth century[4]).

Moreover, while the "establishment" has tended to see education as an essentially conservative force, preserving the true, or immanent, values of American society by transmitting them to the young, those who wanted institutional reform have also regarded it as a powerful instrument of liberation. Some form of the "education strategy" has been woven into the thinking of most of the reform movements that have seriously contested for power in the United States.[5]

At present this faith in educational policy remains strong. It has continued to be employed in the sixties and seventies (some of this education legislation will be discussed in chapters 9 and 10). Thus the use of equal educational opportunity to help resolve or at least ameliorate the present economic and cultural division of the population would be in keeping with a long tradition that has retained its vitality.

The specifically egalitarian character of a more democratic policy would also be consistent with American ideology. A more equal distribution of schooling resources is an obvious extension of the widely accepted slogan "equality of educational opportunity." Of course, an egalitarian schooling policy would come into conflict with other shibboleths. After all, despite the egalitarian rhetoric, the American "tradition" has in reality been one of quite substantial inequalities in educational opportunity. Proposals for reform would necessarily have to cope with the ideologies that have developed around the present unequal distribution of resources—for example, the notion of the freedom of each parent to provide the best education for his children he can afford, or that of states and localities to allocate school budgets in accordance with the communities' resources. Even a policy that simply uses federal money to try to raise education expenditures in the poorest neighborhoods to match the level attained in lower-middle-class areas is resented by the latter as somehow diverting funds from their own schools and hence undermining, or at least slighting, their efforts to provide a better education for their children (cf. the discussion in chapter 9 of the politics of administering the federal aid-to-education legislation of the 1960s). But the ideological adjustment imposed by a more democratic educational policy is still relatively small. The abstract freedom of each parent to dictate the quality of education his children receive has long since been compromised by the public school system. While it is true that *any* change will require some adjustment, a policy of resource equalization in education would probably cause a minimum of ideological conflict compared with other methods proposed for dealing with the problem of poverty.

The introduction of a more egalitarian education policy can thus be regarded as a conservative measure in a double sense. Not only would it bring long-run financial advantages to the wealthier members of the community, but it would also help to meet a challenge to our society with a minimal change in its ideology or values. The new conservative interest in an equalizing education policy will be emphasized in the present work.

This conservative emphasis should not, however, be taken to imply that the rationale for reform must necessarily be limited to such narrow economic and political considerations. Many believe that the poor deserve equal educational opportunity as a right regardless of whether their schooling conveys benefits to the rest of society.

Others see its justification in terms of a particular social philosophy. For example, some liberals retain a faith in the ability of education to develop the intellectual and cultural potential of the individual. They believe in the social value of extending this opportunity to the children of the poor on the grounds that it will make them better citizens and thus will improve the quality of collective decision-making in the years ahead (this point of view is discussed in chapter 7). Socialist thinkers also support a more equal policy. They too believe in equal education for the poor as a right, but their support for change is buttressed by their concern over the political implications of maintaining the present inegalitarian policy. Since the American labor force is stratified along economic and social lines, it is extremely difficult to organize a unified working-class movement. A more equal distribution of educational resources could reduce this stratification.[6]

THE COMPARATIVE EFFICIENCY
OF EDUCATIONAL POLICY

All these arguments for educational reform would be very much weakened if there were readily available alternatives that could accomplish the same goals more efficiently. But this is not the case. On the one hand, schooling for the poor has been shown to have some limited success in helping them, or at least in raising their earning power and increasing their political participation. On the other hand, an examination of alternatives does not reveal any panaceas that could (at least within the framework of our present welfare state capitalism) offer us a ready solution to the poverty problem.

Clearly, equalizing education opportunities—say by removing all racial and class bias in the total educational investment made in children— would not in itself eliminate all the class and racial gaps in academic achievement, social attitudes, or earning power. There is now a wealth of empirical evidence that differences in achievement, whether measured as cognitive learning or as socialization, would remain after resource inputs were equalized.[7] Some scholars (Arthur R. Jensen is the best-known figure here) interpret these findings as showing a biological basis for group differences. They argue that, on the average, the genetic endowment of blacks and lower-class whites provides them with a cognitive learning ability inferior to that of middle-class whites.[8] Other scholars hotly dispute this interpretation of the evidence and insist that the observed racial and class differences in achievement arise from a variety of environmental factors. But they include in this category not only school-related factors but such environmental influences as the quality of prenatal care, the level of literacy in the child's home, and the level of street violence and other disturbances in his neighborhood. Hence even the typical environmentalist interpretation of differences in schooling outcomes would not support the view that an equal distribution of schooling resources would yield equal achievement levels.

Moreover, even if achievement could be equalized by introducing a sufficiently large reverse bias into the distribution of educational inputs, class and racial differences in earnings would still result from discrimination in employment, the isolation of blacks and lower-class whites from employment opportunities, and other socioeconomic problems. Many economists and sociologists, however, would argue today that education could play a major role in increasing the earnings and raising the occupational status of lower-class youths even if it alone could not achieve complete equality.

Consensus is stronger on the relationship between years of schooling and occupational and earnings success than on the contributions of variations in educational quality. An examination of the evidence on the relationship between years of schooling and income (see chapter 5) indicates that important gains in lifetime earnings can be obtained even by black and lower-class white youths. Superficially, the evidence on the effects of educational quality is less clear. There is, in fact, a large, growing literature on how *not* to spend money to upgrade the quality of education offered to the poor—negative evaluations of compensatory education programs that neither improved the learning of children nor, apparently, made any other contribution to their expected economic and social future.

Increases in expenditure per student, however, need not be allocated in scattershot fashion. As empirical evidence accumulates on which quality variations do make a difference, compensatory education can become increasingly effective. The evaluative work of Hanushek,[9] Coleman,[10] Levin,[11] and others suggests that variations in at least one quality input, teachers' verbal ability, does make a significant contribution to learning. Levin, especially, reports that funds expended to hire teachers of higher verbal ability and adequate experience could have a productive effect on the progress of students.

The empirical evidence of these limited though positive gains to be obtained from education would still be much less meaningful if superior alternatives were at hand. But at present such policies as the negative income tax, manpower training, government control (by regulation or subsidy) over industry hiring and promotion practices, or the direct government employment of the "disadvantaged" are either untried or have produced uncertain or disappointing results.

Of course, to some the fact that we have had so *much* experience with education is itself a source of disillusionment. For we do know the effect, say, of schooling received fifty years ago by a black child in a segregated school in Mississippi on his earnings today as an adult. The gain is positive but limited in size (we may hope it underrepresents the gains that will be obtained from the much higher quality education now offered black children).[12] In contrast, each new program suggested as the cure for poverty forecasts great gains at a minimal cost. Unfortunately, as the empirical evaluations of these programs become available such expectations are deflated, and our optimists must suggest still another untried remedy.

While it is useful and necessary to continue to search for new and better methods for dealing with poverty, it would simply be irresponsible to abandon the "education strategy" at this time, given the positive results it appears to yield, the support it has in American tradition, and the lack of any alternative that would make equality of educational opportunity unnecessary.

WHY SCHOOL INEQUALITY PERSISTS

But this positive evaluation of the social value of a democratic education policy simply brings us back again to the original question: Why the persistence of schooling inequalities?

To answer this question and to assess the prospects for a more equal policy, this book will first analyze at some length the structure of schooling inequality in this country. It will then consider in greater detail the changing social, economic, and political conditions of the present welfare state and their implications for change in our educational institutions.

At a high level of abstraction, the explanation of the continued neglect of the education of the poor in the United States in the face of social demands for change is simply that our educational institutions are not structured to advance the interest of society as a whole but rather are subject to a variety of pressures that deflect them from that goal. To carry this analysis forward, a useful if extremely simple device is to divide the demands placed on our schools into three categories: private, group, and social.

Private, Group, and Social Demands

The private demand for education can be defined as that arising from the benefits each graduate and his family derive from his education. These provide an incentive for parents to seek more and better education for their own children.

Education, of course, not only creates benefits for the family of the graduate but indirectly helps (or in some cases harms) many others. Some of these indirect effects are localized in particular groups; others are diffused throughout society as a whole. It is therefore useful to consider group and social benefits as well.

The group benefits of an educational policy can be defined as those obtained only by members of a particular group. Because of the importance of organized groups in American politics, group demands have been of critical importance in determining the actual course of education legislation in this country. Group benefits need not be limited to, or even include, educational benefits to the children of a group. For example, even when the children of the upper class are kept in private schools, the provision of public elementary schools brings net benefits to this group in their capacity as employers (as long as the gains they secure from a better-educated labor force outweigh any tax costs this schooling imposes upon them).

The social demand for education is best defined as that given by the interest of society at large in an educational policy. Unfortunately, insofar as the private or group demands determine the distribution of resources, this social demand may be poorly served.

It will be argued here that the continuation of inequality of educational opportunity today largely results from a conflict between social and private demands on the educational system. That is, the present institutional structure gives greater weight to private or family demands than to the interest of society as a whole. Since these private demands are quite unequally distributed among parents, the result is more inequality of educational investment than is in the social interest.

It will also be argued (in chapter 9 below) that powerful group interests were at one time well served by an unequal distribution of educational inputs; that until quite recently the traditional system was roughly consistent with the interests of taxpayers, including the important employer group. Because of the political power of these groups—more specifically, because of the ability of organized business groups to block education reform legislation at the national level—a structure of educational institutions was retained that now advances private interests rather than those of American society as a whole. The new taxpayer (and employer) interest in reducing poverty costs through lower-class education in the welfare state, however, now provides the wealthy with a more positive rationale for evaluating educational reform and so affords a more realistic basis for optimism about the prospects for a more democratic policy.

This abstract schematization of system demands provides a useful frame of reference for our study. But a full understanding of inequality in schooling can be obtained only from a more detailed analysis of the dominant traditions and institutions of American education. We must examine just how they do in fact produce an inegalitarian distribution of resources and, at least implicitly, how they might be reformed to yield a more equal allocation.

There are, of course, a vast number of particular institutions and customs in our system of schools and colleges whose combined effect generates the present resource inequality. But a study of these suggests that several basic characteristics underlie this distribution.

Decentralized School Finance: A Prescription for Inequality

The American educational system is largely a public school system. Eighty-eight percent of the elementary, 92 percent of the secondary, and 72 percent of the college students attend government schools, colleges, and universities in the United States.[13] Yet inequality in the distribution of educational resources in this country was explained above as a result of the importance of private pressures in allocating educational resources.

The most important single reason for this apparent paradox is that the American educational system is financed by a decentralized state and local system.[14] The lack of a strong federal role in school finance limits the resources available for educating the poor for two reasons. One is that the tax base available for education varies with the wealth of the community or state. Even when poorer school districts charge a higher local tax rate, they are typically not able to match the quality of education offered in wealthier towns or regions. The other reason is that within each state or district the incentive to spend on the resident poor is reduced by the so-called spillover effects due to migration.

Decentralization reaches its most extreme form in the one-class suburb. When a suburban town or village sets zoning and other requirements for residence such that essentially only one small economic class or subgroup is represented in it, the question of the schooling of all other classes is simply eliminated from the practical processes of education decision-making. The residents vote for a school budget that meets their own tastes and budgets. A theoretical model of this suburbanization process designed by Tiebout shows that if it is followed to its extreme interpretation, each suburb and school system becomes little more than a consumer cooperative for the efficient purchase of education.[15] Otherwise, despite an omnipresent public school system, schooling is provided as though it were an ordinary private consumer good of no special consequence to society.

The elementary and secondary school systems of our large cities and suburbs and the state school and college systems are, of course, more diverse in class composition than the Tieboutian one-class village. But here, decentralization of finance encourages the cities, and even the states, to neglect the education of their poorer citizens on account of the spill-over of migration and finance. Because of migration the financial incentives of local districts to make a long-term investment in the education of their poor are undermined. Lower-class graduates who become economically successful move to the suburbs (only a fifth of the women in New York City receiving benefits through the Aid to Families of Dependent Children program were born there, and only 5 to 7 percent had parents born there, most of the remainder having migrated from the South and Puerto Rico);[16] taxpayers move from city to city and from city to suburb. The problem is exacerbated by the much larger role the federal government has been willing to play in underwriting welfare costs than in assisting local efforts to educate the poor.

The effects of decentralization are to be seen in a number of other characteristics of our educational system that in turn help to determine the distribution of schooling resources. It is useful, however, to distinguish at least two other major problems of resource distribution as autonomous factors. While it is true that these problems could be more easily resolved in a federalized system, it would still be necessary to take explicit account of them in designing a centralized structure to ensure that they did not persist as causes of inequality.

School Subsidies for Those Who Can Afford to Pay

The first of these problems is the use of subsidies to provide free (or, at higher levels of education, moderate) tuition charges to all students regardless of their financial need. The same total subsidy that society now allocates to education could provide for far more educational opportunities if it were administered more democratically—that is, if standardized means tests were employed to determine the ability to pay of each parent (using, perhaps, a modification of the measures designed by the College Scholarship Service[17]) so that at each level of schooling no child would receive any more subsidy than would be necessary to permit him to continue to study.

Some remarkable changes would follow. Middle-class students would pay at least some tuition from the elementary school level, and many could and would pay most or all of the cost—the *full* cost—of their higher education. This would release billions of subsidy dollars that could be used to provide room and board, or perhaps even opportunity costs, to those lower-class youths who now drop out of high school or college for economic reasons and who would continue to do so even if their tuition were little or nothing unless provision were also made for their living expenses.

Instead, most education subsidies are now used to provide a simple reduction in tuition. The result is quite inegalitarian: education is, in effect, subsidized in proportion to the amount of education a student can afford. The middle-class student stays in school for more years than the lower-class youth; as a consequence he obtains much more subsidy from the state. The difference is compounded by the fact that education subsidies per student are considerably larger at the higher levels of education and are still greater at four-year colleges and universities than at community colleges, which those working-class youths who do extend their schooling are likely to attend. In effect, the free or low tuition principle serves to underwrite the higher education of the middle class while (at least in comparison with a more democratic distribution of subsidy) restricting the opportunities open to the lower class.

The present use of subsidies may simply reflect the preferences of local constituencies voting within the context of a decentralized system. Yet the low tuition subsidy principle must certainly be regarded as an immediate or proximate cause of inequality in American educational finance.

Middle-Class Bias in the School Bureaucracy

Another immediate source of inequality in the distribution of educational inputs is the middle-class bias in their administration by school bureaucracies. In most of the economy a free market decides, or at least has a very large role in deciding, the allocation of resources. Within school systems, resources are allocated by a bureaucracy. While each school system is dedicated to providing quality schooling for every pupil within its jurisdiction, this abstract resolve must in practice be translated into a number of decisions, each of which will reflect the rules of the system and their interpretation by its employees. If the brighter teachers are permitted to elect to teach the brighter, middle-class students; if old school buildings are allowed to stand in decaying neighborhoods to conserve funds for construction needs in the growing outer city; and if the states use "equalization" formulas to support the cities' school efforts in proportion to the expenditure each community makes, it is obvious that the egalitarian rhetoric of the public school system has been transformed into a rather unequal allocation of resources.

This bureaucratic element would not be very important for our analysis of the distribution of educational resources if all communities approached the ideal of the one-class, single-taste community. All the inequality would then be between communities. But where there is heterogeneity of class and race, as in the big-city school bureaucracy and in the state education system (which directly administers the public college and university system and indirectly influences subsidies to the local school districts and the distribution of resources in the primary and secondary school systems), administrative rules and their interpretation play a decisive role in determining the extent to which schooling inequality is maintained.

In principle, these bureaucracies need not discriminate against the poor. Indeed, they could be a bulwark of protection against hostile market forces—for example, by rigorously overriding private parental pressures for special treatment for their children. But in practice these controls are more typically exercised to favor the middle class, which has brought rather stronger pressures to bear for expensive educational resources than have the poor. Since the education bureaucracy is itself middle class and has held to professional norms which, in turn, have also been found to be oriented to middle-class needs, it has more typically yielded to and in many cases actively supported these middle-class parental demands.[18] Whether one looks at the distribution of funds within cities, at the operation of the state "equalization" formulas for distributing subsidies to local districts, or at the functioning of the college and university system (see chapters 2 to 4 below), one finds the bureaucracy, through a system of seemingly "fair" rules and regulations, devoting more resources to the better-off children and youths.

The tolerance of this discrimination at the city or state level again may, in the final analysis, simply reflect the fact that decentralization of educational decision-making now undercuts the social incentives to provide for the schooling of the poor and gives a disproportionate weight to private demands. Nevertheless, the prevalence of these practices makes it clear that any real hope for a more democratic allocation of resources not only depends on a formal commitment to change at the national level but also requires a reorganization of the "delivery" system to make the schools less responsive to middle-class demands for special consideration.

Thus decentralization of finance, the free or low tuition principle of subsidy, and a middle-class bias in administration each contribute to inequality in the distribution of educational resources by giving undue weight to private demands in the face of a social need for a reduction in inequality. But this discussion of the principles underlying inequality in the distribution of educational resources in this country has been rather abstract. The next three chapters examine in some empirical detail several key dimensions of this inequality. Apart from its intrinsic interest, a more systematic understanding of the structure and underlying causes of inequality affords a useful insight into the obstacles to change and hence will assist us in assessing the prospects for a policy more consistent with contemporary social needs.

2

The distribution of educational resources in American cities: some new empirical evidence

INEGALITARIAN PRESSURES ON THE BUREAUCRACY

The large center-city school system provides a good example of the way in which bureaucratic structures are used to undermine a manifest commitment to equality. If one were to predict the allocation of educational resources in the city simply on the basis of the social crisis in our urban ghettos and the faith of the American people in the capacity of education to solve such social problems, one would certainly expect to find a rather substantial commitment to the schooling of the lower class, or at least of lower-class blacks. Many Americans in fact believe that inequality was abolished within the cities' public school systems by the mid-1960s at the latest and that various special efforts to compensate for past neglect have led to a tendency to favor blacks over others. An empirical analysis of resource allocation in the big cities indicates, however, that on the average neither statement is true. On the contrary, blacks and lower-class whites have continued to obtain considerably less than their share of educational resources.

The immediate causes of this inequality are bureaucratic—a series of rules and regulations the effect of which tends to discriminate against the poor, and a middle-class bureaucracy that tends to interpret these rules to the advantage of their own class. A more fundamental explanation is that, because school finance is decentralized, decision-making in the municipal school system is not shaped by national so much as by citywide concerns or goals, with unfortunate effects for lower-class blacks.

Demographic Factors

Most of the blacks residing in metropolitan areas (now a majority of all blacks) live in the center cities, and a majority of the white middle class in the area typically resides in the surrounding suburbs. The middle-class and upper working-class voters remaining in the center city—often a minority of the nonpoor in the entire metropolitan area—feel, perhaps understandably, that they do not have either the moral responsibility or the financial capacity to deal with the social problems imposed on them by this distribution of population. Moreover, as a result of decentralization, they lack a financial incentive to tackle the problem of poverty by means of a positive education policy. Much of the direct poverty cost—welfare, medical aid, and the like—falls on the federal and state governments rather than the middle-class city dweller.

A more important factor reducing financial incentive is migration. As was mentioned in chapter 1, much of the present poverty population in the cities was born elsewhere and many poor youths who were schooled in the urban centers have moved out. In addition, many taxpayers—businessmen and both middle-class and upper working-class residents—now plan to leave the center city well before the present generation of inner-city students reaches adulthood. One can thus expect the typical ratepayer to regard an increase in the local property tax to improve ghetto schools as lowering the sale value of his house or business and so making it more difficult for him to save the capital needed to move to the suburbs.

These major class migrations generate secondary movements with further deleterious results for the municipal school system. As the proportion of lower-class residents in the city increases, the tax base available for the support of schools declines. At the same time, social problems mount in the schools themselves (to some prejudiced parents the presence of black children is itself a social problem). Many middle-class families then react to what they perceive as a decline in school quality by abandoning the city system and turning to private or parochial schools or moving to the suburbs.

The result is that many of the middle-class whites now remaining in our central cities have no children in the public school system. They are young single people, the elderly or other single adults, and couples who are either childless or who use nonpublic schools. Thus by 1970 only 38 percent of the children in the elementary schools of the nine largest urban systems were white. Among eligible voters in these cities, however, whites outnumbered blacks by margins ranging from 3–2 to 5–1, and voting participation was much lower among the blacks, typically giving the whites very substantial majorities at the polls.[1]

The consequences are predictable. Not only does the general outmigration of the middle class reduce the economic base, but these secondary results—the changing character of the remaining middle-class and upper working-class residents—seriously undercut the political base of those interested in salvaging the center-city school systems. The remaining middle-class residents are much less interested in being taxed for the support of a system so many of them do not use.[2] Those who *do* keep their children in the municipal schools seek to undermine the system's egalitarian commitment by obtaining preferential treatment. These informal pressures placed on the city school bureaucracy have been widely chronicled and need not be doubted.

The Bargaining Model

Actually, once one abandons the notion that a social demand determines the allocation of educational resources—in this case, a national concern of all classes for the education of the poor—it is easy to predict the general outline of what happens. At the most abstract level, it is a consequence of a simple bargaining process in the local system.[3] Thus the mayor or board of education can be regarded as determining that the poorest citizens, possessing only very limited financial resources, would be best satisfied with a combination of inferior schools in their districts and a less regressive tax system. The less poor citizens would be willing to exchange a more regressive tax system for better schools in their neighborhoods. Any attempt by the poor to change these rules of the game could be blocked by the threat of the remaining middle-class and other nonpoor citizens to leave the city and thus further undermine the municipal tax base. The poor usually don't have the option of leaving, and when they do leave their departure actually eases the city's tax burden, so they have no comparable threat to employ. Under these circumstances it is easy to see how the mayor would maximize his own political fortunes by providing an unequal distribution of educational facilities along with a tax system that favored the poor in some way. In this fashion he would in effect be accommodating the allocation of school resources to the unequal private demands of parents.

In practice, the process of distributing educational resources within a city is more complicated than this simple bargaining model.[4] The school bureaucracy itself commands large resources, has its own traditions and customs, and, as a number of authors have told us, is not so easily pressured to change.[5] City hall politics is also more complex than any simple bargaining model would suggest. Finally, a fully realistic model of city decision-making must take into account the effect of racial discrimination and, more generally, the relative powerlessness of the poor in further increasing the bias in the allocation of educational resources.

ASSIGNMENT OF TEACHERS

An abstract discussion can trace the bargaining and political factors that introduce inequality into the distribution of local school resources. But consideration of the processes by which the educational bureaucracy allocates its crucial resource, the teaching staff, is necessary to understand how blacks and poor whites are deprived of an equal share of educational resources. Teachers are the key here because their salaries account for about four-fifths of instructional costs, which in turn are approximately three-quarters of all operating expenses.[6] Moreover, empirical analysis of the relationship between learning and school inputs has found teacher quality to be much more important in determining the educational progress of pupils than the physical quality of buildings and equipment.

In the allocation of experienced teachers and of instructional expenditures, the typical urban teacher assignment system has concentrated the least experienced and lowest-salaried teachers in the slums and ghettos. The average American city teacher's salary is determined almost entirely on the basis of his or her experience. Ordinarily, no financial incentives to accept inner-city assignments are offered, nor can exceptional teaching ability substitute for experience in increasing his salary.[7] In the absence of such rewards, most American cities permit their teachers to request transfer to schools outside the ghetto. In general, teachers find schools in white middle-class or upper working-class areas most attractive. This preference may be the result of racial or class attitudes, of fear or dislike of poor ghetto neighborhoods and working conditions, of the teacher's awareness that he has been prepared to teach upper working-class and middle-class children in a well-equipped classroom and can perform most effectively in such a school, of a simple preference for working near home, or of other factors. Requests for transfer are usually granted on the basis of seniority. It can easily be seen that the combination of a single citywide salary scale and a seniority preference system in teaching assignments, combined with widespread teacher preference for white, nonpoor schools, results in a concentration of inexperienced teachers in poor, nonwhite areas[8] and ensures that the average teacher's salary—and hence the average expenditure per pupil—will be lower in such districts.[9]

Another dimension to the allocation of instructional resources is afforded by the ratio of teachers to students. A persistent tendency for this ratio to be lowest in poor districts will also reduce the instructional expenditures per pupil. This ratio, however, is not consistently correlated with neighborhood economic level. In Boston, for example, it was found that because of an open enrollment policy that attracted pupils from all over the city to the better schools, the teacher-student ratio was higher in the slums than in less disadvantaged districts.[10]

The validity of using any of these three measures—experience, salary, or the teacher-student ratio—to represent teacher quality has been questioned. The Coleman Report has been widely interpreted as demonstrating that a teacher's verbal ability rather than his or her experience or salary is the main factor in determining effectiveness.[11] More recently, Eric A. Hanushek has obtained similar findings with new data.[12] Coleman also found that verbal ability had a rather low correlation with experience and salary. Hence it could be argued that variations in teacher experience or salary may not reflect very important discrimination.

But other features of the teacher assignment system may tend to concentrate the least able teachers in poor or nonwhite areas. For example, the more able teacher will often prefer to teach middle-class or white students, while less able teachers are sometimes more concerned about the pressures placed by principals and the parents' associations than good teaching in a middle-class school.[13]

Teacher Segregation

The role of the black teacher in this assignment process is crucial. There is evidence that most black teachers do not share the white teacher's preference for white students.[14] Moreover, white parents generally have a stronger preference for white teachers than do black parents,[15] and white administrators frequently prefer to place black teachers in predominantly black schools (perhaps partly as an accommodation to the preferences of white parents). These attitudes become important when principals and others divert the teacher assignments from a straightforward seniority system. There is some evidence that they do modify the assignment pattern and, at least in some cities, that they modify it in the direction of encouraging black teachers to remain in predominantly black schools.[16]

For these several reasons, one will expect to find a tendency in this "traditional" system for black teachers to teach black students. If black teachers are equal or superior to white teachers in experience or verbal ability, this racial assignment pattern will constitute a major equalizing force in the city school system, at least in the sense that it will assure black sudents of a supply of able, experienced teachers. If black teachers fall below white in experience or verbal ability, of course their concentration in black schools merely increases the level of discrimination in the system.

ANALYSIS OF DATA FROM
NINE LARGE CITIES

Until recently empirical data on the distribution of educational resources within cities were difficult to obtain. Studies have now been carried out, however, for several individual cities, including Atlanta, Chicago, Detroit, Boston, and St. Louis. These have found inequality in the distribution of at least some educational resources, although the degree of inequality varies from city to city.[17]

The Coleman Report cited above has also made available data on resource inputs in a large number of individual schools within a rather extensive sample of school systems. These permit the analysis of a number of cities using the same methodology and hence can afford a measure of the *average* amount of inequality in the distribution of a variety of educational resources in the typical large American city. Moreover, unlike the several individual city studies, the Coleman data provide information on the distribution among schools of the verbal ability of teachers.[18]

For the present study I drew data from the report on elementary schools and their pupils in nine large cities[19] and supplemented them with published data from the Bureau of the Census and other sources. The distribution within these large cities of several measures of teaching quality—average teacher salary, teacher-student ratio, and teacher experience and verbal ability—was selected for study. A statistical analysis (the estimation of a linear regression model) was used to provide a measure of the extent to which the distribution of each of these variables was influenced by within-city variations in the economic and racial character of the families served by each school. Average family income in the school attendance areas was used as a measure of neighborhood economic level,[20] while the percentage of white students was used to measure the racial composition of the school.

Some observers believe that there is a tendency for racial discrimination to increase as the proportion of whites declines.[21] To test this hypothesis the effect of an interaction measure, (percentage white students in the city) × (percentage white in the school), was also studied. If the hypothesis is *wrong*, then variations in this measure will have no effect on school quality. Any racial discrimination will be traced by the simple measure, percent white in the school. But if the hypothesis is valid, so that the higher the percent nonwhite in the city the more racial discrimination is practiced, it will have a positive effect.[22]

The analysis was standardized for differences in city income per capita.[23] Since the study includes nine cities that varied somewhat in average income, it was important to obtain school income effects that represented *only* within-city variation—that is, that excluded differences in school quality arising from intercity differences in wealth. In the statistical analyses discussed below, the partial effect of school income, with city income held constant, is given in each case.[24]

Table 1 gives some statistical results from this study. The first row analyzes the effect of school income and racial composition on expendi-

TABLE 1. ALLOCATION OF RESOURCES IN URBAN SCHOOLS

Teacher Quality Variable	Real Neigh- borhood Income	% White Students (School)	% White Students (School × City) Interaction	% White Students (City)	Adjusted Corre- lation Coeffi- cient
1. Real expenditure per pupil on teacher salary	.43	.20	−.22	. . .	.45
2. Real teacher salary	.20	.06	−.05	. . .	.46
3. Teacher-student ratio	.24	.04[a]	−.05	. . .	.25
4. Teacher experience	.60	.22	−.12[b]	. . .	.56
5. Teacher verbal ability	.11	.10	−.06	.10	.61
6. Proportion of white teachers	−.01[b]	.39	−.32	.97	.62

Source: John D. Owen, "The Distribution of Educational Resources in Large American Cities," *Journal of Human Resources* 7 (Winter 1972): 171–90.

Note: Numbers in the body of the table are elasticities, calculated at the means of the variables, the percent change in the dependent variable (row head) per 1 percent change in the independent variable (column head).

[a] Not statistically significant.

[b] *t* ratio estimated at 1.96.

ture per pupil on teacher salaries. The results suggest that there is significant discrimination against poor students in the allocation of instructional expenditures: for every 1 percent increase in school neighborhood income (holding city income constant), salary expenditures rise by 0.43 percent.

Expenditure per Pupil

The text table below gives an example of the effect of neighborhood income on salary expenditure per pupil in a typical city in this study. An increase of $1,000 in income per family is accompanied here by an increase in salary expenditure per child of about $18.

Average family income in school area	Expenditure per pupil on teacher salary
$4,000	$158
6,000	193
7,500	219

The distribution of expenditures per pupil is of interest in itself as a measure of the extent to which financial resources are allocated unequally. But the distribution of dollars also reflects differences in school quality in that per pupil salary costs rise both with the ratio of teachers to students and with the average experience level of the faculty.

A significant interaction term, (percentage white in the school) × (percentage white students in the city), is found to support the expectation that discrimination would increase with the percentage nonwhite.

Since there is usually a negative correlation between income and nonwhite population in city neighborhoods, these results suggest that the gap between the poorer neighborhoods (that is, low-income white and black districts) and more prosperous neighborhoods (upper working-class and middle-class districts) is greater than that suggested by the income effect alone, since the latter was obtained by holding racial composition constant.

The measure of variation in salary expenditures per student can be broken down into its two components, teacher salary and teacher-student ratio (since salary expenditure per pupil is simply the product of these two variables). Rows 2 and 3 of table 1 show the effects of economic and racial biases in the distribution of each of these. As expected, these biases are more significant determinants of salary than of the teacher-student ratio.

The variation in instructional expenditures is traced a step further in the fourth row, where teacher experience (the principal determinant of salary differences within the city system) is analyzed as a function of school racial composition and school neighborhood income. Teacher experience has a neighborhood income coefficient of three-fifths. This result implies that a school serving an affluent neighborhood in which average family income is, say, 50 percent greater than in a poorer area will have a faculty whose average experience is about 30 percent higher. The average level of teacher experience is also positively related to the proportion of white students. Moreover, this bias is larger in cities with a higher proportion of nonwhites, as evidenced by the value obtained for the interaction coefficient. Teacher experience has a closer relationship to the economic and racial character of school neighborhoods than does salary (see row 2), perhaps because above a certain level of experience most teacher salary scales provide less than proportional increases in pay.

Thus the results presented in rows 1 to 4 support the view that the social and economic characteristics of the neighborhood are a significant factor in determining instructional expenditures per student. Experience of teachers is higher in the middle-class or white neighborhoods, and hence salaries of teachers and instructional costs per pupil are also higher.

Verbal Ability

Some evidence of the influence of racial and economic factors on the distribution of teacher verbal ability among schools is offered in row 5, where the dependent variable is the average score in the verbal ability examination given to teachers by the Coleman research team. The results here show that both school neighborhood income and racial composition are significant factors in the assignment of verbally able teachers. For every 1 percent increase in neighborhood income, there is a 0.1 percent increase in the verbal ability of the teachers employed. The verbal ability of teachers also tends to be higher in white schools, even when the economic level of the neighborhood is held constant. Moreover, this racial effect becomes more important as the proportion of nonwhites in the city grows.

The hypothesis that white teachers are more likely to select or to be assigned to schools in white, upper working-class neighborhoods is examined in row 6. As might be expected, the proportion of white teachers not only rises with the percentage of white students in the city but also increases with the proportion of white students in a given school. An increase of 5 percent in a school's proportion of white students is associated with an increase of up to 2 percent in the proportion of white teachers.

Teacher Segregation

It is possible to determine the extent to which the tendency for municipal education systems to segregate black teachers and students affected the distribution of teachers high in verbal ability, experience, and salary. Two methods were used here: first, in each city studied, average verbal ability, experience, and salary levels of white and nonwhite teachers were compared. If nonwhite teachers were rated lower on the average, and if they tended to be assigned to nonwhite students, then the lower experience, salary, and verbal ability averages in nonwhite schools are partially explained. As a second measure of the importance of teacher segregation, the statistical analyses of experience, salary, and verbal ability were replicated in the separate black and white teacher data.

In the first comparison, the average black teacher was found to have about 8 percent less experience than the average white teacher and to be paid somewhat less as a result. Moreover, his score on the verbal ability test was considerably lower; the average differential was 3.60 points (this is greater than one standard deviation in the combined sample).[25] The results of the second comparison were equally striking. There was no observed tendency to assign higher quality white teachers to the better-off or all-white schools. Similarly, among black teachers, there was no tendency to assign the lower quality blacks to poor neighborhoods or to all-black schools. This held whether verbal ability, experience, or salary was studied.[26] Taken together, the results of these two tests indicate that in the large cities studied the crucial factor in the lower verbal ability, experience, and salary of the average school teacher in nonwhite areas was the high proportion of nonwhites teaching there.

RACIAL ASSIGNMENT OF
TEACHERS AND STUDENTS

These dramatic results suggest that it is worthwhile to pursue the matter of the racial assignment of teachers further. Unlike data on teacher experience or verbal ability, which are limited to the Coleman Report or other special studies, the assignment of black and white teachers within American cities has been studied extensively by the United States Office of Education. Thus it was possible to obtain the teacher assignment statistics for all the elementary schools in sixty-nine large cities. These statistics also include data on the racial composition of the student bodies of the schools in these cities, making it possible to study the tendency of school boards to assign white teachers to white students in some detail. This much larger sample of teachers and students enables us not only to increase our confidence in the conclusions about the bias in the distribution of educational resources in the typical city but also to examine systematic differences in the character of this bias among different types of cities.

In addition, these data afford an interesting critique of the typical city school board's claim that the segregation of their school system reflects racially separate housing patterns rather than any official segregationist or discriminatory tendencies. The familiar argument is that, given housing segregation, the racial integration of schools requires the busing of children to neighborhoods of a different racial composition. This course, the argument goes, is unacceptable: the children's spare time should be used for homework or play rather than in riding a bus, they should be able to come home for lunch, they should have an opportunity to play with their class-mates rather than being carried promptly back to their neighborhoods, and so forth. However, none of these arguments apply to teachers. It is generally assumed that city employees are capable of bearing the stresses and strains of commuting on the municipal transportation system. Upper-class districts of our cites are staffed with policemen, firemen, sanitation workers, and the like, all of whom have to "bus in" from working-class districts. Hence the extent to which the school systems systematically as-sign their white teachers to their white students is a useful index of the degree to which they are actually bowing to the preference of white parents for white teachers and of white teachers for white students.

Teacher Segregation

Table 2 presents measures of teacher and pupil segregation in non-southern cities in 1966 (southern cities are analyzed separately in chapter 10). The first column in the table gives a measure (*b*) of the extent to which black teachers were assigned to black students; it shows the average increase in the percentage of black teachers in a school per 1 percent in-crease in the blacks in its student body. This measure averaged 0.54 in the sixty nine cities studied, although there was considerable variation among cities. Discrimination increases sharply as the percentage of black students in the city rises. The measure is 0.14 in cities with 10 percent or fewer blacks and 0.77 in those with a majority of blacks in the school sys-tem. This is consistent with the finding in the nine-city sample of a posi-tive interaction between the proportion of blacks in the city and the ten-dency of white teachers to be assigned to white students.

Part of the explanation for this correlation between discrimination and proportion of black students is found in column 5, which gives the ratio

TABLE 2. RACIAL COMPOSITION OF STUDENT BODIES AND TEACHING STAFFS IN PUBLIC ELEMENTARY SCHOOLS IN NONSOUTHERN CITIES

% Black Students in the City School System	*b* (1)	*D* (2)	*S* (3)	*E* (4)	Black Teachers/ Black Students (5)	Probability of a Black Student's Having a White Teacher (6)
1–10	.139	.052	.339	.371	.448	.937
11–30	.354	.248	.652	.721	.477	.681
31–50	.419	.268	.627	.861	.501	.607
51+	.766	.591	.765	.882	.866	.203
All 69 cities (including South)	.535	.677	.737	.950	.686	.593

Source: Unpublished worksheets of the U.S. Civil Rights Commission, Washington. Cities weighted by elementary school populations to obtain averages in each case.

Note: See text for definition of symbols. Derivations of measures are presented in ap-pendix 1.

of the percentage of black teachers to percentage of black students for each category. There is a distinct tendency for city school systems with small proportions of blacks in their student populations to have still smaller proportions of black teachers on their staffs. Thus, the black teacher–black student ratio is positively correlated with the proportion of black students in the system. Since a large proportion of black teachers is usually assigned to black students, an increase in the black teacher–black student ratio will typically reduce the probability of a black student's having a white teacher.

However, this staffing policy does not explain all the correlation between discrimination and proportion of black students. Column 4 gives a new measure, E, equal to b *divided by* the black teacher–black student ratio. This measures the percentage increase in the proportion of black teachers associated with a 1 percent increase in the proportion of black students in a class. E can thus be regarded as a measure of discrimination adjusted for variations in the black teacher–black student ratio. Yet E is still positively related to the proportion of black students in the system, indicating that *given* the number of black and white teachers hired, a more discriminating assignment pattern will be found when the proportion of black students is higher.

Pupil Segregation

These data can also be used to bring out the relationship between pupil segregation and discrimination. Clearly, if there were no pupil segregation whatsoever, so that each school had exactly the same proportion of white and black pupils, there would be no way in which an administrative preference for assigning, say, more experienced white teachers to white students could be practiced.[27] Similarly, if the proportion of whites varied within relatively small limits—say, between 45 and 65 percent in a school system that was 55 percent white, a more realistic goal for pupil integration than an absolutely invariant proportion of white students—the effective pupil discrimination that the school system could carry out on racial lines would be quite limited. Even if all the experienced teachers were assigned to schools in which whites were a majority and all the less experienced teachers to the schools in which whites were a minority, many black students attending majority-white schools would benefit and many white students attending minority-white schools would be adversely affected.

Column 3 presents a measure of pupil segregation, S. This measure estimates the difference in the proportion of white schoolmates that a typical white and a typical black child in the school system would have. It has a scale from 0 to 1. Thus, in our ideal example of a fully integrated system with 55 percent white students in each school, each child, black or white, would obviously have 55 percent white schoolmates and the segregation measure would be equal to zero. If the school system were fully segregated, on the other hand, the white child would have 100 percent white schoolmates and the black child none, giving S a value of unity.

S had an average value of 0.74 for the sixty-nine-city study but varied widely among northern cities. It rose from 0.34 where blacks were less than one-tenth of the pupils to 0.77 where they constituted a majority.

This pupil segregation measure enables us to translate the teacher assignment principle into its effects upon pupils. Column 2 of table 2 gives the difference, D, in the probability of a white and a black child's having a white teacher (algebraically, $D = b \times s$). The average value of this measure of pupil discrimination is 0.68, but in northern cities it is highly sensitive to the proportion of blacks in the system, increasing from 0.05 in cities with less than 10 percent black students to 0.59 in majority black school systems.

For some further comparisons, column 6 gives the probability of a black child's having a white teacher. Outside the South this was very high, close to unity, in mostly white communities but shrank to one-fifth in majority-black school systems. (The probability of a white child's having a white teacher was more stable, ranging only from 0.79 to 0.99.)

This racial segregation of teaching staff might be defended on the basis that, quite apart from the usual objective measures—verbal ability, experience, and so forth—the color of a teacher is important in a child's learning. It has, in fact, been argued that a black child will derive a special learning benefit from having a black teacher. The evidence for this effect on cognitive learning is inconclusive. The Coleman study itself found that when student background and teacher quality variables, *including* teacher verbal ability, were held constant, a small but positive effect on the learning of blacks was obtained by the presence of a *white* teacher. More recently, Ohberg reported a study of black learning that found that while middle socioeconomic status blacks learned better with black teachers, low socioeconomic status blacks performed better with white teachers.[28]

In the light of these inconclusive empirical results on the effects of a teacher's color on his or her job performance, it is difficult to reject the view that the racial segregation of teachers is less helpful in the furtherance of a democratic policy than one that assigned teachers on a color-blind basis—insisting that each school receive a minimum number of highly able teachers regardless of their race.[29]

ALLOCATION OF
PHYSICAL RESOURCES

The key variables in any analysis of educational inequality are those associated with teacher quality, both because of their significance in the educational process and because of the importance of teachers' salaries in the educational budget. But, it is also useful to see whether nonwhite or

TABLE 3.　SCHOOL PLANT QUALITY IN NINE LARGE CITIES

Physical Quality	School Neighborhood Income Effect	Adjusted Correlation Coefficient
Age of school	−.75	.26
Land area per student	3.04	.26
Special facilities of school	.44[a]	.19

Source: Data collected for James S. Coleman *et al.*, *Equality of Educational Opportunity* (Washington: Government Printing Office, 1966); statistical analysis by the author.

Note: Numbers in the body of the table are elasticities calculated at the means of the variables.

[a] *t* ratio estimated at 1.81.

poor students are afforded inferior physical facilities in their schools. Even if it does not make a critically important contribution to a student's educational progress, a well-equipped and well-maintained physical plant can make his education a more pleasant experience. Moreover, there can be indirect educational benefits: a better school environment might discourage early school dropouts and attract better quality teachers.

Data from the nine-city Coleman sample on three measures of physical quality—age of plant, area of school ground per student, and special facilities (a weighted average of auditorium, cafeteria, and athletic facilities)— were each subjected to the same statistical tests used to determine whether there was bias in the assignment of teachers.[30] No relationship was found between the racial makeup of the city or the student body of the school and these physical factors, but there was a significant positive association between each of them and income in the school neighborhood. The results of a simple statistical analysis are given in table 3.

These data suggest that, within our large cities, there has been a systematic tendency for the poor to be educated in older schools with smaller play areas and with fewer special facilities to assist them. Although no special racial effect is found in the allocation of physical plant, the fact that nonwhite incomes are less than those of whites would, in conjunction with the results shown in table 3, suggest that the facilities offered to blacks are inferior.

IMPLICATIONS OF THE
EMPIRICAL ANALYSIS

Taking the results of these several statistical analyses together, it is apparent that less has been spent on the education of poor and black children even *within* the large center cities. Even more important than these financial differences, less experienced teachers with lower verbal ability typically have been assigned to these students.

This inequality or discrimination is so firmly implanted in the bureaucratic norms of the big city school system that they appear to be quite "natural." Thus the right of the experienced ghetto teacher to request transfer to a more pleasant environment is respected; it is presumably regarded as a form of compensation for several years of service in a "difficult" school. Similarly, the assignment of black teachers, often themselves trained in segregated institutions, to black students—once simply seen as an accommodation to the prejudices of white parents and white teachers—can now be regarded as a way of paying tribute to black nationalist feeling. Or again, many of the physical disabilities of the lower-class school can be attributed to the facts that they are in older neighborhoods and hence tend to be older than is typically the case in the newer, expanding outer city; that land values are higher in these inner-city neighborhoods, making land for school recreation an expensive "luxury"; and that vandalism takes a heavy toll of the equipment installed in the slum school.

Together with the very fundamental middle-class bias in the demands placed upon the school system, the well-established, "normal" customs and traditions that underlie discrimination in the allocation of resources in large city school systems underscore the need for truly organizational reforms. It is apparent that a few special programs for the inner-city schools, or other superficial if well-intentioned tinkering with this system, will not produce full equality. Not only does the basic incentive system have to be changed—an innovation that almost certainly requires federal subsidy and control—but the bureaucratic norms that have developed within the decentralized system will also have to be thoroughly overhauled to bring them into accord with this new system of school finance.

3

Inequalities in the allocation of educational resources among cities and states

THE IDENTIFICATION OF
INTERAREA INEQUALITIES AND
THEIR CAUSES

Considerably greater economic bias is found in the allocation of educational resources among cities and states than in their distribution among schools within a city. It is in this interdistrict comparison that one observes the full inegalitarian effects of the decentralization of school finance.

Some twenty-eight years ago the National Education Association, the major organization of teachers and education administrators in the United States, surveyed differences among the states in the quality of education offered in this country and concluded:

At the doors of many American children the ladders of educational opportunity rise high; at the doors of many others, they scarcely rise at all. Whether a child will receive a good or a poor education depends, in large measure, upon the community in which he happens to be born and reared.[1]

Unfortunately this judgment still applies today. Yet interarea differences in educational quality have become much more obviously important for public policy, partly because it is now apparent that the migration from the less developed areas of the country to the leading metropolitan centers has been a significant factor in the present urban crisis, contributing to the high level of unemployment, family desertion, welfare dependency, crime, and many other social problems.

In a federal structure it would, in principle, be a relatively simple matter to redirect the allocation of teaching resources so that our educational system would make a positive contribution to the resolution of this problem. In districts where the quality of labor available for teaching is low, the federal government could ensure that local standards did not fall below national norms by obtaining teachers from among the very best of the locally available labor force, by encouraging immigration of good teachers from more developed areas, or both. These policies would require both the use of extra funds in the poorer states and a determination to use these funds to advance national goals.

It will be argued here that neither of these prerequisites for a sane national policy is to be found in our state and local system of school finance. In those regions of the nation where the quality of labor is poorest, per capita income generally is also low. The state and local system links educational spending to the local level of wealth and hence ensures that less rather than more is spent to attract good teachers in those areas where the supply is limited. Moreover, the determination of teachers' salaries and the recruitment of teachers is constrained by local bureaucratic rules that do not permit the district's administrators to use the resources at its disposal to maximum advantage either for its local interests or in pursuit of a national policy.

In one respect, documentation of this argument is simpler than the analysis of inequality within districts in the previous chapter. Within-city variations in school expenditures have often been difficult to obtain, partly because administrators do not wish to reveal the extent to which their allocation of resources departs from the stated egalitarian commitment of the public school system. But all districts publish systemwide reports on average expenditures. Thus it has been easy enough to make interdistrict comparisons of financial outlays.

A number of studies have shown that teachers' salaries and average expenditures per pupil are higher in wealthier states and counties.[2] The first and third columns of part A of table 4 present such an analysis. When the average teacher salary in the ten states in the continental United States that pay the lowest salaries to teachers is compared with the ten states where salaries are highest, a 61 percent salary gap is observed. Moreover, the states paying higher salaries are, on the average, more affluent than those paying less. There is a 65 percent difference in per capita income between the two groups of states (see column 2). This relationship would tend to support a simple income-effect explanation of differences in teacher salaries.

But the *interpretation* of such interarea data is much more difficult than this simple analysis implies. The allocation of educational resources within a city or a metropolitan area takes place, of course, within a single labor market. Variations among cities and states, on the other hand, cut across a number of such markets.[3] For this reason, many believe that the higher teacher salaries paid in the wealthier states are offset by a tendency of the cost of living or the cost of labor to be higher in these areas. If this is so, the quality of teachers hired in the wealthier states may not actually be higher than in the poorer states despite the higher salaries. A more sophisticated methodology must therefore be used to study these variations.

Some empirical evidence of the force of these objections is given in the second column of part A of table 4, which presents data on the wages of

TABLE 4.   INTERSTATE AND INTERCITY ANALYSES OF TEACHERS'
SALARIES

	A. INTERSTATE ANALYSIS OF TEACHERS' SALARIES		
	Teachers' Salaries	Competitive Salaries	Per Capita Income
Average for 10 states in which teachers' salaries are highest (average in lowest 10 states = 100)	161	130	165

	B. INTERCITY ANALYSIS OF TEACHERS' SALARIES			
	Teachers' Salaries	Competitive Salaries	Per Capita Income	Cost of Living
Average for 3 cities in which teachers' salaries are highest (average in lowest 3 cities = 100)	140	124	128	110

	C. INTERSTATE ANALYSIS OF TEACHER QUALITY			
	Teacher Verbal Ability	Quality of Local Labor Force Measure	Teachers' Salaries	Per Capita Income
Average for 10 states in which teacher quality measure is highest (average in lowest 10 states = 100 for teacher salaries and per capita income)	25.0	90.3	113.0	126.0
Average for 10 states in which teacher quality is lowest	19.9	65.3	100.0	100.0

Source: See appendix 2.

a set of occupations roughly comparable to teaching.[4] The fourth column of part B presents cost-of-living indicators for those cities for which these indexes are calculated. These comparisons show that both the cost of living and the cost of labor do tend to be higher in the wealthier areas, where teacher salaries are also higher.

This argument is partly refuted, however, by an interstate comparison of the quality of teachers. Data on teacher characteristics (averages by state of several teacher quality variables) made available to the author by the Coleman Report research team permit such a comparison. Column 2 in part C of table 4 gives data on one of these characteristics, teacher verbal ability, in the highest and lowest ten states in the continental United States. The average score ranges from 19.9 in the lowest ten states to 25.0 in the highest ten (in four states the average score exceeded 25; in two it was less than 19). These are quite large differences, especially when one considers that the results in the table are statewide averages that exclude variations among schools within a given state.[5] Moreover, these quality differences are systematically associated with variations in state real per capita income (see column 4) and in the average salary paid to teachers (column 3), thus supporting the notion that financial variables contribute to differences in educational quality.

These data do *not* show, however, that the financial wealth of the state, or higher teacher salaries, are the *cause* of higher teacher quality in the wealthier states. The quality of the labor pool from which this labor is drawn is also generally higher in the more developed regions. An index of this labor force quality (percent of military recruits passing the Armed Forces Qualification Test) is seen to be closely associated with the quality of teachers hired (see column 2 of table 4, part C).[6]

Hence two questions of relevance to our examination of the role of the state and local system in maintaining inequality must still be resolved. First, do interarea variations in teachers' salaries reflect differences in the cost of living and the cost of labor alone, or do they also respond to differences in area wealth? Second, does teacher quality respond to these differences in teachers' salaries, or is it determined simply by the quality of the local labor force?

STATE AND LOCAL INSTITUTIONS
FOR ALLOCATING SCHOOL RESOURCES
The Process of Salary and Quality Determination

To answer these questions one must take a closer look at the institutions that determine teacher salary and quality and other dimensions of educational expenditure.

It would indeed be useful if a survey of these institutions led to a theory of their behavior such as that of the profit-maximizing business or even that of the utility-maximizing consumer employed in economics. The theory could then be used to rule out at least some of the alternative explanations of local school district behavior offered above as obviously implausible and to ignore some of the empirical relations presented in table 4 as spurious. The analysis could thus be greatly simplified.

However, the complexity of these public institutions does not encourage such theorizing. In the first place, local educational systems must make political decisions in allocating and distributing school resources, so that one cannot use a simple rationale derived from the study of individual behavior to predict community outcomes. Most communities do not follow the one-class Tieboutian model discussed in the last chapter but rather are quite heterogeneous with respect both to class and race. Hence the decision to provide a certain average level of educational quality, one that can strike some sort of balance among the very different groups that compose the community, is the outcome of a complex political process (see the discussion of the case of the large city in chapter 2).

Resource allocation in public education is further complicated by the number of official and unofficial bodies that contribute to decision-making in our decentralized system. At the local level, the school system itself usually has considerable power in determining *how* instructional expenditures are to be allocated. But the *amount* of funding itself is decided elsewhere—by the mayor and city council or even by local referendum. Local funds are also supplemented by state subsidies, so the role of the governor and the state legislature must also be considered. At each of these levels, moreover, various organized pressure groups—not the least of which is the "education lobby" itself—try to influence the allocation of educational resources in their favor.

For this reason our empirical analysis of the determination of local variations in teacher salary and quality will be advanced if decision-making in the typical public school system is treated as a two-stage process. In this model the budget for teachers' salaries and other educational expenses is set by a "legislature," but this budget is allocated among teachers by an "agency." While not excessively complicated, this two-stage model takes into account the separation that typically exists between the political bodies that determine the budget and the school officials, down to the level of principal, who actually allocate the different components of the budget.[7]

Recruitment of Teachers within the Salary Budget Constraint

After the budget for teacher salaries is set, the school system (here the agency) can use the money to recruit personnel. An equalizing policy for the nation would require that the least developed areas use their funds to seek out the most qualified candidates wherever they might be found. But the agency is typically restrained from doing so by a number of bureaucratic or legislative rules. The effect of these constraints is generally to make the quality of teachers hired more closely dependent on the quality of the local labor supply and hence to maintain regional differences rather than to make any contribution to egalitarian goals.

These difficulties will be exacerbated if court rulings prevent school boards in the less developed areas from using objective standards to select teachers and insist that they instead use quotas in hiring so as to make the teaching force even *more* representative of the quality of the local labor force. Thus Judge O. R. Smith has decreed that the requirement of a Mississippi school district that all teachers score 1000 or better on the National Teacher Examination to keep their jobs was discriminatory. Judge Smith declared: "Under this standard, 90% of the white graduates from Mississippi institutions of higher learning are eligible to teach in the Columbus (Mississippi) school district and 89% of the black graduates from Mississippi are disqualified. This amounts to racial classification." Arguing that such tests measure the learning of the teacher but not his ability to teach, the judge ordered the school district to restore the same racial balance that had existed before the introduction of the requirement.[8]

Whatever the merits of this legal thinking in protecting the jobs of members of different groups or in advancing other local purposes, it is demonstrably counterproductive to efforts to reduce interarea variations in educational quality. The failure rate on the AFQT in Mississippi was 37 percent in 1966, compared with less than 10 percent in thirteen of the forty-eight continental United States.[9] If regional differences in the supply of labor from which teachers are recruited are to be overcome, those states where the quality of labor is less well developed must recruit from those where it is higher.

Local school systems are already saddled with several constraints that make this impossible. The size of the salary budget itself restrains the poor district from effectively exploiting the local supply of human resources. Because the conventional teaching technology today prescribes one teacher per classroom, this effect is magnified. Given the existing supply of classrooms and the number of students to be taught in them, the salary budget in effect determines the average salary paid per teacher.[10] This is very different from some other government operations—for example, clerical or other office work—where the agency, though given a fixed budget, may be able to vary the number of its employees as well as their quality. With this freedom it can minimize the effect of budget constraint by, say, substituting a smaller number of higher quality people for a larger number of less skilled employees.

Another hiring constraint is imposed on the schools by the typical bureaucratic requirement that the teacher be a college graduate. At the elementary school level an additional de facto constraint is imposed by the fact that very few males are attracted to the profession. As a result, the state school system is sometimes quite limited in its choice. In some states the school system has in effect been constrained to hire as many as one-half of all employed female college graduates (although this proportion declines as the proportion of the female population with a college degree increases). Under these circumstances the dependence of the school board on the quality of the local labor supply is obvious.

The effective use of the salary budget is further reduced by the fact that most school systems are not free to pay higher salaries to teachers of higher quality. They must conform to a rigid salary scale that bases pay differentials almost entirely on length of service (although many school systems provide a small additional premium for graduate work and for a master's degree).[11] Yet recent empirical research on teacher effectiveness suggests that other qualities, especially verbal ability, are more appropriate measures of teaching competence or quality than are advanced degrees or long experience.[12] There is some empirical evidence that school hiring officials agree with this assessment. Witness the difficulty the teacher with long-term service frequently has in finding employment in adjacent school districts; in a competitive labor market the excessive experience premium in her salary overprices her services. However, because they are not usually permitted to pay a salary premium to a teacher who demonstrates superior verbal ability or shows other evidence of above-average skill, and because the number of posts is given, a school system that wishes to hire teachers of high quality can only set a high salary for all its teachers, rank applicants in quality, then hire them in descending order of ability until staffing requirements have been met.

This single-salary-scale restriction is not limited to the school system. It characterizes many categories of public employees. But its effects are more serious in the case of teachers, since school systems provide a major source of employment for the labor pool of female college graduates from which most school teachers are drawn. When the public employer is hiring, say, computer programmers, it is entering a field in which public employment is a relatively small user of labor. A single-salary-scale retriction here need not lead to a serious misallocation of resources, since employees can then be drawn from a fairly homogeneous group at an authorized standard salary that will, perhaps, attract personnel of middling quality. But when the public agency is a large employer in the market in which it hires, as in the case of school systems,[13] it must hire not only the best applicants but also many others of much lower quality at the same salary.[14]

This single-salary-scale restriction has a special application to the problem of regional differences in equality of educational opportunity. It not only makes it more costly for the poor district to provide education but specifically discourages it from using salary policy to upgrade the quality of the local teaching force. Without this constraint the school board in a poorly developed area where the supply of highly able graduates was also restricted could get the most from its limited budget by paying a premium salary to a number of the most able female college graduates in the area and offering a lower wage to the more typical applicants, who would fill the remaining teaching posts. But a single salary scale eliminates this option by requiring the board to offer the same higher wage to all applicants regardless of their relative quality.

This listing of constraints does not imply that school officials cannot or do not seek to use their salary budgets to maintain or improve the quality of their teaching staff within these limits. For example, an increase in the school budget will lead to a gain in teacher quality if school officials use their improved salary scale to hire the best among those applicants who have the formal qualifications and if better teachers are attracted by the higher salary scale. If these two conditions are *not* met, then of course an increase in salary budgets may not result in improved teacher quality. This may be the case if applicants are accepted on a first-come, first-hired basis, or on the basis of quotas or some other arbitrary condition, or if, on the other hand, higher quality teachers are not attracted by higher salaries.

One would expect that, in practice, these two conditions (which we will call agency-teacher rationality) will be met. Most school boards do try to find good teachers; written tests and interviews are used to screen applicants for teaching positions in a large number of communities, indicating concern with the teacher's intelligence and ability to express herself. And there is no a priori reason to assume that teachers are any less responsive to financial inducements than are doctors, nurses, or any other group.

Determination of the Salary Budget

In considering the options open to the agency it has been reasonable to regard the level of the teacher salary budget as fixed. But since this budget level can be changed by the legislature, it should be considered as a variable for the system as a whole. At least four hypotheses of legislative salary determination appear to be plausible.

1. Salaries of teachers will be higher where per capita income or wealth is higher. Even if legislative bodies are not concerned with the quality of teachers, one might hazard a guess that, in a decentralized system of financing, wealthy communities will pay higher salaries than others simply because they will offer less resistance to higher expenditures. An alternative explanation, however, would imply an explicit concern with quality. In a decentralized system, if the public demand for the quality of education provided by local government is positively related to income (that is, if it follows the private demand in this respect), then, since improvements in quality must be made largely through improvements in teacher quality rather than through increased numbers, one would expect wealthy communities to strive to raise the quality of this service by paying higher salaries.

2. Salaries of teachers will be high if money wages are high in competing private employment. Whether or not the legislature is concerned about the quality of teachers, it may be forced by higher salaries in the private sector to raise its wages in order to fill positions. The government is a large employer relative to the supply of those who meet the formal requirements for employment as teachers. It must therefore pay a wage close to the median in comparable private employment or else face empty classrooms. A smaller employer, on the other hand, could set a low wage and still meet its staffing needs by recruiting from the lowest quality applicants among those who do not meet the minimum formal requirements. But teacher salaries will have to be fairly responsive to changes in competitive salaries if teaching positions are to be filled at all.

Salaries of teachers also may be raised in response to increases in the private sector if the legislature is explicitly concerned with their quality. If a government is hiring and wishes to retain personnel of average or above average quality rather than simply to minimize its salary costs, an increase in private wages will stimulate a competitive increase in the public sector. Hence this hypothesis, like the first, is consistent with both legislative concern and indifference for the quality of education.

3. Salaries of teachers may vary with the quality of the supply of labor available locally. If high-quality labor is scarce, one would expect that relatively higher salaries will have to be paid to obtain it. Unlike the first two hypotheses, this is not only consistent with but also requires an explicit concern with quality in salary determination.

4. The cost of living could have an important independent effect on teachers' salaries if, for example, a paternalistic concern with the welfare and morale of public employees leads government to raise wages in response to increases in living costs.

Of these four hypotheses of legislative salary determination, the first and second are the most plausible. One would expect wealthier communities to provide higher quality education for their children, and because teaching absorbs such a large proportion of the qualified labor supply, teaching salaries would be expected to be competitive with wages in private employment. The fourth hypothesis is also reasonable although somewhat less plausible, since it relies on the concern of voters and legislators with the teachers' struggle to meet a high cost of living. The third hypothesis requires an explicit concern with teacher quality—for example, that salaries might be raised when a falling-off in quality in the local school system becomes apparent through, say, a decline in the average teacher score on a standardized test. Hence it requires a minimum amount of professional sophistication on the part of the legislature.

EMPIRICAL ESTIMATES OF THE ALLOCATION OF TEACHING RESOURCES

The hypothesis of a paternalistic cost-of-living salary determination is the simplest to examine empirically—and to reject. In a study of the determination of teacher salaries in the thirty-three metropolitan areas for which local living cost indexes were available, little support was given to this hypothesis. Once the local level of income was taken into account, little or no additional explanatory power was gained by introducing the cost-of-living index as a determinant of teacher salaries. Other statistical tests on these data also failed to support the cost-of-living hypothesis of salary determination (see appendix 2).

The other hypotheses of teacher salary determination and that of what we have called agency-teacher rationality (that the agency seeks to hire high-quality teachers, who in turn are attracted by high salaries) was tested with the explicit teacher quality data supplied by the Coleman Report research team.[15] Table 5 gives the interstate correlations of per capita income and these measures of teacher quality. When teacher salary is correlated with these quality variables, rather similar results are obtained. No relationship is observed between the highest degree attained by teachers and either state income per capita or average teacher salary. The teacher experience results are even more striking. A strong negative relationship is found between experience and both salary and income.

This negative relationship in the interstate analysis was confirmed by a study of variations of teacher experience by county in Illinois, one of the few states for which such data are available. In the poorest districts of that state, salaries were low and experience levels high; in the richest districts the reverse was true. In general, experience levels were highest in districts that had lost population (usually rural districts or those characterized by a declining industrial base) and lowest in those that had experienced the most rapid gains in population (often the more affluent suburbs).[16] A full empirical explanation of interarea variations in teacher experience would require a dynamic analysis of such demographic changes, an effort beyond the scope of the present work.

Table 5 also indicates a strong positive relationship between the local level of teacher salary and income and the average level of teacher verbal ability, which is very probably the better index of teacher quality and certainly the simpler variable to study in an interarea analysis. The emphasis placed on teacher verbal ability relative to experience that is apparently observed in the table is not inconsistent with the large positive experience differentials in salaries that were found *within* cities. An obvious and plausible explanation is that while the structure of salaries within school systems reflects the internal bureaucratic needs of those systems (for example, to reward as well as to retain older teachers) rather than any

TABLE 5. SIMPLE CORRELATIONS BETWEEN TEACHER
CHARACTERISTICS AND STATE PER CAPITA INCOME

	Coefficient of Determination	
Measure of Teacher Quality	State Per Capita Income	Teacher Salary
Verbal ability	.61	.56
Experience	−.47	−.44
Highest degree	.00	.05

Sources: Data on teacher verbal ability, experience, highest degree, and salary are from tapes for 1964–65 from James S. Coleman *et al.*, *Equality of Educational Opportunity* (Washington: Government Printing Office, 1966). State per capita income for 1964 from *Survey of Current Business* 48, no. 8 (Aug. 1968): 15. Correlations obtained from data in logarithmic form.

positive evaluation of the productivity of long-term teachers, local variations in the level of teacher salaries are used to recruit better quality teachers as measured by their verbal ability.

Because of the common correlations problem (among teacher verbal ability, state average per capita income, teacher salary, salaries in competing occupations, and the quality of the local labor force) discussed earlier and the resulting ambiguities of interpretation, it is necessary to go beyond the simple correlation analysis of table 5 to test this hypothesis of the determination of teacher verbal ability or the several hypotheses of teacher salary determination. A relatively simple statistical model can be used here: if the level of teacher salary a school board is willing to offer is determined by the per capita income of the area it serves and by the quality of teachers which can be obtained at that salary (the first and third salary hypotheses), and if, similarly, the salary required by teachers is regarded as a function of their quality relative to the quality of the labor supply in the area where they are employed (consistent with the agency-teacher rationality hypothesis), the common correlation problem can easily be resolved by the use of a standard statistical technique, two-stage least-squares regression. As a variant of this model, the salaries demanded by teachers can be regarded as a function of salaries in competing occupations as well as of teacher quality and the quality of the local labor force.

These two models posit a modicum of sophistication on the part of the legislature, since they specify an explicit concern with teacher quality. When they were tested statistically (the results of these tests are described in some detail in appendix 2), little support was found for this interpretation. Teacher quality was statistically insignificant as a determinant of the school board's willingness to pay higher salaries either in the first model or in the variant.[17] Moreover, when a simple direct analysis of the joint effects of per capita income and the quality of the labor force on teacher salary was carried out (using the technique of multiple regression of the reduced form), the quality of the labor force was found to be statistically insignificant.

Thus the available data do not support the second salary hypothesis. If teachers' salaries are not responsive to local quality conditions but are posited to be determined by local school systems simply as a function of local per capita income and possibly of salaries in competing occupations (that is, if only the first and second salary hypotheses are valid); and if the quality of teachers the school system can hire is regarded, as before, as responsive to the level of salary offered as well as to the quality of the local labor supply (as would be expected from the agency-teacher rationality hypothesis); no explicit concern with teacher quality on the part of the legislature need be assumed. A somewhat simpler model of salary and quality determination is indicated. This model can be schematized as a "causal chain" (see appendix 2) in which a line of causation runs from teacher salary to teacher quality without any feedback from quality to salary, as shown in the figure below.

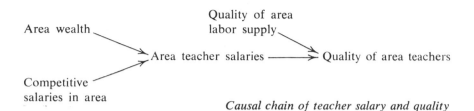

Causal chain of teacher salary and quality

Statistical results obtained from this model (see table 6) strongly support it. Teacher salaries[18] are determined by community income and, to some extent, by salaries in competing occupations. Thus the higher per capita income is in an area, the more willing its legislative body will be to pay high salaries to teachers; and, in any event, as a large employer of labor, the school system will be forced to raise teacher salaries if salaries are high in competing private occupations. At the same time, the quality of teachers hired is a function of salaries paid as well as of the quality of the local labor supply, suggesting that school system officials do use their salary budgets to seek high-quality teachers and that such teachers are attracted by higher salaries.

IMPLICATIONS FOR
EDUCATIONAL INEQUALITY

This analysis of quality determination has immediate and important results for a study of educational inequality. It points up the significant area differences in the quality of teachers, shows that these quality dif-

TABLE 6. DETERMINATION OF TEACHER SALARY AND QUALITY IN A CAUSAL CHAIN SYSTEM

	STEP 1: TEACHER SALARY DETERMINATION		
	Income Effect	Competitive Salary Effect	Coefficient of Determination
Teacher salary	.45	.69	.82
	STEP 2: TEACHER QUALITY DETERMINATION		
	Teacher Salary Effect	Quality of Local Labor Supply Effect	Coefficient of Determination
Teacher quality	.21	.36	.81

Note: Effects in table are elasticities. See appendix 2 for details of this statistical estimation.

ferences are systematically related to differences in the cultural and economic levels of the states, and measures the effect of the decentralized system of finance in maintaining this educational inequality. It of course refutes the notion that area expenditure differentials simply reflect variations in the local cost of living or of labor.

The quality of teachers is higher, other things being equal, in the better developed states where the quality of the local labor force is better. But other things are generally not equal. These data indicate that the decentralized school systems do not use salary policy to equalize teacher quality. Rather this system of finance leads the wealthier, more developed regions to set *higher* salaries for teachers (and to raise them still further, if need be, if the competitive costs of labor are higher there) so as to exacerbate the effects of local differences in labor force quality.

These findings give little support to those who resist a more egalitarian, federally supported system of school finance on the grounds of the efficiency and, especially, of the responsiveness to local conditions of the present decentralized system. Even within the numerous institutional constraints to which the system is subject, there is no evidence that the typical school system, with its authority fragmented among a number of agency and legislative bodies, takes teacher quality into consideration in determining teachers' salaries. Rather the ability of the community to pay and the necessity of finding college graduates appear to be the principal causes of salary variations.

Yet these results do provide some grounds for optimism to those who want change. The strong support given to the agency-teacher rationality hypothesis (that teacher quality is responsive to salary changes) means that, despite the many institutional restraints imposed on the school systems, an increase in the salary budget at the state or local level by, say, the federal government can be expected to lead to a significant improvement in the quality of instruction in the local system.

In fact, the measures of the responsiveness of teacher quality to salary changes are likely to be underestimates of the gains that could be obtained from a truly egalitarian federal policy that concentrated assistance on the poorest districts within each state. The estimates in table 6 are based on statewide data; but when teacher salaries are raised throughout a state, most of the gain in quality must come by attracting college women from other occupations or from housewife status. For economic reasons there is relatively little interstate migration of elementary school teachers. But when a poorer community raises salaries relative to those in adjacent districts within the same state, it can hope to attract many more teachers by migration or commuting as well as to attract local college graduates who are not presently teaching.[19] Hence the interstate results presented here are only minimal estimates of the quality gains to be obtained from a more egalitarian salary policy.

EMPIRICAL ANALYSIS OF THE
DISTRIBUTION OF NONTEACHING
RESOURCES

The data presented to this point are for teaching resources. A similar (though very much simpler) analysis can be carried out for nonsalary instructional expenditures. These expenditures are for textbooks, library supplies, photographic equipment, and the like—mostly goods sold in interstate commerce. Any price variations stem largely from transportation costs, and there is little reason to believe that the delivered prices of such goods are significantly affected by local differences in either the cost of living or the cost of labor. Consequently a very straightforward analysis can be used.

Table 7 presents the result of an empirical study of interstate differences in nonsalary instructional expenditure per pupil in average daily attendance. For every 1 percent increase in state per capita income, expenditures rise by 1.3 percent. This is a considerably greater income effect than was found in the analysis of teaching resources. Thus this analysis affords evidence of the very real differences in educational quality that exist among states and cities and of the relationship between state wealth and maintenance of these quality differences.

COMPARISON OF INTRADISTRICT
AND INTERDISTRICT INEQUALITIES

Finally, the interarea analysis presented in this chapter can usefully be compared with the study of inequality within large cities presented in chapter 2 to provide further measures of the effects of decentralization.

Unlike the within-city case, in which a heavy premium was placed on long-term service, no evidence was found that the wealthier communities or states have more experienced teachers. The relationship between wealth and teachers' verbal ability is much stronger in the interarea comparison, however, than in the within-city analysis. A direct analysis of the effect of variations of area income on teacher quality (one that abstracts from the intermediate effects of political and bureaucratic forms on salary determination) is offered in appendix 2 (table 28).

When the quality of the local labor supply was held constant a coef-

TABLE 7. INTERSTATE DIFFERENCES IN NONSALARY INSTRUCTIONAL EXPENDITURES (50 STATES)

	Income Effect	Coefficient of Determination
Nonsalary expenditures	1.31	.511

Sources: State per capita income: *Survey of Current Business* 48, no. 8: 15. Nonsalary instructional expenditure per pupil in average daily attendance: U.S. Office of Education, *Statistics of State School Systems*, Office of Education Circular No. 751 (Washington, 1964), p. 46, table 21, col. 4, and p. 61, table 35, cols. 11–13.

ficient of .18 was obtained, and when the local cost of labor was also held constant an income coefficient of .27 was found. Within cities, an increase in neighborhood income of 1 percent gave rise to an increase in teacher verbal ability of 0.11 percent—about one-half the interstate effect.

A comparison also shows that wealth has a much stronger influence— roughly twice as much—on teacher salaries *among* districts than *within* districts. Within large cities, for every 1 percent increase in average family income, an increase of 0.2 percent in teacher salary was obtained. But across state lines an increase of 0.43 percent was found per 1 percent increase in average income, even when the effect of local variations in the cost of labor was taken into account. The interstate effect is again twice the within-city effect.

The comparison thus supports the view that, despite the bureaucratic distortions in the big-city school system—the segregation of teachers and pupils and the underlying financial problem of finding a rationale for educating the local poor in a society characterized by a high rate of geographic mobility—there has been some egalitarian benefit derived from the formal commitment to equal education for all students within the municipal school district. Moreover, such comparisons demonstrate the futility of striving for equality of educational opportunities simply by seeking to eliminate differences within cities by administrative fiat while much larger differences among communities are ignored as products of our traditional decentralized system of school finance.

4

Economic and racial barriers to higher education in the United States

INEQUALITY IN DURATION OF
SCHOOLING AS A CAUSE OF
UNDERINVESTMENT IN EDUCATION
OF THE POOR

Inequality of educational opportunity is not limited to the variations in schooling quality discussed in chapters 2 and 3. A second, and very important, dimension of inequality derives from class differences in years of schooling. The fact that lower-class people generally spend fewer years in school increases the underinvestment in their education for two reasons. One is that there are fewer years of investment in their schooling. The other is that education costs rise sharply with years of schooling, and so the poor miss out on the most expensive years. Since quality differentials continue into the higher education levels, the two dimensions—expenditures per student year and duration—interact in a number of ways to compound the inequality. Moreover, the fact that many lower-class youths are culturally disadvantaged, learn to read much later than middle-class children, and then often continue to acquire skills more slowly means that a shorter duration of schooling for this group may have a critical negative effect on their educational attainment.

Underinvestment in postsecondary education of the poor is partly a result of social and cultural factors, but it is also a result in part of financial obstacles to their further schooling. At the secondary level, the absence of a living stipend while in school leads many lower-class youths to yield to the lure of paying employment, and the poorer quality of education often offered them further contributes to class differences

But the financial obstacles become much more important in higher education. Tuition at the average large private college is about $2,500 and is continuing to rise sharply. At the large public universities the average fees are about $600 per year for residents and $1,500 for out-of-state students. For the many youths not within commuting distance of a college, room and board fees—now averaging about $1,200 per year—must also be paid as well as travel expenses and other miscellaneous costs of living away from home.[1] Apart from the minority who are fortunate enough to obtain scholarship aid, these fees provide a formidable barrier to college attendance for the lower class. Moreover, the opportunity costs of forgone earnings are much more important for college-age high school graduates than they are for high school students.

Even without these financial barriers, the poor would be likely to be underrepresented in college (see the discussion in chapter 5 below of the social and cultural bases of class differences in family or individual demands for education). A national policy that was dedicated to equality of educational opportunity might try to offset the effect of nonfinancial obstacles not only by eliminating all financial barriers to lower-class education but also by diverting resources to the design of curriculums that would be more attractive and useful for them. Instead we find that through both the duration of schooling and the variations in quality, monetary factors are used not to counteract the cultural disadvantages of the lower class but to reinforce them.

A survey of the institutions providing higher education in this country shows that many of the factors that produce inequality at the elementary and secondary levels are also operative here. Financing is decentralized; most funds come from state and local governments or from privately endowed colleges. The larger part of the subsidy is allocated in accordance with the low or zero tuition principle, which favors the middle class, rather than with the assistance of a means test. The administration of the various subsidy programs is typically characterized by a thoroughgoing middle-class bias, the academic value system. An additional obstacle to a democratic higher education policy is the popular resistance to the idea of universal higher education.

LACK OF CONSENSUS ON EQUAL
HIGHER EDUCATION

At present about two-fifths of all American high school graduates go on to college. Among the more affluent upper-middle-class youth only a small minority don't obtain some college training. Yet the idea still persists among many that, unlike secondary schools, *all* institutions of postsecondary education, even those offering appropriate curriculums for the disadvantaged, should impose selective academic standards. Perhaps this idea is not held regarding admission; most Americans readily accept the idea that there should be colleges into which even the least able sons of the rich can purchase admission. But it certainly is held for granting the full scholarships, tuition *plus* a living allowance, that poor youths often require.

These attitudes have made the task of extending the duration of schooling, at least beyond the high school level, more difficult than that of providing equal quality in elementary and secondary education. We are disturbed at the remaining inequalities within our municipal systems. Moreover, because of the "spillover effects," the traditional defense of the right of each community to determine the quality of the public education it offers appears to be an increasingly ineffective argument for the maintenance of important intercommunity differentials. But no such commitment has emerged at the college level.

Later chapters in this book discuss the economic, social, and political advantages and disadvantages of extending lower-class educational opportunities. To understand the inequality that at present pervades our educational practices, however, it is necessary to take into account the influence of the lack of a national consensus about universal postsecondary education in forestalling a more democratic outcome, whether or not this policy would be socially desirable.

It is easiest to understand this "ideological gap" in historical terms. For generations postsecondary education was the prerogative of a small elite. But because of the recent very rapid expansion of higher educational opportunities, we are quickly approaching a point where the absence of some form of post-high-school training becomes a competitive handicap in the labor market (see the discussion in chapter 5). Hence, while democratization of higher education opportunities could once have been interpreted simply to mean their extension from a small to a larger number, it now implies a systematic attempt to reduce the schooling gap between the near-majority and the lower class. Yet many still think of the problem as one of providing majority education.

Moreover, the effects of this earlier development are to be found in policies on the resources allocated per student at postsecondary institutions as well as on attendance. In the rush to expand opportunities to a majority, the fact that the institutions in which the working class and lower middle class have been enrolled have generally had a smaller resource base despite the special educational needs of many of their students has received comparatively little attention.

This problem of developing a democratic commitment for post-high-school education has a clear historical parallel in the history of secondary schooling in the United States. Today, high school dropouts, and class or racial biases in the quality of secondary schooling obtained by those who do not drop out, are generally regarded as major social problems. But this consensus has taken over a century to develop. By the middle of the nineteenth century, elementary education for all Americans (or at least all white Americans) had gained widespread acceptance as a norm, although many were in fact still unschooled. But when the first public high schools were introduced they were attended by an elite. At that time there was still a labor market demand for young teenagers, and adult wages were low enough that the workingman's family typically required the children's earnings to maintain itself. The "free" public high school was in fact beyond the means of most of the working class. As a result, public high schools were actually opposed by a majority of workingmen in many areas on the grounds that the entire citizenry would have to pay taxes for schools that only an elite could afford to attend.[2]

With further economic development, high school enrollments increased and attitudes changed. In 1902, a forward-looking professor of education could write: "Primary education . . . is the education needed for all; which, for the sake of the general good, no citizen can be permitted to do without. Beyond this is the region of difference, or divergence, and it may be added, of very great uncertainty and dispute. Occasionally, one hears the prophecy that what we call secondary education will eventually be an education for all."[3]

By the mid-1920s, further gains had been made in secondary school enrollment,[4] and Ryan and Crecellius, themselves educators and advocates of universal secondary education, could put the case for high school for all to their more snobbish colleagues in these rather aggressive words:

> If secondary education is to be extended to include a majority, the educational world will have to develop a new conception of human worth—a conception partaking of the nature of that now held by the workaday world.
>
> The fact that the community pays the realtor $20,000 a year and the college professor $4,000 should strike us as a rather broad hint that society in general places a value upon academic intelligence which is somewhat different from our own estimate. We shall need to broaden our sense of values.
>
> Once the academic mind has definitely conceded the right of the non-academic mind to education, the door is open and the time is ripe for the study of ways and means.[5]

Of course, the nature of the schools changed with their class composition. As the president of the board of education of "Middletown" told the Lynds, again in the mid-1920s, "For a long time all boys were trained to be President. Then for a while we trained them all to be professional men. Now we are training boys to get jobs."[6]

And, as the children of the less affluent began to be enrolled in larger numbers, more differentiation in the type of public secondary schooling offered was introduced. Thus, Ryan and Crecillius explicitly advocate ability tracking in the junior high school as a way of *reducing* educational inequality. (The argument was that if the poorer students were taught and graded separately their very high failure rate would be reduced, making possible their further education.)[7]

In the following decades high school attendance became recognized as a prerogative for all. The egalitarian critics of the secondary system are now concerned with the inequalities in the quality of secondary education and with the minority of youths who still do not finish high school.

There is evidence that a similar process has also been at work, slowly changing attitudes toward mass college (or at least postsecondary) education. The post–World War II G.I. Bill of Rights provided college tuition and living cost allowances to millions of veterans, changing the ideas of many about the potential for a permanent increase in college education opportunities.[8] In 1947, the President's Commission on Higher Education compared the academic skills of those attending college with those deprived of this opportunity, using Armed Forces Qualification Test scores as a measure of the capacities of those not in college. It calculated that a radical increase could be obtained in the proportion of youth attending college with no reduction in academic quality if only financial obstacles were eliminated. The commission set as a national goal an increase to 49 percent in the proportion of the youth population enrolled in the first two years of college and to 32 percent in the last two years of college by 1960.[9]

The goals of the commission are now close to full realization as a result of long-term gains in the purchasing power of the average citizen and of the very considerable governmental effort to expand educational opportunities. If the trend toward increased college attendance continues, it is very likely that a national consensus on the need for universal postsecondary education can gradually be developed over the next several decades. It will be argued below (see chapter 6), however, that there are now pressing reasons for accelerating this historical process and upgrading the educational levels of lower-class youth relative to the average immediately.

In this situation the historical experience is of small comfort. Secondary schooling was extended to the poor very slowly and is still not universal. Moreover, as high school attendance for the working class rose, college attendance for the middle class also increased, so that there was not a very significant decline in the overall inequality of years of schooling completed (historical changes in the distribution of educational opportunities are discussed in chapter 10 below). To obtain fuller equality, national policy must not simply seek to increase educational opportunities for the poor but must ensure that these opportunities rise even more rapidly than those open to the average student. But if this is to be done and done with the requisite dispatch, the historical trends have to be accelerated. The "ideological gap" must be closed quickly, and an immediate, definite commitment must be made to universal postsecondary education.

MIDDLE-CLASS BIAS IN COLLEGE
STUDENT ASSISTANCE POLICIES

The principal financial obstacles to a more democratic distribution of college opportunities now appear to lie not so much in the level of funding for the colleges as in the way the available subsidy is allocated. As we have seen, there is not yet a full national consensus on universal postsecondary education, and funds are allocated by decentralized authorities (state and local governments and the private colleges). As a result, national concerns are minimized in their distribution, and subsidies are used largely to underwrite the education of the middle class and, to a lesser extent, that of the upper working class. As at the lower levels of schooling, the proximate causes of inequality are the low-tuition principle and middle-class biases in the administration of subsidies.

The Low-Tuition Public College

The low-tuition principle has particularly detrimental effects at the college level because other costs of education—the opportunity cost of forgone earnings and the out-of-pocket expenses required to live away from home—are so much more important there. But the pressures for low tuition are considerable within the present decentralized system of education finance. Because public colleges are funded locally or by states, the national need for upgrading the educational level of the poor can obtain relatively little support in this system. Taxpayers and voters demand low tuition, at least for state residents. Moreover, both public and private colleges fear that if they act alone to raise tuition they would lose their middle-class students to other colleges that continued to subsidize tuition for all students.

Of course, one cannot deny that tuition subsidies have helped make higher education available to a much larger student body. The private colleges often claim that without this subsidy their tuition charges would have to be increased dramatically, perhaps as much as tripled. It is extremely difficult to verify such calculations since many of the college expenditures for research, fund-raising, and the like cannot properly be regarded as teaching costs. However, about three-fourths of all college students are now enrolled in public colleges where tuition is indeed heavily subsidized. In the 1973–74 academic year, average tuition at a large public college was about $556 per resident, much less than the $2,523 charged at the average large private college.

These public college tuition subsidies do have some effect on broadening college opportunities. For example, 39 percent of the freshmen entering public colleges in 1971 had parents with incomes below $10,000, as compared with 25 percent of those at private four-year institutions.[10]

The democratizing effect of the public college in the postwar period has probably resulted as much from the proliferation of local state college units, which has reduced the relative importance of the nontuition costs of college attendance, as from the low tuition itself. Most state universities originally had a single "downstate" location far from the state's major population centers. These locations were generally inconvenient to the average potential student. More important for an analysis of inequality, the room and board charges, now more than twice as large as the average tuition charge at the typical American state university, provided a formidable obstacle to the poorer student. But in the past twenty years many state systems have established public colleges in their major urban centers, enabling more working-class youths to attend as commuting students.[11] Moreover, the number of two-year community colleges has mushroomed in the same period; their enrollment rose from 308,000 in 1955 to 1,630,000 in 1970.[12] Partly because they offer a degree (the Associate of Arts) after only two years of study and partly because their curriculums have been better organized to meet the needs of the working class, these institutions also attracted large numbers from less affluent student groups.[13] Obviously such reforms have enabled many more working-class and lower-middle-class youths to attend college. However, their positive effect should not be overestimated. Many communities are not served by either two-year or four-year colleges; some set admissions standards the lower class cannot meet; most charge some tuition; and they offer relatively few living stipends to help the poorest students, the lower-class youths, to attend. The very large subsidies now invested in underwriting tuition at these public colleges could be much more helpful in removing class barriers to college attendance if they were administered with the help of a means test, with the middle class charged what they could pay and the lower class afforded living stipends where needed. For example, they could be used to enable poorer youths residing in the smaller communities of the state, where it may not be economical to build even two-year colleges, to attend a down-state or metropolitan college.

College Scholarship System

Actually there is a widespread system of college scholarships which does utilize a means test and which provides for living expenses as well as tuition costs for poor students. This system is the second major method used to liberalize college opportunities in the United States today.

At present more than eight hundred colleges, enrolling the majority of the nation's college students, report they allocate their student aid funds according to the rules of the College Scholarship Service. Some of these colleges charge very high tuition to those who do not need subsidy, but as members of the service they are committed to charging the family of each needy student at their college a "price" that is determined strictly by the family's financial means. Tuition is set on the basis of a thorough examination of the family's income, assets, and other financial needs—for example, whether it has other children of college age. This tuition can be negative: if the CSS finds the family to be sufficiently poor, the student can receive a cash amount up to his full need for room, board, books, and miscellaneous expenses.

The average scholarship awarded to those receiving aid is $234 at the member public colleges and $1,031 at the private colleges. These grants are supplemented by loans and work opportunities offered by the colleges, so that the average student receiving aid obtained a total of $1,633 at private colleges and $1,068 at public colleges. About two-fifths of the freshmen at private colleges and one-third of those at public colleges received some form of aid; the remainder paid full tuition.[14]

These programs represent an important departure from the low-tuition subsidy principle and deserve close scrutiny as possible models for a more democratic policy.

A superficial reading of the college scholarship literature might convince one that the financial barriers to college attendance (at least for those who have graduated from high school) have indeed been eroded, that now students can be judged solely on the basis of their ability. However, the CSS system as it now stands must be characterized as inadequate to this task of providing equality of college opportunities.

A recent empirical analysis commissioned by the CSS itself showed that scholarship offers actually made by the member colleges were far smaller than those provided by its rules. Only 45 percent of the additional financial requirements of poor students were met by any form of aid (including loans or work offers) by the private colleges and 43 percent by the public colleges. Still more significant, the investigation found that those students requiring substantial amounts of aid were very much less likely than others to be admitted. For each $1,000 of calculated need (that is, of about $450 in actual total "aid," including jobs and loans, or less than $300 of scholarship), the probability of admission declined by 7 percent in the private and 11 percent in the public institutions (with student ability held constant).[15]

The rationale for these departures from the stated egalitarian values of the CSS is obvious once one understands the institutional framework in which subsidy funds are allocated. The service is not and cannot be a substitute for a federal higher education policy. It is a voluntary association of member colleges without the sanctions or taxing power of the central government. Obviously it cannot be expected to obtain fundamental changes in the college system, especially if such change, however desirable it may be for the larger society, runs counter to the collective interests of the colleges. When seen in this light, both the positive contributions of the CSS and its shortcomings from the point of view of egalitarian policy are much more easily understood.

The CSS rules, which set the amount of each scholarship at a level determined by the central association's analysis of the family's ability to pay, clearly advance the colleges' collective interests. They prevent the individual colleges from using all their funds to subsidize low-cost tuition, which would effectively *under*charge the middle-class families that could pay more. They also prevent colleges with scholarship funds from dissipating them on very large grants to compete for the most able students regardless of their financial need. Insofar as the colleges can obtain students by paying them *less* than the CSS needs analysis dictates (for example, by taking advantage of the student's preference for a nearby school or his willingness to work relatively long hours at "part-time" work), the collective interest of the colleges is also advanced, not diminished.

Similarly, reducing the admission chances of students who need more financial aid advances the colleges' collective interest. The money allocated to scholarship funds is not adequate to meet the needs of all poor but able students. It is therefore reasonable from the colleges' point of view to set higher academic admissions standards for those who need scholarship aid than for those who do not and for those who need more than for those who need less. According to CSS rules, the amount of the student's scholarship is determined strictly by his financial need. But this scholarship then becomes his "price" to the college and to the college system and so has an inverse relationship to his chance of admission.[16] Essentially, in selecting scholarship students for admission, the college (and the system, through the CSS) must mentally compare the scholarship cost of each student with some index of his attractiveness as a candidate and then rank students in terms of the ratio of the latter to the former—that is, in terms of their academic value per dollar of scholarship. In this ranking many candidates who are more attractive in terms of nonfinancial considerations will be rejected in favor of others, less well qualified, who require less scholarship aid or none at all.

Of course, if an adequate level of funds were allocated to scholarships either by the colleges themselves or by governmental or other outside sources, the subsidy requirement of the student would be irrelevant, and students could be admitted on the basis of academic considerations regardless of financial need. But under present conditions of inadequate scholarships budgets, discrimination against the poor but able student is "rational."

Scholarships and Academic Values

The financial need of the poor is only one factor in their rejection by many colleges. Empirical work has found the academic ability of applicants to be a key determinant of college admissions when financial need and race are held constant.[17] But academic ability, as measured by the colleges, tends to be much lower among the poor. For example, Project Talent found that over one-half of those high school graduates whose families earned less than $3,000 a year had below-average academic aptitude compared with only one-fourth of those from families with incomes above $12,000. Similarly, only a little more than 1 percent of the poor children were in the top 2 percent in aptitude in comparison with 7 percent of those from the more affluent group. Such findings have been confirmed in a large number of other studies.[18]

This differential in academic ability operates against the poor not only when they apply for scholarships but also when they seek admission to the better endowed institutions without aid. Institutions that can offer both a high level of resources per student and heavily subsidized tuition generally ration the demand for places by setting very high academic admission standards. The most expensive divisions of a number of state university systems have typically followed this practice. This use of academic ability tests to determine college admission has gained wide public approval. Acceptance of this academic value system must, however, be considered an important aspect of the "ideological gap" that obstructs a more democratic policy, for the result has been to bar the majority of lower-class youth.

Whatever its drawbacks as a social policy, this value system makes a great deal of sense from the point of view of the individual college and perhaps even advances the interest of the college system as a whole, given its academic orientation. The *objective* interests of the administrations and faculties of the individual colleges are caught up in a system of academic values that provides them with an obvious basis for preferring able students. The institutions are rated by academic standards, which examine the quality of a school's *graduates*. Clearly the best way to ensure high-quality graduates is to admit highly able freshmen (and to weed out any "mistakes" you have made as soon as they are discovered). Given the wide variation among applicants in academic ability, this course will guarantee a relatively high-quality crop of college seniors no matter how inefficient the college is at its task of education. But it is not adequate as a basis for public policy. The academic emphasis on the graduates' quality overlooks the difference between the quality of education (as measured by the improvement in the capacities of youths as a result of their schooling) or its efficiency (as measured by the quality gain per unit of education resource input) and the quality of final output. Thus the colleges' institutional needs tend to lead them not only to ignore broad social values such as minimizing the number of poorly educated voters but to emphasize the quality of the "raw material" much more than does, say, the successful businessman, who knows that a fortune can as easily be made in processing guano as in cutting diamonds.[19]

Of course the public does not allow the academy a free rein in admissions and scholarships policy. For example, legislatures require state colleges to set much higher tuition charges for out-of-state applicants of equivalent quality.

Many colleges have also departed from the traditional value system to favor black applicants as consequences of the social disturbances of the sixties and of the widely held view that it was now necessary to recruit a well-educated black elite. A special study by the CSS found that by 1969 some colleges appeared to be practicing what must be called blatant reverse discrimination against poor whites. The study found that "in six of the seven private colleges that provided racial identification of applicants, being black improved the probability of being admitted. If Standard Achievement Test (scores), high school grade point average, and financial need are held constant, a minority applicant's probability of being admitted in those six colleges was higher by 15 to 20 percentage points."[20]

More typically, however, the middle-class and academic biases of the administrators and faculty and the pressures on the individual institutions to maintain and improve their academic standings have tended to favor the applications of those youths who are either superior in academic ability or above average in economic resources or both.

In summary, despite a number of exceptions such as scholarships to the very bright or black poor, college subsidies are still directed to a considerable extent to middle-class students. This bias occurs either directly, through scholarships policy, or simply because these youths tend to attend the better-endowed, highly subsidized institutions while the poor either don't attend or go to the least expensive schools. As a result, student subsidies at the higher as at the lower levels of education are used to a large extent to complement the middle-class-oriented individual demand for schooling rather than to try to shape it toward egalitarian ends.

INEQUALITY IN THE DURATION OF SCHOOLING AND IN THE QUALITY OF HIGHER EDUCATION

The empirical study of duration of schooling is quite simple compared with the analyses of inequality in the provision of educational quality presented in chapters 2 and 3. Very few young people at present do not finish elementary school, but significant variations begin to appear at the secondary level. Thus even today two out of five *young* blacks (those in the 25–29 age bracket) lack high school diplomas, compared with only one out of five whites in that age group.[21]

A number of studies have related high school dropout rates to economic class. For example, an interesting study by Master illustrates the influence of class on high school completion even among whites. He estimates the net effect of such class factors as low family income, poor housing quality, and low parental educational levels as well as racial factors. His results imply that a white boy whose family is low in all these measures (has a broken home, a dilapidated house, and a father who earns less than $3,000 and has less than eight years of schooling) had a 50 percent chance of becoming a high school dropout while a higher-class youth with none of these disadvantages had only a 5 percent chance.[22]

Some ideas of the obstacles to full participation in higher education faced by lower-class youths can be gained from the work of the Project Talent survey. These data deal only with the high school graduate group, so the class factor that operates through high school dropouts is not included. A strong class bias is still observed. Only 32 percent of the sons of farm laborers (and 43 percent of the sons of nonfarm laborers) who did finish high school went on to college, while some 83 percent of those whose parents were in professional or technical occupations did so. A similar gap was found between those whose family income was less than $3,000 per annum and those for whom it was $12,000 or more. College attendance was 39 percent for the first group and 79 percent for the second. For those whose fathers' educations were less than twelve years, college attendance was 46 percent, and for those whose fathers had graduated from college it was 84 percent.[23]

A more current estimate can be gained from the American Council on Education data on incoming freshmen for the 1971 year. These data show that blacks were only 5.5 percent of the college student body and 3.5 percent of the students at private universities, although they constitute about 11 percent of the general population. Similarly, 43 percent of all freshmen had fathers with some college, as did 67 percent of those at private universities, while only 21 percent had parents whose income was less than $8,000 and only 26 percent had fathers who were blue-collar workers (the figures at private universities were 10 and 14 percent).[24]

Regional differences are also important in determining duration of schooling. Thus about 30 percent of ninth graders in the southeastern United States went on to college in the mid-1960s, compared with 61 percent in the far west.[25] The smaller rate of college attendance among children of rural or southern backgrounds is caused partly by the lower level of average income in these areas. But it also reflects a failure of the public higher education system either to provide colleges within commuting distance of rural or small-town youths or to provide them with living allowances that would permit them to board away from home.

Data on variations in the quality of higher education have been studied less, but the available work indicates that those working-class youths who do go to college tend to have less expended on their education there. The California system of public higher education has probably been analyzed most extensively. It is well known and widely admired for the opportunities it has given to the youth of that state. But in an important study of this system, Hansen and Weisbrod found considerable inequality along class lines.

Hansen and Weisbrod determined that the two-year colleges and the senior colleges distributed throughout the state served a somewhat lower income group than did the state university. Median family income at the two-year colleges was $8,800, at the senior colleges $10,000, and at the university $12,000. (These figures must, however, be compared with an average of $7,900 for parents without children in any branch of the California system of higher education.) The discrepancy arose partly from higher academic admissions standards, partly from higher tuition, and partly from inconvenient locations requiring room and board payments. Costs and standards were generally higher at the university than at the four-year colleges and at four-year than at two-year schools. Hansen and Weisbrod also found that more was spent per student per year in the institutions serving the more affluent families. Thus $720 was spent per student at the junior colleges, $1,500 at the senior colleges, and $1,700 at the universities.[26]

Quality variations are not confined, of course, to the public sector. Among the private colleges, recent empirical work has found that the higher quality schools charge higher tuition[27] and that this higher tuition discourages attendance by the poor.[28] Moreover, subsidy per student has also been found to be greater in the more expensive schools, demonstrating yet another middle-class bias for the system.

The available empirical data provide abundant and convincing evidence of the effects of the postsecondary education system in maintaining class differences in the duration of schooling as well as in its quality. While there has been a rapid expansion of enrollments in higher education in the post–World War II period, the working class is still sharply under-represented there and many lower-class youths still do not finish high school. Moreover, when the working class is found in college, they are most likely to be found in the less expensive institutions where fewer resources are allocated per student.

It is apparent that, given the structure of our system of higher education, only a very thoroughgoing reform will lead to the provision of equal opportunity for all in postsecondary education. This reform would rethink the effects of middle-class bias and bureaucracy, including the "ideological gap" built into the academic value system. It would reevaluate the decentralization of subsidy allocation to private colleges and the state or local public college systems. Finally, it would reassess the use of subsidy to underwrite low tuition for all rather than to provide adequate scholarships for the truly needy.

PART II

The welfare state demand for a less unequal policy

5

The private demand
for schooling: pressure
for continuing inequality

THE MIXED PUBLIC-PRIVATE
SCHOOL SYSTEM

The empirical analyses in chapters 2, 3, and 4 described how education subsidies at each level of schooling are allocated in a way that favors the more affluent over the poor. We have seen that the low-tuition principle and a middle-class bias in the education bureaucracy are important factors in explaining this allocation in a number of specific instances. More fundamental is the decentralization of school finance to the states and localities (and, at the higher level, to private colleges). Decentralization permits the educational system to minimize national concerns and hence to put comparatively little emphasis on meeting social demands, and it gives maximum scope to private considerations in educational decision-making. Both the low-tuition principle and middle-class biases in administration, moreover, are accommodations to private demands for education.

Private demands—that is, those of each parent for the education of his own children—are, then, an important determinant of the distribution of education subsidies. Further, the force of these private demands is not limited to subsidy effects, since the American system permits a fairly wide role for individual parental incentives in education. For example, since the student and his family bear the brunt of education costs once the youth is past the age of sixteen or so (at least if the opportunity costs as well as the direct costs of schooling are considered), the family's estimates of the private benefits relative to the private costs of further education play a critical role in determining the duration of a child's schooling and, if college is decided upon, the quality of his further training.

There is also ample room in our system for private choice at the lower levels of schooling. If an urban parent is dissatisfied with the quality of the public school and is willing to pay for options, he can transfer his children to a private school or he can move to a suburb or even to a "better" section of the same city.

When the force of these individual decisions is considered together with the effect of private demands on collective decision-making, private demand emerges as a very powerful determinant of the distribution of educational resources. Despite the fact that most of our education is provided by public bodies, in a very real sense the United States has a mixed system, with private and social (or group) demands each influencing resource allocation.

Of course, collective decision-making is also important in shaping the allocation of educational resources in this country. Through a system of regulations requiring minimum schooling for all and by the collective provision of highly subsidized education, the nation's total investment in education is raised much beyond the level that could be obtained without government intervention—that is, under a system of unsubsidized, unregulated private academies.

It is not so clear, however, that governmental actions are, on balance, such a powerful force in determining the *distribution* of educational resources among middle-class and poor people. Government subsidies to education often appear to be used to underwrite the private demand for schooling rather than to shape it to some other end, so that subsidy policy may have little net redistributive effect in the United States. It is possible that the many government subsidies that assist the education of the deprived youngster are in this sense offset by others that help to pay for the more expensive schooling of the middle class. A number of instances in which the government's education subsidy was higher where individual expenditures were greater—in college tuition, for example—were mentioned in chapters 2 to 4. This feature encourages the inference that the government's subsidy policy is influenced by private pressures.

Tables 8 and 9 provide further evidence at a very high level of aggregation. Table 8 shows that government subsidies to education are highest in those areas of the United States where the opportunity costs of attending school are the greatest. Table 9 indicates that per student subsidies are higher on the average at the college level, where private costs are higher, than at the secondary level. It is not obvious from these various comparisons that government subsidy policy helps significantly in equalizing the distribution of schooling resources.

TABLE 8. REGIONAL VARIATION IN PRIVATE AND PUBLIC COSTS OF EDUCATION IN THE UNITED STATES

Region	Average Annual Public Expenditure per Student	Private Opportunity Cost
Northeast	$730	$735
South	458	603
Other	574	627

Sources: Expenditure data from U.S. Department of Health, Education, and Welfare, *State Data and State Rankings* (Washington: Government Printing Office, 1967), p. S-34. Private opportunity costs were estimated by average annual income of male youths with income, 16–17 years old, who completed only eight years of school. These data are given in *Educational Attainment*, a subject report of the *U.S. Census of Population, 1960* (Washington: U.S. Bureau of the Census, 1963), table 6.

TABLE 9. PRIVATE COSTS AND SUBSIDIES PER STUDENT IN AMERICAN HIGH SCHOOLS AND COLLEGES

Level of Schooling	Tuition	Other Direct Costs	Opportunity Costs	Total Private Costs	Subsidy
High school	$ 10	$ 31	$534	$ 565	$354
College	245	142	955	1,342	556

Source: Derived from W. L. Hansen, "Total and Private Rates of Return to Investment in Schooling," *Journal of Political Economy* 81, no. 2 (1963): 128–40.

These subsidy data, however, do not take into account the public controls that in effect *force the poorer citizens to invest in themselves.* State compulsory schooling laws, together with the laws banning child labor, now effectively impose schooling on almost all youths to age sixteen regardless of the preferences of their parents. In addition, state legislation requiring minimum quality schooling in even the poorest districts further constrains the choice of the poor.[1] It would seem, then, that while the major thrust of public policy in American education undoubtedly has been to increase educational investments rather than to work systematically to change their distribution, it probably has had some egalitarian effect through these and similar regulations, which put a floor under the educational level of the poor.

Nevertheless, the more important force shaping the distribution of educational resources in this country (and certainly the key factor in explaining schooling inequalities) has been the major role assigned by the American system to private demands for education.

WHY THE PRIVATE DEMAND FOR EDUCATION IS INEGALITARIAN

It is now possible to carry our analysis of schooling inequality one step further. Previous chapters presented considerable evidence concerning the private demand for education in the United States and its role in generating an unequal distribution of schooling resources. The next step is to examine systematically the underlying sources of this class bias in the private demand for schooling. Apart from its intrinsic interest in helping to explain the etiology of schooling inequality, this analysis will be useful both in the subsequent discussion of a socially optimal policy for school resource distribution and in considering the practical political obstacles in the path of a reformed policy.

Group Inertia Model

Perhaps the simplest explanation of unequal demands for schooling is the superficially plausible "group inertia model." It interprets lower-class underinvestment simply as a result of the social and psychological pres-

TABLE 10. MEAN EDUCATIONAL LEVELS

	Whites	Blacks
Younger people (29–34 years old in 1973)	12.31	11.10
Older people (69–74 years old in 1973)	9.18	5.91

Source: Christopher Jencks *et al.*, *Inequality: A Reassessment of the Effect of Family and Schooling in America* (New York: Basic Books, 1972), p. 21.

sures of the lower-class family, neighborhood, and school that make it difficult for a poor youth to rise to a higher educational level than his parents.[2]

But this is not an adequate explanation. Indeed, the facts flatly contradict it. The average young person now gets about three to five more years of schooling than his relatives did forty years ago. Table 10 shows that the educational attainment of whites has increased by over three years, while that of blacks, a group that contains a far higher proportion of lower-class people, has almost doubled. These figures imply a definite break in the average family's educational "tradition." Today the working-class high school graduate is likely to have a father who did not have a high school diploma, while the middle-class college graduate may well have parents who did not finish high school.

Model of Individual Choice

The economists' model of individual choice can provide a useful alternative to the "group inertia" concept. This model endeavors to explain differences in education by emphasizing the response of individual families to economic and other incentives.

The equation below presents a somewhat simplified version of the now-standard economic analysis of individual or family decision-making.[3] Here a student and his family are considering another year of education for the youth. By emphasizing the multiplicity of factors influencing private decision-making, this individual family investment model helps us to avoid any simplistic interpretation of the problem of unequal private demands for education. For example, it is clear here that it would not be enough to say that higher education is a luxury the poor cannot afford. In this equation, schooling is an investment that, under some circum-

EXPECTED ANNUAL VALUE OF GAIN IN CONSUMPTION BENEFITS
AFTER EDUCATION IS COMPLETED

$$\frac{\text{VALUATION OF EXPECTED GAIN IN ANNUAL INCOME FROM ADDITIONAL EDUCATION} + \overbrace{\underset{\text{prestige}}{\text{Status,}} + \underset{\text{conditions}}{\text{Working}}}^{\text{Job Benefits}} + \overbrace{\underset{\text{gains}}{\text{Cultural}} + \underset{\text{in consumption}}{\text{Efficiency}}}^{\text{Other Consumption Benefits}}}{\text{RATE OF DISCOUNT OF FUTURE BENEFITS (TIME PREFERENCE)}}$$

stances, can raise the poor out of that condition and hence is an expenditure they "can't afford" to neglect.

The model is also proof against those critics of the class approach who argue against its validity by pointing to those individuals within each class who behave very differently from the others in the group. By focusing our attention on the determinants of individual decision-making, it also emphasizes the role of differences among individuals (even within the same socioeconomic group) in intellectual ability, preference for study, attitudes toward the future, and other factors that influence educational investment. In fact, its individualist bias can lead to the opposite error of ignoring group influences on family decisions unless careful attention is paid to class differences in such social pressures.

Application of the Model

Nevertheless, while certainly not a social class model in design, a close scrutiny of the economists' paradigm does help to explain why there is a systematic *tendency* for the poor to invest less in themselves, on the average. The most obvious class differential here derives from differences in the finances available to families for education. These generate class differences in the effective *assessment* of the future benefits of education relative to their present costs. To take an extreme example, consider a family of agricultural laborers that is considering schooling a gifted child to become a brain surgeon. Its discounting of the future income and other benefits that could be obtained by having a brain surgeon in the family would be infinite. No matter how high the future gain, the family would have no way of reducing its present consumption to pay for such an expensive education. The plan would therefore have to be dropped, at least without very extensive scholarship support.

In the more typical decision, a working-class family can make an additional investment in its children if it is willing to cut its consumption to the bone. For example, a skilled worker can often manage the financial cost of an Ivy League college education for his son if he is willing to sacrifice his family's living standard. But this decision may not appear to him to be reasonable or worthwhile. Why should his family sacrifice what he regards as consumption *necessities* now so that the son can enjoy extra luxuries after his graduation? If the family's rate of discounting

$$\frac{\text{Cost of the Year of Schooling}}{\text{(Tuition + other} \quad \text{Forgone}} + \begin{array}{l} \text{Consumption value of a} \\ \text{year in school (by} \\ \text{comparison with a year} \\ \text{in the labor force)} \end{array} = \begin{array}{l} \text{Present value of the} \\ \text{additional education} \\ \text{to the family} \end{array}$$
$$\text{direct costs} \quad + \quad \text{earnings)}$$

future benefits is fairly high and its evaluation of luxuries relative to necessities is low, it may be more reasonable for the family to enter the boy in his father's trade or to enroll him in a local commuter college.

In contrast, the average middle-class family is in less straitened financial circumstances. It can often afford to pay for college education from savings or by borrowing, using securities and equity in a home as collateral, and so can consider the additional education strictly as an alternative investment. Even a middle-class family that has been less thrifty and now must sacrifice current consumption to afford a college education for its children is much less likely to find that spending on actual necessities has to be reduced. In either case, education does not impose as large a real sacrifice on the middle-class family as it does on the poor.[4]

Some economists would argue that class differences in educational investment level which result from differences in financial wealth should be regarded as an "imperfection" in the workings of the private capital market rather than as an inevitable result of what we have called the private demand for education. But this argument rests on a rather strained usage of the word "imperfection," at least as it is used by the layman. A large-scale *governmental* initiative would be required to remedy this defect in the private market at the higher education level, because poor people can't obtain loans from banks on the scale required for higher education without government guarantees and subsidies. Fixed repayment loans would also threaten financial bankruptcy to those college graduates who, because of illness or some other reason, failed to obtain the average earnings gain from their education. It is probable, however, that the financial obstacles to college education could be eliminated if the government would, as many economists have suggested, make sufficient loan funds available to students, repayable as a percentage surtax on postgraduation earnings.

Moreover, a truly revolutionary reorganization of the state and local system of public school finance would be necessary for the loan principle to be used to eliminate differences in educational quality resulting from financial obstacles at the elementary and secondary school level. Otherwise small children would have to be permitted to mortgage their lifetime earnings to obtain a good first grade education. As adults they would also be expected to remit funds to the towns in which they had received their education rather than to the community in which they reside and in which their children attend school.[5] No system that will permit such arrangements seems at all likely to evolve in the United States. Class differences in financial resources must therefore be considered an important reason why the private demand for education now generates schooling inequality and why it will probably continue to press in that direction.

Nonfinancial Sources of Inequality

Even if all financial obstacles to schooling were somehow eliminated, class differences in the private demand would arise because the poor are not willing to pay to obtain the consumption benefits of higher education. The economists' education decision equation includes several nonfinancial benefits from education—better job status and working conditions, cultural and other benefits as a graduate, and the student experience itself, which many consider a benefit if the alternative is factory work or unemployment. Such benefits are in some ways similar to ordinary consumer goods, the demand for which also generally increases with family income. Of course the poor may appreciate fraternity life or training in music appreciation just as much as the middle class. But the lower-class family can still be expected to put a lower *dollar* value on such benefits, since it has fewer dollars and must reserve them for more pressing needs. Hence one would expect the poor, other things being equal, to be less likely to invest in education to obtain its consumption benefits.[6] (Obviously the student loan solution doesn't work here since the graduate cannot use his nonfinancial benefits—what economists call his "psychic income"—to repay his loan.)

Moreover, other things are very definitely not equal between the middle and the lower class with respect to at least one of these benefits—the prestige, status, and better working conditions associated with middle-class employment. The value the middle class places on these benefits provides them with an important additional incentive to pursue higher education. The difference can be seen most sharply today in comparing attitudes toward college education, the level now regarded as meeting the standard requirements for middle-class jobs. An educational investment at this level permits an upward occupational movement for the working-class family. But a decision not to invest is very likely to result in *downward* mobility for the middle-class family—and there is considerable empirical evidence, collected by the sociologists, that families will pay a much steeper financial price to resist a downward movement in their occupational status than they will to move upward.

The sociologists Blau and Duncan conclude from their study of intergenerational mobility that the lowest white-collar occupations

provide a refuge for the downwardly mobile from higher origins (inasmuch as downward mobility into them exceeds theoretical expectations considerably more than does downward mobility into any lower occupations), thereby enabling unsuccessful sons of nonmanual fathers to maintain their white-collar status.

These lower white collar occupations, according to the Blau and Duncan data, pay much less than the higher blue collar jobs. To take an extreme case, the median income of craftsmen exceeds that of low-grade clerks by about 80 percent. Blau and Duncan conclude that:

The skidder from a white-collar home, unfamiliar with the working class and possibly threatened by the prospect of becoming part of it, appears to be willing to pay the price of the lesser income offered by the lowest non-manual occupations to preserve the cherished symbol of the white collar.[7]

Since in our "credentialist" society the college degree is rapidly becoming the minimum requirement for white collar status, the middle-class family is urged on by a much more powerful social or psychological stimulus to invest in higher education than is the blue collar working-class family. Hence, even if the middle-class family did not possess any greater wealth or income, one would expect it to be more likely to send its children to college and to send them to more expensive institutions.

Rising Educational Levels

This social mobility argument does not contradict our earlier judgment that the parents' education level typically does not provide an upper limit to a child's attainment in the United States, since the educational attainment required to maintain the same job status has increased over the past generation.

Despite a remarkable expansion in the number of professional, technical, sales, clerical, and other white collar jobs,[8] the great increase in the educational level of the American people over the past several decades has resulted in an upgrading of the schooling requirements of most occupations. Some indication of the size of this upgrading is provided in table 11, which compares the educational levels of large occupational classes in 1940 and 1970. The rise in schooling requirements ranges from about one to almost three years. Moreover, the comparison of changes

TABLE 11. MEAN EDUCATIONAL LEVEL OF EMPLOYED LABOR FORCE

	1940	1969
Farmers (including farm laborers)	6.7	9.4
Laborers, nonfarm	7.1	9.6
Domestic servants, other private household workers	7.5	8.6
Service (except private household)	8.6	10.4
Operatives	8.3	10.0
Craftsmen	8.4	10.6
Managers, officials, proprietors	10.2	12.8
Sales and clerical	11.0	12.1
Professional and technical	14.2	15.3

Sources: U.S. Bureau of the Census, *1970 Census of the Population, Subject Report, Occupation by Industry* (Washington: Government Printing Office, 1972), and U.S. Bureau of the Census, *Sixteenth Census of the U.S., 1940 Population. The Labor Force. Occupations* (Washington: Government Printing Office, 1943). Categories of 1940 were adjusted to conform as closely as possible with occupational definitions in use in 1970.

in average educational levels in table 11 understates the pressures on young people to acquire education. Employers now often impose much stricter schooling requirements on new workers than could be met by their older employees. New factory workers, for example, are increasingly expected to have a high school diploma in establishments where many older employees have finished only eight years of school. The student and his family when making school plans must also try to forecast the still higher educational requirements that may be set during his career in the labor force. Consequently the pressure of an increased supply of better-educated youth throughout the labor force requires that American families at each socioeconomic level now "run much faster just to stand still."

This process tends to reinforce the class bias in the private demand for schooling in that the middle class must more than match the schooling gains of the working class to maintain its class status. The working-class youth today typically must finish high school to have a reasonable chance of finding decent, well-paying, and permanent work. The middle-class family must therefore go beyond this level and obtain an additional four years of higher education for its children if they are to retain white collar status.

Financial Rates of Return

An additional factor skewing the demand for education toward the children of the middle class is the probable higher financial rate of return to their education (measured, approximately, by the ratio of the average increment in earnings due to additional education to the financial costs—including direct and opportunity costs—it imposes).[9] The evidence for this bias is based more on empirical work than on theoretical analysis, since the theoretical argument for expecting the middle class to obtain a larger relative earnings gain from education is not very strong. Even if it is posited that the middle-class child tends to be a better student and hence to learn more in the years he spends in school, it need not follow that his more rapid progress is due to his schooling as such. His growth is also supported by powerful positive home and neighborhood influences. The *relative* importance of formal schooling could be greater for the child living in more deprived circumstances.[10]

Recent empirical evidence collected by economists does tend to support the view that, at a given level of schooling, additional education will on the average be a better financial investment for middle-class than for lower-class youth. But these findings are much too tentative to be regarded as more than preliminary judgments or "guesstimates." They do not show that class *as such* importantly affects the rate of return (possibly because no accurate measure of social class has yet been developed). But this work does afford some very preliminary evidence that the return to education may be less for the less able[11] and for blacks. Given the strong positive correlation between measured ability and social class, and given the generally lower class status of blacks, a lower rate of return to the education of these two groups would imply that education returns are smaller for the lower class even if no further class effect was observed when the ability and race factors are taken into account.

The empirical evidence of a racial difference in the financial rate of return to education is partly based on a number of studies in which blacks and whites were studied separately. Because of differences in statistical methodology these studies are not strictly comparable. However, several studies that used data on both blacks and whites (and hence employed the same econometric technique to analyze the earnings of both groups) have also found smaller education returns for the former. Thus, Becker obtained a rate of return of 14 percent for the college education of white males and 8 to 12 percent for nonwhite males. Higher returns to the schooling of whites have also been found by several other investigators.[12]

Table 12 presents preliminary results of a study that affords a comparison of the effects of *both* ability and race on earnings. These results, based on data for white and black males in their thirties, demonstrate a positive relationship between both ability and race and the earnings return to education. Low-ability blacks had an estimated 3 to 9 percent return to their schooling in comparison with a 7 to 13 percent return to schooling for high-ability whites.[13]

The majority of economists doing research in this area would probably agree with this assessment: that the financial return to lower-class education—or at least the return of the less able and the blacks—though significant, is less than that obtained by the middle-class or average American. Several, however, have a different interpretation. At least one economist, Welch, argues that improvements in the quality of public education offered blacks since the 1954 Supreme Court decision have raised the earnings potential of better-educated *young* blacks to the point where their schooling return exceeds that of young whites.[14] Similarly, Chiswick maintains that the rate of return to the education of less able youths is now quite high. He obtains a 12 percent figure for a group of young males rejected by the armed forces for intellectual deficiency.[15]

TABLE 12. EARNINGS RETURNS TO EDUCATION BY ABILITY AND RACE

	Whites	Blacks
High ability	7–13%	4–10%
Medium ability	5–11	4–10
Low ability	4–10	3–9

Source: The Coleman–Rossi Continuous Life Histories Study. See John D. Owen, "Ability, Race, and the Earnings Return to Education," mimeographed (Baltimore, 1971).

On the other hand, some writers still argue that the educational reforms of the past twenty years have been a dismal failure—that, while education appears to improve the earnings of the average youth, it has very little if any positive effect on those of the lower class.[16]

Economists obviously need to do additional empirical work to determine to what extent, if any, the majority view—that schooling for the lower class is productive but less so than it is for the middle class—requires modification. But however this statistical controversy is resolved, when one considers the combined effect of *all* the factors determining the private demand for schooling it is easy to understand why it is such a powerful force for inequality in education. The financial resources of the middle class, their greater demand for the consumption benefits of education, and their resistance to the downward mobility their children would suffer if they did not attain a high education level complement a probable tendency for the financial rate of return to their education to exceed that of the lower class. The overall result is a definite expected class bias in private education demands—an expectation that is fully supported by the statistics of class differences among families in educational investment.

This analysis of the causation of unequal schooling opportunities is incomplete in one very important respect. We must still ask *why* our society has permitted such a large role to be given to private demands in determining the distribution of educational resources, while intervening, through government regulations and subsidies, to ensure that the total *amount* allocated to education is much larger than the level dictated by private concerns. The next several chapters carry the discussion of schooling inequalities a step further by considering whether the dominant position of private demands in some sense reflects the interests of the larger American society or at least advances the interests of important groups in an unequal distribution of schooling opportunities.

6

The economic benefits
of lower-class education
in the welfare state

THE SOCIAL DEMAND FOR
EDUCATION
Neither the sharp class differences in quality of education, described in
chapters 2 to 4, nor the determining influence of private demands in generating this inequality, described in chapter 5, can now be regarded as in
the best interest of American society. This and the two succeeding chapters will argue that the maintenance of educational inequality hinders the
pursuit of a number of widely accepted social goals, including economic
growth and the improvement of the quality of our political life. Inequality
in educational opportunity and the institutions that support it may once
have served such social requirements well enough—at least, a rather conservative interpretation of these requirements, which emphasized the need
for economic growth over the demand for improving the quality of our
political democracy, was probably advanced fairly well by the traditional
system. But the thesis of these chapters is that as a result of recent social
changes the public interest, even in this conservative interpretation, would
be advanced by a reduction in educational inequality.

However, an optimal distribution of educational resources will not result from any laissez faire policy or from one that simply subsidizes the
private demand for education. Rather it will require an explicitly egalitarian government education policy. The root of the problem here is that
the social demand for education does not equal the sum of private or individual demands. Of course there is an overlap between the two types of
demand for schooling. For example, increasing the growth of national income through investment in education is a widely accepted social goal,
yet a higher national income also makes it possible for millions to increase
their private consumption of goods and services. There is, however, no
simple, one-for-one relationship between social contribution and private
reward. The social value of an individual's education typically exceeds his
private gain from it. The avant-garde painter, the poorly paid teacher, and
the scientist engaged in basic research provide obvious examples of the
educated man whose private earnings fall far short of rewarding his social
contribution. But better education for the average man also yields economic, political, and other benefits to society in excess of those captured
by the individual. Hence economists from the time of Adam Smith[1] have

recognized that schooling deserves financial support from the state. If education is not offered at subsidized rates, they reason, many people will not invest adequately in their own schooling and society will be the worse for it.

Yet this concern over general support for education has been extended in only a limited way to its *distribution*. The political and economic well-being of a modern industrial society, it is agreed, requires that illiteracy be abolished and basic education extended to all. But no real consensus exists on further reductions in schooling inequality.

It will be argued here that the effort to equalize should now be directed to a much higher average level of educational investment. Because of the dramatic social changes of the past decade, the pursuit of such generally agreed-on goals as the promotion of economic growth and the improvement of the quality of our political decision-making (discussed in chapter 7) now requires a reduction in educational inequality through further upgrading of lower-class educational levels.

It will also be argued that a more egalitarian education policy is now likely to bring net gains even to the "taxpayers"—that is, to those non-lower-class citizens who must provide the subsidy for the education of the poor. A very conservative view of the interest of society would be that a gain in total social output is not an unmixed blessing if there is a substantial group that loses from a policy even though these losses add up to a smaller sum than the total gains to some other groups. The fact that *both* donors and recipients are net gainers means that social welfare can conservatively be regarded as likely to gain from a more democratic education policy, since there is no identifiable group of "losers."[2] This point may have considerable political relevance as well as interest to economists concerned with the abstract measurement of social welfare, since the inclusion of the large, politically dominant taxpayer group obviously could be a crucial political factor in developing an effective consensus in favor of increasing educational opportunities for the poor.

ECONOMIC BENEFITS OF LOWER-CLASS EDUCATION UNDER PRE-WELFARE STATE CONDITIONS

In our developing welfare state, a substantial expansion of the educational opportunities of the lower class would increase economic growth and yield net benefits to both taxpayers and graduates. Yet neither of these statements could have been made (at least with very much confidence) under pre–welfare state conditions.

The contribution of a better-educated labor force to national economic growth is well known. For example, Denison estimates that about one-half of the *total* increase in productivity per man-hour in the United States in recent decades has resulted from schooling gains by the labor force.[3] This is in addition to some further gains that may have accrued because of technological innovations contributed by this better-educated workforce but not captured by the conventional measurements.

But increasing the educational level of the population also imposes costs that may inhibit economic growth. Educational and other social expenditures can be thought of as taking place at the expense of either consumption or physical capital investment. The latter is usually considered the more sensible alternative because even if an educational expenditure is in fact financed by a reduction in consumption, the same sacrifice may yield a still greater increase in economic growth if used for an *alternative* investment in physical capital. Under this assumption the simple economic growth argument for spending on education is no longer so obvious. The net effect will depend on the productivity of the investment in education relative to that of investments in physical capital.

The conventional measure of an investment's productivity is its rate of return. The rate used for a social analysis differs from the private rate-of-return calculation in that the expenditures of the state and the student subsidies by private institutions must be included as costs. As a result a somewhat lower yield is calculated.

Empirical estimates of the average rates of return to higher education and to physical capital indicate that the two may be roughly competitive. At least one can say that there is sufficient controversy over the correct measure of each to make it difficult to find convincing evidence that one rate exceeds the other. But many estimates of the rate of return to lower-class and middle-class education have found a *lower* yield for the former at the same level of schooling (see the presentation of the "majority view" in chapter 5). Thus it would be very difficult to maintain on the basis of the simple rate-of-return argument that economic growth would be advanced by raising the poor to the educational level of the middle class if this were to be accomplished by transferring resources either from expenditures on middle-class education or from investment in physical capital.

Criticisms of the Rate-of-Return Criterion

Moreover, many would argue that the observed rate of return to education, especially to the schooling of the poor, actually overstates the return to society, thus affording further reason for not investing in lower-class education. These critics maintain that in a capitalist society the true economic value of different types of labor corresponds poorly to the financial values of the labor market, which are used to estimate the earnings rate of return. If they are correct, the economic argument for schooling for the poor is weak even under welfare state conditions. It is very difficult, however, to assess the effect of this type of criticism on our problem.[4]

Of course it is true that earnings differences often do not measure real differences in social productivity. For example, an ambitious young janitor may save his money until he can go to college. At the end of four years he joins an advertising firm and spends his life writing copy for cigarettes and other products. Society has lost a good janitor, but it is not clear what of positive value, if anything, it has obtained. Here the calculated private earnings rate of return obviously overestimates the gain in social productivity. But similar distortions operate to underestimate the social return to education, for the poorly educated also enter parasitical, hustling occupations. For example, it has been estimated that there are now literally hundreds of thousands of persons employed in prostitution, gambling, and the narcotics traffic in the ghettos of one city, New York. And of course there are low-paid but productive occupations, such as teaching, that employ college graduates. Hence it is hard to discount the social benefit of education on such general grounds.

More pertinent is the currently popular criticism that lower-class education is often relatively more successful in developing good work habits— or at least those that are regarded as desirable in our capitalist system— than it is in increasing skill levels.[5] However, the force of this criticism rests upon essentially philosophical grounds—that a rebellious or lazy "wage slave" is a freer man than one who is punctual, hard-working, willing to take responsibility, and above stealing from his employer. Whatever our attitude toward the moral and social value of a personal rejection of the work ethic, it is hard to controvert the view that, given our capitalist institutions, economic growth is advanced by the development of what employers regard as good work habits. (Cf. the discussion on pages 97–99 below.)

In a similar vein, other critics have argued that much of lower-class education makes the graduate more socially acceptable to his employer and to his fellow employees but has little bearing on his productive skills. But again, given the existing social relations of capitalism, the acquisition of productive skills is not economically useful if the graduate is barred by prejudice from using them. If skill training is accompanied by other schooling designed to lower the social barriers that would otherwise prevent the trainee from utilizing his skills, it follows that the resulting de facto increase in his productivity and earnings can still be regarded as a result of both types of education. This is so even if the supplementary training is in dress, speech, and other middle-class social appurtenances irrelevant to the technical performance of his craft. Admittedly, however, the same productivity gain could presumably be obtained much more cheaply by society if employers and their customers would overlook the social graces and allow schools to concentrate on increasing technical skill levels and good work habits.

Not all criticism of the private rate-of-return measure discounts the social value of education. Some economists have argued that the observed rate of return to education underestimates the social return because of the positive correlation of the education of a nation's labor force and the rate of technical progress it enjoys, a benefit not fully captured by the conventional calculation. But this analysis does not provide a strong argument for equality of educational opportunity. These technological benefits would be obtained by investing in middle-class as well as lower-class education. Moreover, investments in physical capital are also thought to make an important contribution in stimulating technical change. Hence, in the absence of adequate empirical evidence on the relative size of these different effects, the technical change argument cannot be used to alter the *ranking* of the social gains to be obtained from investments in people and machines.

Thus, while these criticisms indicate that the earnings rate of return to education is not a very accurate measure of its economic productivity, they do not offer a convincing argument that the rather low estimated rate of return from lower-class education is systematically biased either upward or downward. They clearly do not support the argument that increasing expenditures on lower-class schooling to raise them to the middle-class level would advance economic growth.

The simple rate-of-return argument does, however, point to two areas where some increase in lower-class opportunities would foster growth. First, there are many children of the poor who compare favorably with the middle class in motivation and intellectual capacity despite cultural deprivation and the alleged class biases in the tests used to measure attitudes and intelligence. These children typically do well in school and as adults profit economically from their education. In other words, they receive a high financial rate of return to their schooling. Yet some of these talented young people do not pursue their studies because of economic difficulties. Scholarships, loans, and other assistance for this group would obviously be expected to advance economic growth.

Second, there is a similarly persuasive argument for encouraging the average lower-class child to finish high school. The average rate of return to completing high school is much higher than that to college. Yet many poor people drop out, partly for economic reasons. Thus there is a clear economic rationale for helping the poor to finish their secondary education even if it were felt that college training for them were not economically worthwhile.

But apart from these two cases, the simple rate-of-return evidence does not provide an obvious economic argument for the sharp reorganization of educational priorities that would be required for full equality of educational opportunity.

RESULTS OF LOWER-CLASS
EDUCATION IN THE WELFARE
STATE

As a result of basic social and economic changes over the past decades in the treatment afforded the poor in the United States, the simple rate-of-return analysis of the economic benefits of lower-class education is out of date. When account is taken of these new conditions in a more appropriate analytical framework it becomes clear that the traditional system of inferior education for the poor is no longer adequate as a growth strategy.

This new environment—the developing American welfare state—has two characteristics that are of key importance in evaluating lower-class educational opportunities: a welfare system that commits the federal government to support the living standards of the poor at ever higher levels, and a structure of minimum wages that sets a relatively high floor under the price of labor.

Development of the Welfare State

The new structure has its origins in the New Deal period, although it has only become fully articulated during the past decade, especially in the years of President Lyndon B. Johnson's "Great Society" legislation. In 1962 Michael Harrington could still write with some accuracy:

> The [American] welfare state was designed during that great burst of social creativity that took place in the 1930's. . . . [I]ts structure corresponds to the needs of those who played the most important role in building it: the middle third [the upper working class], the organized workers, the forces of urban liberalism, and so on. . . . The poor get less out of the welfare state than any other group in America.[6]

Harrington is correct in his assessment of the New Deal insofar as he judges by the original level of funding of the different programs, examines carefully which groups of workers were actually covered in the pioneering legislation of the thirties, and so forth. But the origins of the present structure of benefits and controls, which now do directly affect the lower class (and hence our analysis of lower-class education), can be found in these New Deal reforms even though subsequent amendment was usually required to expand them to the point where they had a more important effect on the "lower third."

For example, the Fair Labor Standards Act of 1938 set a minimum wage for only 11 million workers, excluding millions of low-paid workers in retail trade and in the service sector. But subsequent legislation steadily increased coverage so that by 1966 43 million workers were covered. At the same time, the impact of the law on those covered has also been increased by subsequent legislation: the 1938 minimum of 25 cents an hour was 40 percent of the average manufacturing wage in that year, but the $1.60 figure set by Congress in the mid-sixties was 54 percent of the contemporary average.[7]

Similarly, while the New Deal legislation encouraged an immediate rise in trade union membership, its impact on the lower class has been more gradual. But it has had an effect. For example, black workers, largely excluded from the craft-dominated labor movement before the founding of the CIO in the mid-thirties, are now actually somewhat *more* likely to be union members than whites.[8] This is partly because blacks have entered traditionally unionized occupations as the whites moved on to the expanding white collar sector and partly because the unions did make some effort to organize the more poorly paid occupations, especially in the public and the private nonprofit sectors.

The origins of the present Aid to Families of Dependent Children and other federal welfare programs also can be found in the measures taken to relieve the economic distress of the thirties (before the New Deal, the destitute had recourse to local poor relief and private charity, or they starved). The New Deal federal welfare relief measures were primarily designed to help the temporarily unemployed "average" American rather than to put a permanent floor under the consumption levels of the poor. As the unemployment level receded in the late thirties, benefits to the remaining poor were cut sharply, although the continuing program was, of course, a significant change from the laissez faire federal policy of the pre-Depression period. Hence one can identify a second distinct break in policy in the middle and late sixties when, in response to social unrest, the welfare rolls were opened to additional millions of the lower class. Per family payments increased significantly in a seven-year period and so qualitatively changed the nature of our economic commitment to the poor.[9]

Effects on Optimal Education Policy

These welfare state innovations have had three economic effects that require a reevaluation of the conventional wisdom that the taxpayers' interest lies in lower education taxes and of the standard rate-of-return analysis of the effect of increased lower-class education on economic growth. First, largely as a result of liberalization in the administration of the AFDC and other welfare programs, there has been a massive increase in the subsidy cost of poverty for the rest of society. In a very obvious sense, the economic costs of low earning capacities are now shared by all. Second, increasingly high legal and union minimum wages now reduce the *demand* for low-skilled workers. Unless their productivity is somehow increased to match these higher minima, many workers have difficulty in finding employment for their labor services, which are then lost to society. Third, the provision of alternative means of support through the liberalized

AFDC program (or, a fortiori, through the passage of the generous negative income tax program favored by many) also reduces the financial work incentive of the low-skilled and so tends to diminish the *supply* of labor services offered by the poorly educated workers.

As a result of these three economic changes, it is now very likely that a long-run commitment to educating the poor serves both to increase total economic growth and to advance the economic interest of the taxpayers (by increasing their after-tax income) who provide the funds for both welfare and education programs.

This argument can be made more concisely if a commitment to increase the educational level of the poor is described quantitatively. A Poverty-Reducing Education Policy (hereafter abbreviated as PREP) can be defined as a long-run commitment either to provide a given additional number of years of schooling, or to improve the quality of educational personnel per student by a specified amount for a given fraction of the poverty population. An example of a PREP would be a long-term commitment to increase by two years the education of all (or, say, one-half) of the poverty group youth and to maintain this increase with each successive generation of teenagers.

INCOME MAINTENANCE AND THE
ECONOMICS OF A PREP

The recent dramatic increase in the subsidy cost of poverty (the first of the three social changes adduced above) has obvious and important results for the evaluation of a PREP.

Since the welfare state has made a commitment to provide a government subsidy to support the living standards of the poor—that is, to make up the difference between lower-class earnings and the minimum consumption standards—it is now very much in the state's interest to train young people so that as adults they can attain this minimum consumption level on their own. In effect, government subsidies to the education of lower-class children can, in the long run, be regarded partly as a substitute for welfare or other income maintenance subsidies. To the extent that the children of the poor can be integrated into the economy through education, the welfare bill in subsequent years will be reduced.

Of course, not all the welfare cost reduction can be passed along directly as a tax cut. A long-run commitment to lower-class education requires that funds be set aside for improved schooling for each successive generation of poor youths. But insofar as the continuing flow of fiscal benefits in the form of a reduction in welfare expenditures exceeds the recurring reinvestment costs of the PREP, a permanent cut in the tax rate is possible. It will be argued here that, in the welfare state conditions developing in the United States, these reinvestment needs will be met even if the rate of return to investments in the education of the poor is as little as 3 or 4 percent, the long-term national economic growth rate. Since most studies of this rate of return for the poor obtain a result of at least this size, a solid argument is afforded for the taxpayer's fiscal interest in lower-class education.

The new income maintenance commitment will not only reverse the conventional wisdom about the taxpayer interest in lower education taxes but also provide the basis for using the same generous criterion for judging the effects of investments in lower-class education on economic growth —that its rate of return exceed the national growth rate. Hence it can now be argued that increasing the level of expenditures on the education of lower-class children would be likely to advance, not retard, economic growth. Moreover, this conclusion holds even if the government's expenditure on lower-class education were paid for by a tax that did not affect consumption but rather was levied strictly on investments in physical capital. With such a tax, each dollar of expenditure on education investment by the government would be matched by an equal reduction in private investment in physical capital. The tax would be reduced only insofar as subsequent declines in welfare costs permit the financing of the future needs of the education program without a higher tax.[10]

Now physical capital is said by some economists to yield 10 to 20 percent, and human capital investments in the lower class may return only a fraction of this rate. Yet a tax on the former to subsidize the latter could advance economic growth. The basic explanation for this apparently paradoxical result is that the surtax on physical capital would be only temporary. If in the long run the program were successful and the tax rate reduced, then the accumulation of physical capital could be resumed at an accelerated rate. Not only would there be a better-educated labor force to supply profits and production, but the total welfare and education tax on these profits would be reduced, allowing a higher rate of reinvestment in physical capital. The resulting eventual increase in physical capital stock accumulation, plus the permanently enhanced labor supply quality, would yield a higher long-run level of economic growth, since this growth is a function of the labor supply, the *rate* of investment in physical capital, and the rate of technical change.

In effect, reducing the expenses of the welfare state through better education for the lower class would shift the fiscal cost of a PREP from investment in physical capital (or, for that matter, in the taxpayers' consumption) to reductions in welfare spending. After an initial period in which a tax would be levied, a "revolving fund" would be established, with "payments" coming in the form of reduced welfare costs and outlays going to lower-class education. If the plan were financially successful, the "fund" would eliminate the need for continuing the higher tax rate and could even reduce taxes, encouraging a higher rate of investment in physical capital.

Under welfare state conditions, the plan would be fiscally successful if it yielded a rate of return large enough to allow this "revolving fund" to expand at the same rate as the economy. In comparison, the rate of return to physical capital necessary for the latter to grow at this rate[11] is much higher, since only a fraction of net profits is reinvested, with much of the remainder going to stockholders' consumption, government taxes for military spending, and the like.

Threshold for a Welfare State Evaluation of Education

Of course, the income maintenance characteristics of the welfare state must be developed to a certain minimum level for this generous criterion to be applicable to investments in lower-class education. This requirement would be met (and, it will be argued below, met by a substantial margin) if two conditions were satisfied. First, the proportion of the PREP graduate's education-based earnings gain that returns to the state as a reduction in welfare and other poverty costs must be at least as large as the proportion of education costs (including the opportunity costs of forgone earnings) paid by the rest of society to underwrite his additional schooling. If this condition were not fully satisfied, a larger total earnings return from lower-class education would be required for the welfare tax reduction to be sufficiently great to meet the education cost.

Since a PREP is a long-term program, a second condition must be specified: welfare costs must rise at least at the same rate as national income and the education costs of the program. If welfare costs were forecast to be constant, a PREP would have but limited value in a growing economy even if a static cross-sectional analysis appeared to justify the program.

If these welfare state conditions were met, a PREP with a 3 to 4 percent earnings rate of return would yield a sufficiently large stream of welfare cost reductions to provide for the investment costs of schooling the next generation. If more than this were earned, a fiscal surplus would permit a reduction in taxes and a further stimulus to economic growth.

The empirical evidence strongly suggests that the establishment of a PREP now could indeed be expected to lead to a long-term reduction in the total burden of welfare and education expenditures for the taxpayer. This conclusion follows from either of two methods of analysis. One is a direct study of the relationship between educational attainment and welfare incidence. This is the more practical method, as we shall see, if one believes that the present welfare system will be maintained. The other is the indirect calculation described in the preceding sections, which uses the earnings payoff to lower-class education together with its feedback to poverty cost reductions under our welfare state conditions. This is the more practical method if passage of a negative income tax is expected during the lifetime of today's students.

The Growth of Welfare and Education Costs

It is useful to begin the empirical study with the conditions on the rate of change of education and welfare costs. It is an easy point to make, since a forecast of long-term increases in welfare costs is well supported by the historical record. But it is also necessary for the argument under both the direct and the indirect methods.

Failure to take account of the secular increase in welfare costs has led a number of investigators to underestimate the fiscal gains from lower-class education. Investments in schooling have a period of social and economic payoff extending over the lifespan of the graduates—perhaps fifty years or more for each cohort of students. Hence to estimate the total welfare savings from educating a lower-class youth, one must forecast the future level of the welfare payments the youth will *not* require, because of his education, over an extended period. In the absence of some reasonable forecast it has been common simply to extrapolate the schedule of welfare benefits at their current levels.[12] This method yields a hopelessly biased result. Once the notion is accepted that the current "poverty line" will be retained, it is almost inevitable that education will appear to be an inferior method for dealing with the welfare problem.

The argument is simple. A large proportion of the lower class now depends on poor relief to maintain its living standards. But if real wages continue to increase at about 2 percent per annum, this proportion will become quite small within a generation. Under the constant poverty line assumption this effect appears to be a simple algebraic result of the "compound interest" principle of economic growth. Moreover, those few whose family earnings would fall below this minimum would probably be mentally, physically, or emotionally handicapped people for whom education might not be economically efficient. Thus, so the argument goes, with higher real prices of labor expected to rule throughout the economy in, say, twenty or thirty years, there would be relatively little welfare incidence that could legitimately be attributed to inferior educational attainment. Under these circumstances, it would seem much cheaper to provide a dole to the diminishing minority of losers in an ever more affluent society than to invest heavily now in the education of the entire lower class. For most of the poor each decade would bring an increase in living standards as the wage rate for unskilled labor increased, even if no special effort was made to assist them. Moreover, the same conclusion is reached with any suitable constant poverty line. If the standard is more generous than the present one—if, for example, either the Democratic Party's $4,000 or the National Welfare Rights Organization's $6,500 minimum income for a family of four is adopted—it simply takes somewhat longer for the compound interest law apparently to reduce the problem of substandard earnings to relatively minor proportions.

The notion of a constant poverty line has obvious appeal to those who wish to set a target for the elimination of the *physical* suffering of the poor (although some observers insist that the psychological and social distress of the poor will grow when the average living standard increases and expectations rise in consequence unless the incomes of the poor increase at the same time).[13] The historical record, however, disproves the hypothesis that Americans are in fact committed to a constant poverty line. Welfare payments have not only increased but have actually risen more rapidly than average income or the average wage. The ratio of payments per family under the Aid to Families of Dependent Children program (the largest single program for providing cash welfare benefits) to average spendable earnings of employees in private nonagricultural employment rose from 32 percent in 1950 to 42 percent in 1970 despite a rapid increase in real wages. Furthermore, the proportion of the total population that was supported by this program increased from 1.5 to 4.7 percent in the same period, largely because of a less restrictive attitude toward eligibility. As a result of these two factors, AFDC payments per capita rose at 7 percent per annum, in constant dollars, a much faster rate of increase than the 2.3 percent growth rate obtained in real disposable income per capita.[14]

This trend has continued in the past three years. While the federal government now forecasts that "outlays for the AFDC program are expected to begin levelling off," reflecting "management reforms begun in 1973 to assure that welfare recipients receive only the benefits to which they are entitled," it still projects a level of expenditure that is almost *60 percent* above the 1970 level.[15] Moreover, a recent study by the Joint Economic Committee of the U.S. Congress points out that AFDC and other cash welfare payments are only a part of the fiscal cost of income maintenance. A very rapid rise in the late sixties and early seventies in payments in kind has introduced a new momentum into the growth rate of subsidies for the poor. These noncash benefits were projected to rise twice as fast as AFDC in the 1972–74 period. The total cash value of the federal contribution to three of these in-kind benefits—medical care, food subsidies (food stamps, surplus foods, and school lunches), and subsidized housing (largely public housing)—already is almost two and one-half times as great as is the federal outlay for the much more publicized program of AFDC benefits.[16]

Of course, a conservative administration could stem the increase in payments in kind as well as put a ceiling on cash outlays for income maintenance, at least temporarily. But the data for the past twenty-five years do appear to indicate a long-term trend toward higher levels of welfare payments.

This secular growth in welfare benefits challenges the constant poverty line idea as a guide to future welfare costs. It appears rather to support the social theories of those who see the increase in the social minimum wage set by an advancing capitalist society as an outcome of a political and economic process that raises the minimum "target," or socially acceptable minimum consumption level, at least as rapidly as the average wage (more rapidly, they would argue, since they believe that affluence is likely to make the electorate more generous to the less fortunate among them).[17] On that reasoning, a forecast of a constant long-term ratio of welfare expenditures to national income is conservative, inasmuch as it implies that the trend toward a narrowing of the relative gap between the minimum and average standards of living will cease. But even if one makes this conservative prediction, a far more positive evaluation of the long-run fiscal and economic benefits of a PREP is obtained than if a constant poverty line is assumed.

Of course the costs of education have also risen in the long run, although at a rate less than that of welfare expenditures. The expense of training each new age cohort of lower-class youths is rising, reducing somewhat the net tax gain from a PREP. Hence a reasonable if somewhat conservative forecast is that the reinvestment costs of the PREP will rise at the same rate as the wage bill or the national income, the rate assumed for the poverty reduction benefits.

Economic analysis would predict that costs per student will increase over time quite apart from any general inflation. Education is a very labor-intensive activity, and the cost of the time of students, teachers, and others working in this field can reasonably be expected to rise at about the same rate as the average wage of labor—that is, to exceed the general rate of inflation by the amount of secular growth in real wages. Hence, unless there is some unexpected technical revolution that permits a dramatic decline in the ratio of teachers to students, one should also anticipate secular increases in costs per student. Time series data confirm this expectation. The average expenditure per student in daily attendance in the public schools has risen, in constant dollars, by more than 4 percent per year in the past thirty years largely because the real salary per member of their instructional staffs more than doubled.[18] This rate of increase in per student cost is actually larger than the 2.6 percent rate of growth in real gross national product per capita in the same period. Hence, taking into account the population growth of the poverty group as well, it is more reasonable to forecast that educational costs will rise at the economic growth rate than to assume that they are static, as is often done.

Empirical Evidence of the Fiscal Effects

The argument that the nation's expanding welfare commitment implies that a Poverty-Reducing Education Policy will in the long run probably be at least self-financing can now be made in two ways. First, one might assume that during the lifetime of today's students the present cumbersome welfare system will be replaced by a rationalized system of income maintenance based on the negative income tax principle. Virtually all the plans for an NIT call for marginal tax rates on lower-class earnings of at least one-half (in other words, the government reduces its subsidy to the worker as the latter's earnings increase; in the most popular plans, the reduction is 50 to 70 cents for each dollar earned). Furthermore, since the income floor set by the plan can be expected, on the basis of our earlier discussion, to rise with national income, the earning "ceiling" beyond which the NIT's 50 percent tax rate would no longer apply would also be expected to increase with the average wage. Hence this high marginal tax rate could be considered to be a permanent condition for lower-class graduates.

Moreover, the official rate would undoubtedly be a gross underestimate of the state's share from lower-class earnings gains under an NIT since it is unlikely that all other poverty-related programs would be eliminated. For example, subsidized medical care would probably continue to be made available to the poor. Hence 50 percent would be a quite conservative figure.

But this one-half share implies that the proportion of education-based lower-class earnings gains received by the government would exceed the fraction of lower-class education costs paid by the "taxpayers." The state now generally pays 50 percent or so of education costs, at least at the upper secondary and college levels (see table 11 in chapter 5). Moreover, this figure overestimates the tax costs to the rest of society since the poor also pay local sales and property taxes and so contribute to the state's expenditure on their education.

Hence, if the forecast of a comprehensive NIT policy is accepted, the conditions for a welfare state analysis of education finance are clearly met. The earnings rates of return from lower-class education are generally at least 3 to 4 percent, the criterion under welfare state conditions. One can then conclude that if an NIT is likely to be adopted in the next decade or so, a PREP could be expected to succeed in reducing taxes and stimulating economic growth. This conclusion illustrates the indirect methods, mentioned above, of demonstrating the tax advantage of a PREP.

It is not necessary, however, to rely on this prediction of a reformed welfare policy. Much the same conclusion can be reached directly if retention of the present system is assumed (with the scale of benefits increasing with the average wage rate, as we have also assumed).

Cross-sectional data are available on the relationship between welfare incidence and educational attainment under the present system. In conjunction with our analysis of the growth trends in welfare and education costs, these data permit a direct calculation of the effect of lower-class education on the tax rate.

This direct method is quite simple. One compares the welfare reduction that would be obtained if all lower-class adults (or a stated percentage of them) had more education, with the current costs of giving that education to all lower-class children (or the same percentage of them). If the former exceeds the latter, a tax reduction is possible.

The validity of this interpretation depends on our second welfare state criterion—that is, our forecast that the growth rates of welfare and education costs will be the same. But the lower-class birth rate could fall, reducing the ratio of PREP children in school to adults on welfare. Or per case welfare payments could rise relative to per student education costs. In either case, the use of the current cross-sectional relationship between welfare payments and education costs would tend to underestimate the tax-reducing effect of a PREP. On the other hand, if the *constant* poverty line assumption were correct, this cross-sectional method would grossly overestimate the benefits of the PREP. If benefits per recipient did not increase with average per capita income, welfare dependence would become increasingly unattractive. Welfare incidence might decline as a result, reducing the magnitude of poverty costs. But even if welfare incidence were stable, so that both total welfare costs per capita and the reduction in these costs as a result of a PREP were fixed, the rising trend in the *education* costs of the program would eventually swamp its reduction in poverty costs, which would be constant, and so would require the continuance of a higher tax rate.

This direct method is more practical than the indirect, since under the present system—unlike the NIT—most benefits are paid to those who are not currently employed. As a result it is most difficult, in the absence of retrospective data on the lifetime family earnings of recipients, to measure accurately the relationship between earnings and incidence. But this measure is necessary under the indirect method, which first relates earnings to education, then poverty costs to earnings, to determine the education-poverty cost relationship.

Apart from its simplicity and practicality, this direct method has another advantage. Families that break up, especially large ones, are more likely to need and to obtain welfare assistance than others even when the earnings capacity of husband and wife are unchanged. Hence, insofar as education leads to better family planning or marital stability, poverty costs are reduced. Similarly, the so-called stigma effect, which has deterred many families from applying for public assistance, may be a greater disincentive for the better educated. The direct method captures all these education effects as well as those of increased earnings on welfare incidence.

Cross-sectional data relating welfare incidence to low educational attainment are available for a very large sample of recipients in the federal Aid to Families of Dependent Children program. This program now assists more than 11 million people, most of whom are members of fatherless families.

Unpublished survey data were obtained for a 1 percent sample of the AFDC program for 1969. Women recipients were classified by race, age, and educational attainment. The data for black women are more helpful than those for whites for inferring the effects of education on welfare incidence, since it is not possible to standardize the white data for social class here. There is wide dispersion in social class among whites, and there is also a high correlation between the social class of adults and the educational attainment of their children. It would therefore be difficult to infer empirically the separate effects of social class and education as such on welfare incidence for this group. Data for blacks, a largely lower-class, minority group, are less subject to these difficulties. Table 13 gives welfare incidence among black families by education of mothers in 1969.

The strong negative association between education and welfare incidence observed in the 1969 AFDC data is also found in a more detailed study of a sample of 1,390 black women thirty to forty-four years of age carried out in 1966. Moreover, the detail available in this second data source does enable us to standardize for social class. Part A of table 14, derived from these data, shows that when the socioeconomic level of the respondent's family background (as measured by her father's educational attainment) is held constant, the respondent's education continued to exert a strong welfare-reducing effect. In fact, it is approximately as large as that obtained when class background is ignored and the simple negative relationship is calculated between educational attainment and welfare incidence.

Further, the statistical estimates offered in the first two lines of Part D of table 14 show that the education effect retains its strength even when a longer list of background variables—the education of the respondent's father and mother and the social prestige of the occupations they pursued —is held constant.

Other results from this detailed study serve to illustrate the mechanisms that account for the negative education-welfare incidence relationship. Part B of table 14 shows that the proportion of black women with children but without a husband reported present declined markedly with the women's educational level, even when family background was held constant. An even more striking education effect is observed when one examines welfare incidence among the group of women with children but no father reported present. As expected, incidence was quite high here, reaching 40 percent or more among those respondents with less than high school education. But incidence fell sharply with education, even when the data are stan-

TABLE 13. PROPORTION OF BLACK FEMALE POPULATION RECEIVING U.S. AID TO FAMILIES OF DEPENDENT CHILDREN BENEFITS —1969

Age	Education (Years of School)			
	0–11	12	13–15	16+
20–24	22%	8%	2%	0%
25–29	22	8	5	0
30–34	25	8	5	0
35–44	14	7	4	0
45–54	6	2	2	0

Source: Unpublished worksheets of the National Center for Social Statistics.

TABLE 14. DETAILED ANALYSIS OF THE RELATIONSHIP BETWEEN WELFARE INCIDENCE AND EDUCATIONAL ATTAINMENT AMONG BLACK WOMEN

A. WELFARE INCIDENCE AMONG BLACK WOMEN 30–44 YEARS OF AGE
(PERCENT RECEIVING BENEFITS IN BODY OF TABLE)

Educational Attainment of Her Father (Years of Schooling)	Educational Attainment of Respondent (Years of Schooling)			
	Less than 12	12	13–15	16 and over
8 or less	18	11	8	0
9–11	18	9	0	0
12 or more	19	8	0	0
All women in sample	18	11	5	0

B. PERCENT OF BLACK WOMEN 30–44 YEARS OF AGE WITH CHILDREN PRESENT
BUT NO FATHER REPORTED PRESENT

Educational Attainment of Her Father (Years of Schooling)	Educational Attainment of Respondent (Years of Schooling)		
	Less than 12	12–15	16 and over
Less than 12	30	25	23
12 or more	33	32	12
All women in sample	29	26	19

C. WELFARE INCIDENCE AMONG BLACK WOMEN 30–44 YEARS OF AGE WITH
CHILDREN PRESENT BUT NO FATHER REPORTED PRESENT (PERCENT
RECEIVING BENEFITS IN BODY OF TABLE)

Educational Attainment of Her Father (Years of Schooling)	Educational Attainment of Respondent (Years of Schooling)			
	Less than 12	12	13–15	16 and over
8 or less	42	38	22	0
9–11	40	29	0	0
12 or more	40	15	0	0
All women in sample	39	30	17	0

Source: Calculated from the NBER tape of the 1967 National Longitudinal Survey of Work Experience for Women 30–44 (U.S. Department of Commerce, Bureau of the Census).

TABLE 14 (Continued)

D. STATISTICAL ESTIMATES OF THE EFFECT OF EDUCATION ON WELFARE INCIDENCE

Women Studied	Education Effect*	Variables Held Constant
All in the sample	−1.33†	Respondent's residence in metropolitan area, father's education, mother's education, father's occupational prestige, mother's occupational prestige.
All in the sample	−1.57†	Residence in metropolitan area.
Women with children present but no father present	−1.16†	Age, father's education, mother's education, father's occupational prestige, mother's occupational prestige.

* Education effect is an elasticity calculated at the means of the variables. It measures the percentage decline in welfare incidence per 1 percent increase in the respondent's educational attainment.

† The t ratios obtained for the education effects were −5.00, −4.00, and −2.62 for the first, second, and third equations, respectively. The first two equations were estimated by the logit method; the third was estimated by multiple regression. (The first two were also estimated by multiple regression. Very similar results were obtained: education effects of 1.46 and 1.50, and t ratios of 4.04 and 3.06 for the first and second equations, respectively.) The correlation coefficients obtained by multiple regression in the three equations were, respectively, .19, .20, and .34.

dardized for social class background, dropping to almost zero for those with a college degree.

The statistical estimate presented in the third line of Part D of table 14 shows a large education effect on welfare incidence, even when the educational attainment and the occupational prestige of both of the respondent's parents are held constant. Economic explanations of this relationship are suggested by the findings in this detailed sample study that better-educated black women enjoyed better earnings opportunities than women with less schooling and that they were more likely to be able to use the courts successfully to obtain financial support from their former husbands. Among those with children but no husband present, 38 percent of those with some college education reported that they were receiving alimony or child support payments, in comparison with 21 percent of all those with less education and only 16 percent of those with less than elementary school education. Moreover, within this group of mothers with children but with no father present, the *number* of children present declined with the mother's educational attainment, while the probability of her being on welfare rose with the number of children present, thus suggesting another way in which education reduced welfare incidence.[19] These results suggest that the reduction in welfare incidence among better-educated black women observed in the 1969 AFDC study reflects a meaningful rather than a spurious statistical relationship.

Such data on the relationships between welfare incidence and educational attainment, together with data on the number of black women in each age and education category[20] and our assumption of equal welfare and education cost growth rates, enable us to calculate the welfare cost portion of the poverty-cost-reducing effects of an upgrading of the black education distribution. The most dramatic gains are obtained here if a PREP is assumed to improve schooling levels at certain key points in the distribution. For example, simply using the PREP to eliminate high school dropouts obtains a maximum welfare reduction for the increment in schooling. But this method clearly overestimates the expected gain. It would be very difficult to eliminate *all* high school dropouts without a very expensive program. Moreover, it is unlikely that the high school diploma will retain its present effectiveness over the lifetime of the present generation of students. If current trends continue, twenty years hence some higher level of education may well be required for the sharp drop in incidence now associated with high school completion. Hence a more conservative but reliable estimate of welfare savings can be obtained if each group of blacks is simply assumed to be given some additional amount of schooling. Calculations based on the larger 1969 sample data indicate that if schooling levels of black women in each education-age subgroup were increased by just two years, a 41 percent reduction in AFDC incidence among blacks would have been obtained.[21]

When this welfare reduction gain is converted into a dollar saving and is compared with the number of children of school age in this category, an estimate of $1,200 per child is obtained. This is the maximum figure that could have been spent per year to encourage these students to remain in school and still reduce total subsidy costs of the AFDC program as of 1969.

In a recent study for the U.S. Congress, Henry Levin found that the fiscal benefits to the nation of eliminating high school dropouts that would accrue from a reduction in AFDC incidence were equaled by those expected from the total of education-based savings from three other welfare programs—medical assistance, general assistance, and unemployment insurance. An equal savings would also result, he argued, from cuts in the *fiscal* costs of crime (law enforcement and judicial outlays) alone, so that the AFDC benefits would at most represent, in Levin's reckoning, only one-third of the total fiscal gain to the state.[22] Levin, moreover, omitted the fiscal costs of food distribution and public housing for the poor, which were emphasized in the more recent Joint Economic Committee study cited earlier. These results indicate the extent to which $1,200 would underestimate the fiscal benefit.

But the government spent much less than $1,200 (or $3,600 or more) per child on the education of blacks in 1969. The figure was only $900 for the *average* child,[23] and there is considerable empirical evidence (some of which was presented in chapters 2 and 3 above) that the typical school system spends less on blacks than on whites. Moreover, this figure overestimates the cost to the rest of society, since blacks also pay taxes. In fact, since the primary basis for educational expenditures is regressive local taxes, they pay a significant proportion of this cost despite their low average income. Hence the gap between actual state expenditures on a black child and black school taxes paid per black child is probably much less than $900.

Thus this direct evaluation gives considerable support to the view that a long-run tax reduction could result from a PREP that encouraged these children to stay in school. It also suggests that, given the relatively low earnings payoff from education for blacks, the proportion of that gain which would effectively return to the state as a reduction in poverty costs would be quite large indeed—easily larger than that required to meet our condition for a welfare state.

These empirical calculations can only be regarded as providing a tentative estimate of the tax gains from a PREP. Apart from the problems of accurately measuring either the net reduction in welfare incidence associated with higher educational levels or the net cost of lower-class education to the rest of society, questions also arise about the assumptions underlying this cross-sectional analysis.

These assumptions generally give a downward bias to the empirical estimates. For example, constant birth rates are assumed here. Yet there has actually been a marked decline in the birth rate among both blacks and whites in the past several years. It is therefore likely that in the future the ratio of educable children to adults will be lower than it was in the 1960s. Relaxing this assumption reduces the expected cost of a PREP and hence increases its likely net fiscal benefit. A second conservative assumption used here is that there will be no further upward trend in the ratio of welfare costs to national income. This is probably appropriate for the short run, given the present concern over the recent jump in these costs. But it may well prove to be too conservative as a long-run projection of American social trends.

Effects on Wages of the Remaining Low-Skilled Workers

Moreover, there are several reasons to believe that this cross-sectional method of establishing the effects of a PREP would lead to a serious underestimate of the benefits no matter how refined the analysis or how accurate the forecast of future income maintenance policy. The cross-sectional method implicitly assumes that if the educational levels of the poor were raised, the incidence of welfare or other social costs would remain the same at each educational level. This is unlikely, however, if wage rates were raised and unemployment rates reduced at each of the lower educational levels. But these are probable results of a PREP.

A more democratic education policy would in the long run be expected to compress the wage structure. A PREP would tend to reduce the gap between the wages of the average and the poorly educated worker by reducing the supply of the less well educated and increasing the supply of those with average educational attainment. As a result, a PREP would not only alleviate poverty by giving some of the poor the education necessary to rise out of that condition, it would also benefit the remainder by making their unskilled labor more scarce and thus increasing its price.

Since income maintenance payments are geared to meet the gap between lower-class earnings and some consumption floor, this increase in lower-class earnings itself could reduce poverty costs significantly. The empirical importance of this factor would depend on how expensive it was for employers to substitute machinery and, perhaps, better-skilled workers for the diminished supply of low-skilled employees. If this cost were high, one would expect employers to be willing to compete for the remaining unskilled workers, raising their wages. Little is known empirically about the responsiveness of the wages of the unskilled to changes in their supply, but some hypothetical calculations (given in appendix 4) indicate that, under plausible assumptions, these indirect, wage-increasing savings could be quite large—easily as large again as the direct savings from reducing the number of the poor. The estimates, together with the unemployment rate analysis of the next section, imply that the calculations based on the cross-sectional analysis of welfare incidence statistics are a gross underestimate of the actual welfare reduction that could result from an upgrading of lower-class educational levels.

RISING MINIMUM WAGES AND
THE ECONOMIC BENEFITS
OF A PREP

A number of economists have long regarded rising minimum wages as a major cause of unemployment among marginal groups of workers. They see the policy as affecting the low-skilled in general but especially those with some special disability in the market place—the nonwhite or other minority group member, the resident of an industrially backward state or county, the housewife interested only in part-time or temporary employment, the older worker, the inexperienced teenager, and so forth.

They believe the increase in the minimum wage relative to the average over the past twenty years and the extension of minimum wage coverage in the same period are important factors reducing the demand for poorly educated, marginal workers and hence have led to a relative increase in their unemployment rate. Moreover, several empirical studies by economists have found a more specific cause-and-effect relationship between the well-intentioned effort to put a floor under the price of labor, and high unemployment rates for the low-skilled.[24]

Widespread unemployment among the low-skilled has an obvious significance for evaluating a PREP, since unemployment rates decline with increasing educational levels. Some measure of the effects of education on unemployment for adult workers (twenty years of age or more) is given in table 15. It compares the educational level of those among the unemployed who have been laid off or fired from their jobs with the schooling attainment of those who have quit their jobs and with that of the entire labor force. The "job losers" have almost a year and a half less education than the "job keepers," on the average.

This inverse relationship between schooling and unemployment rate alone requires a reevaluation of educational policy. This is so even if the poor employment prospects of the less-educated, marginal worker resulted altogether from other influences such as the rigidity of company hiring and wage policies, although minimum wage legislation does appear to be at least partly the cause. Whichever interpretation is adopted, this relationship indicates that cross-sectional estimates of the benefits from lower-class education both in increasing economic growth and in reducing poverty costs (such as those calculated in the preceding section) should be revised upward.

The conventional measurement of the rate of return to education captures some part of the employment benefit to the economy from lower-class education since it uses annual rather than hourly earnings estimates. When a worker is unemployed he does not earn income and his annual earnings are reduced. But this method underestimates the *social* gain in that it implicitly assumes that a reduction through education in the number of low-skilled will not reduce unemployment *rates* themselves.

The conventional measurement of the social costs of education is probably more seriously biased by this assumption than is the estimate of benefits. In fact, several economists have defended the assumption of a constant unemployment rate in measuring such benefits. They reason that since moderate adult unemployment typically exists at each educational level, an increment in education will most likely place the graduate in a market where there is still some unemployment (though probably a

TABLE 15. EFFECT OF EDUCATION ON UNEMPLOYMENT OF ADULT WORKERS

Category in Labor Force	Median Years of School Completed by Persons 20 Years Old and Over, 1968
Total civilian labor force (employed plus unemployed)	12.3
Job leavers	12.2
Job losers	10.9

Source: Manpower Report of the President, March 1970 (Washington: Government Printing Office).

lower level than that prevailing in the labor market he would have entered without the additional education).[25] Unemployment rates may increase in the market for graduates as a result of his entrance as well as decline in the market for low-skilled labor, which he leaves. Since it is not clear which effect would be the larger, these economists argue that a reasonable and simple compromise is to ignore both changes, assuming, in essence, that the two effects cancel each other.

The problem is quite different, however, in the measurement of the *cost* to society of educating lower-class youths, since schooling removes these youths from the labor market altogether. Because employers are reluctant to hire inexperienced and immature workers at the prevailing minimum wage, these lower-class youths now face truly startling unemployment rates. In 1971, while the average unemployment rate was 5.5 percent for the entire labor force and only 2.8 percent for married white males, it was *38 percent* for black males, sixteen to nineteen years old, living in urban, low-income areas, and was still over 30 percent for members of this group who lived in higher-income urban areas.[26] Under these circumstances it is more plausible to argue that a withdrawal of their labor would have little or no effect on total employment than to insist that there would be no reduction in the black teenage unemployment rate. But a constant (or new constant) employment assumption would imply a more positive evaluation of a PREP than is obtained by assuming a constant unemployment rate. If the *social* opportunity costs from forgone earnings of these lower-class groups are to be regarded as close to zero, because their place in the labor market is taken by others who would otherwise be unemployed, the total social costs of their education are much less than the estimate used in the conventional method. The data in table 9 indicate that private opportunity costs may constitute about one-half of the total cost of education in high school and college. This would mean that the conventional estimate of the social return from educating these lower-class youths could be as much as doubled if the opportunity cost of their time could be treated as having no value to society because of institutional barriers to hiring minority teenagers.

Another reason for upgrading the conventional calculation of the social rate of return to lower-class education is that such estimates are based on the current relationship between education and unemployment. If present labor market trends continue, as seems very likely, the poorly educated will face increasing difficulties in finding employment in the years ahead. This trend may result from a too-high rate of growth in the minimum wage, from technical or organizational changes in the economy, or, as some fear, from a simple irrational refusal to employ the labor of the less well educated. But whatever the cause, cross-sectional data based on current labor market conditions must underestimate the actual gain that society—or, for that matter, the graduate himself—can expect to gain from the education of a lower-class youth over his lifetime.

Finally, consideration of the low market demand for poorly educated labor also leads to an upward revision of the estimates of the *fiscal* gains from a PREP in reducing welfare and other poverty costs, which are based on a cross-sectional calculation. Unemployment imposes fiscal costs on the state not only during the period of the individual's idleness but for years afterward, since unemployment is a contributing factor to family breakups and hence to welfare dependency. Moreover, high unemployment among lower-class teenagers, and the resulting idleness and poverty, are widely believed to contribute to delinquency and related social ills, imposing further costs on the state. The reduction in youth unemployment rates obtained by keeping lower-class youths in school thus provides special fiscal gains. But calculations based on a current cross-sectional analysis underestimate the fiscal gains to society from reducing lower-class employment by an undetermined though probably important amount for the same reasons that the production gain is underestimated. An upgrading of educational levels should lower unemployment *rates*, and unemployment rates among the poorly educated should also increase over time, rendering present cross-sectional estimates obsolete.

EDUCATION AND WORK
INCENTIVES IN THE
WELFARE STATE

The development of a welfare state in the United States threatens to undermine work incentives, especially for its lower-class citizens. But since education helps to shape individual choice toward work and away from leisure, a lower-class-oriented education policy can be used to ward off this threat to the traditional work ethic and hence to help maintain the supply of labor to the economy over the years ahead.

Many would disagree with these arguments, especially with the first statement. A more popular view is that the whole work incentive argument is a bugaboo conceived by conservatives to protect their pocketbooks from the humane but expensive programs of the welfare state. Frances Fox Piven and Richard Cloward argue in an influential book that the maintenance of work incentives has traditionally been second only to the minimizing of tax costs as a goal of American welfare policy. They point out that while the welfare rolls have grown very considerably over the past ten years, the recipients have continued to be almost exclusively children, the aged, mothers with children to care for, and others whose potential labor has a small market value in any event.[27] Furthermore, supporters of welfare reform argue that the proposed negative income tax would, if adopted, reduce work disincentives still further by permitting recipients to keep as much as half of their earnings above an income floor. But both the supporters of the present system and those who advocate an NIT minimize the work incentive problem.

A full treatment of this controversy is obviously beyond the scope of the present work. But to see the special function of education in shoring up lower-class work incentives in the welfare state it is first necessary at least to summarize the thinking of those who are less than sanguine about the fate of these incentives in the United States.

AFDC and Work Incentives

Under the present AFDC program, work disincentive effects are not confined to female recipients and their children. The impact on adult male work input, however, has to be seen as a two-stage process. First, it appears likely that the financial premium given to fatherless families under the present system encourages family dissolution and discourages conventional family formation. Second, adult males without family responsibilities have less need for income and so are likely to work less than those with children to support. Hence the effect of the AFDC program may be to create a large group of "familyless fathers" whose attachment to the labor force is more or less marginal.

The available empirical data on this two-stage relationship are fragmentary but interesting. It has been observed that while the welfare rolls expanded in the second half of the 1960s the proportion of single-parent families remained constant among whites at about 12 percent but rose from 28 percent to 32 percent among blacks.[28] Similarly, in a cross-sectional study of American cities, Marjorie F. Honig has found—not too surprisingly—that cities with more generous welfare payments have had, *ceteris paribus*, a higher incidence of welfare cases. Of more interest for our argument, however, is her finding that *80 percent* of this induced increase in welfare incidence apparently came from an increase in the proportion of female-headed households (the remainder being explained by an increased tendency of eligible households to apply for and obtain assistance).[29]

The relationship between family responsibility and male work input is more obvious and is better established empirically. Among nonwhites in the prime age groups, 25–54, 95 percent of the married men but only 72 percent of the others are in the labor force (that is, are either employed or are seeking work). The corresponding figures among whites are 97 and 83 percent (see table 16).[30] Moreover, unemployment generally runs at a much lower rate among the married.

The combined effect of these unemployment and labor force differentials is a significant difference in the number of weeks actually worked per year by married men and by others. For example, the census of 1960 found that nonwhite males in their thirties and early forties who were married and living with their wives worked an average of about one-third more weeks per year than those who were single or separated. Furthermore, married men tended to put in longer hours per week of work; the census found a 7 percent difference in weekly hours between married and other nonwhites in these age groups. Adding together the hours of work,

TABLE 16. LABOR FORCE PARTICIPATION OF MALES

| | White | | Nonwhite | |
Age	Married (Wife Present)	All Others	Married (Wife Present)	All Others
25–34	97.9%	86.4%	96.1%	74.7%
35–44	98.0	82.2	96.1	72.5
45–54	96.9	79.2	91.1	68.8

Source: U.S. Bureau of Labor Statistics, *Special Labor Force Report 144* (Washington: Government Printing Office, 1971), p. A-11.

unemployment, and labor force participation effects, nonwhite married men worked over 40 percent more man-hours per year than did single and separated nonwhite males in these prime age groups. Many have also observed that the married worker is a better-motivated and hence more productive employee when he is on the job. Some indication of the force of this aspect of the superior work input of married workers is given by their generally higher earnings.[31] Thus there is a good deal of statistical evidence that married workers supply more labor than others.

Since the case for the first point in the argument, the negative effects of the AFDC program on family structure, is not so well established, it would be prudent to reserve judgment on the extent to which this program does in fact damage male work incentives. But these statistical comparisons should at least explain why some economists doubt that the AFDC-imposed work loss has been restricted to effects on women and children.

Multiple Welfare Benefits and Work Incentives

Recent changes in welfare practice now challenge male work incentives more directly. Some working males now receive fairly large subsidies as a result of the recent rapid growth of in-kind payments to the poor—especially medical care, food subsidies, and subsidized housing—for which the working poor are eligible even when a husband is present. Another factor of this sort is the relaxation of the "man in the house" rule that now permits a "stepfather" to live with an AFDC family.

The effect of the welfare structure on the working poor family has aptly been termed chaotic and anarchic. Many poor families receive no aid at all because of local eligibility rules or simply pride, while others obtain benefits from five or more programs. The recent study by the Subcommittee on Fiscal Policy of the Joint Economic Committee of Congress found that this multiplicity of benefit programs constituted a definite threat to work incentives. The chairperson of the subcommittee was concerned about:

what the financial incentives are for people with low incomes to work. By adding one program on top of another, we have made it possible for some people to derive as much or more income from welfare programs than they could earn in a full-time job and than their neighbors currently are earning. And since many of these programs reduce the benefit amounts as earnings rise, being in several programs often means that the recipient who increases his work effort may have very little gain in net income to show for it. . . . If you look at the families who are in a number of programs and who are not working you find that their total benefits [are] close to the average working-man's wages after you deduct taxes and work expenses to figure take-home pay.[32]

Welfare Reform and Work Incentives

Because of the anarchy that characterizes our system of poor relief, many of the working poor are not reached by federal programs and hence are still not subject to these heavy work disincentives.

The proposed NIT scheme for welfare reform could substitute a more rational scheme for this chaos, at least if it were accompanied by the termination of subsidized food, housing, and other in-kind benefits. But it is very likely that such reform—however desirable it might be on other grounds—would actually exacerbate the work incentive problem simply because it would affect far more workers, and much more productive workers, than does the present welfare system. By making payment automatic and so eliminating the "stigma" deterrent, and by raising payment levels in the poorest counties and states to the national average, the scope of poor relief would be considerably enlarged.

Moreover, these plans all call for a high rate of (in effect) marginal taxation on millions of workers who are well above the poverty line. Under a typical plan, for example, if a floor of $5,000 were set for a family of four, recipients would retain some of their earnings, say 50 percent, in order to give them some incentive to work. Thus a family earning $4,000 would actually have an income of $7,000. But then, subsidies would have to be extended to those earning *over* the floor amount or the low earners would receive more income than the higher, eliminating the financial incentive to work altogether.

To cope with this problem, the typical plan calls for a constant marginal tax rate up to the point where no subsidy would be payable. In our example, that point would be reached at a take-home pay of $10,000, or a gross income of, say, $12,000 or $13,000. All workers below this level of earnings would pay an effective 50 percent marginal tax rate; those above would continue to pay the usual lower rate. But this means that a 50 percent tax rate would be applied to the labor earnings of the *majority* of workers, including some of the most productive, all supposedly in the interest of restoring the work incentives of the welfare mothers.

It is difficult to forecast the long-run effect on work input of the high marginal tax on labor earnings imposed by these negative income tax plans (or by the present chaotic system). In this country, only a small minority of very well-paid executives and professionals have had to face such high tax rates on their earnings. It is true that this group has continued to work hard, despite the tax system; but their experience is of little value to us here because of the differences between the position of the executive and professional group and that of the lower class. The former is highly socialized to work; it is selected partly on this basis. It does interesting work that is rewarded by power and prestige as well as by income, and it faces an opportunity structure in which still further promotion can be obtained only by continued hard work. The lower class, on the other hand, consists of those who have been least successful economically. They do unpleasant and uninteresting work and are typically trapped in secondary labor markets that offer neither security nor opportunity for advancement. It is unlikely that their work ethic would be similarly resistant to a change in financial work incentives.[33]

Hence it is easy to see why some economists are concerned about the labor supply effects of both the proposed NIT plan and the present welfare system. The simple truth is that it is extremely difficult if not impossible to design a plan that will put a floor under the consumption of all without reducing the financial incentive to work of those with the smallest earnings capacity.

Education and Work Incentives

A Poverty-Reducing Education Policy hence becomes more attractive because schooling raises the earning power of the poor so that the work incentives of fewer people are weakened by the income floor set by society. But it also has value because education tends to bias choice toward working more and taking less leisure.[34] The arguments for a work bias effect from schooling are fairly well established. Indeed, there are at least four separate reasons for expecting a positive relationship between education and labor input.

One widely accepted argument is that schooling in the United States trains or "socializes" a child to accept the values of a work-oriented society and to develop habits that will enable him to adjust readily to work disciplines—to show up on time, take orders, cooperate with others, and generally postpone immediate gratifications on the promise of future rewards. In fact, it is just this feature of our school system that has been attacked by many of its critics. They argue that the child's choice is distorted at an early age to the advantage of his future employers but at the expense of his capacity to enjoy the fruits of his labor in an affluent, technically advanced society. The critics have been especially harsh on the inculcation of the work ethic in the lower-class child since, they say, his schools tend to train him to accept limited career opportunities and in the process deny him a more liberal education. But there seems to be little disagreement as to the role the schools endeavor to play in encouraging a positive attitude toward work.

Education also increases work incentives by opening up new, more attractive job possibilities to the graduate. The availability of a highly educated work force encourages the development of the white collar and especially the professional and technical occupations, which offer less onerous, more interesting work than the unskilled tasks to which the poorly educated are often confined.

A third explanation of the schooling-work relationship is that a longer period of schooling tends to increase the graduate's financial incentives to work.[35] Schooling affords an individual an opportunity to increase his income, but only through hard work. Upon graduation he receives a higher wage per hour and will usually find opportunities to increase that wage through on-the-job training and eventually promotion. But the extent to which he profits from these advantages depends largely on his own effort. In order to obtain this education in the first place, moreover, the student's family had to make a considerable financial sacrifice (even in our subsidized system). In that sense the new graduate is less well off economically than the dropout who has been earning consistently for several years. Thus, investment in education simultaneously reduces the family's wealth and increases the potential for recouping this expenditure by raising the value of the graduate's work time.

Economic theory predicts that a reduction in income or wealth tends to increase an individual's interest in work. For example, if he incurs a large gambling debt, he may seek out a second, moonlighting job to pay it off. Theory also expects that an increase in his "price of leisure"—the opportunity cost of his leisure time in terms of goods and services—will tend to increase his work offering, which is why many employers found it useful to pay bonuses for overtime—to get longer hours from their work force—long before a law was passed requiring them to do so. Since education both requires an initial sacrifice of wealth *and* yields increases in the market value of a graduate's time, economic theory has a ready explanation of the long hours often worked by highly educated professionals despite their high income. Using the same reasoning, the provision of education subsidies to the poor can be regarded as a way of increasing their prospects for earning a good living and thus strengthening rather than reducing their financial incentives to work.

Finally, economists have argued that employers for their own reasons tend to set longer hours for their better-educated workers—for example, by rewarding them with promotion or at least job security. The economists' expectation is based on the observation that employers tend to invest more in their better-educated workers through on-the-job training and by other means. The employer's return to this initial investment is recaptured from the subsequent labor services of his employees. Hence, the economists argue, the employer has a special interest both in setting longer hours for the more highly educated (either directly or by rewarding long hours by promotion) and in extending their employment so that the total return to the company's investment will be maximized.

As a result of these four effects of schooling, the work input of the better educated is in fact generally higher than that of others, at least when other factors such as income are held constant. Several studies have found this to be true of hours of work and of the labor force participation rates of both males and females. For example, Mincer calculates that each additional year a white American male spends in school leads him to delay his retirement by approximately six months.[36] When the effects of education on hours of work and on other dimensions of the labor-leisure decision are taken into account, it is apparent that the greater part of the potential work effort that is sacrificed to schooling by the student is subsequently made up by the educated man.

Implications for Evaluation of Lower-Class Education

If one accepts both terms of this argument—that welfare state legislation tends to undermine lower-class work incentives and that education shores them up—a further reinterpretation of the conventional measure of the economic returns to education is required. An important implication for evaluating lower-class education is that welfare state conditions may now be considered to *legitimize the work bias in schooling.* Under pre-welfare conditions the argument of some libertarian economists that the state had no business encouraging the young to work had considerable philosophical merit. In fact, insofar as the conventionally measured earnings rate of return to education reflected this inculcation of the work ethic, one could assert that it was an overestimate of the gain either to society or the individual and could insist on a rate-of-return calculation that used only the gain in hourly earnings rather than the effect on hours worked per year. But when a capitalist welfare state is simultaneously providing strong financial disincentives to work and footing the bill for those who choose not to, this objection is seriously undermined and the early inculcation of a work ethic is put in a more favorable light.

A second result derives from the expectation that welfare state trends will continue, inducing further declines in lower-class work incentives. Since this forecast obviously is not reflected in current cross-sectional analyses of adult earnings, they will tend to underestimate the social payoff to the education of today's lower-class children.

EVALUATION OF LOWER-CLASS
EDUCATION IN THE WELFARE STATE:
SUMMARY AND CONCLUSION

The logic of a developing welfare state requires a very different critique of the economic costs and benefits of lower-class education from that of a pre–welfare state economy. A national commitment to income maintenance (even at the present ungenerous level) shifts a large portion of the economic costs of substandard earnings to the state. Hence a PREP, which would raise many out of the low-skilled category and help raise the wages of those who remain by reducing their supply, now is very likely in the long-term interests of the rest of society. Further, insofar as the program is in the long run self-financing, it need not be at the expense of either consumption or investment in physical capital. It would thus make a contribution to economic growth even though the observed rate of return to lower-class education is somewhat less than the pretax return to investment in physical capital.

Moreover, the catastrophically high unemployment rates among lower-class teenagers—believed by many to be at least in part an unwanted result of minimum wage legislation—undermines the view that economists should give full weight to the forgone earnings of these teenagers in calculating the social cost of their schooling. The result can be a sharp upward revision of our estimate of its net economic value.

Finally, education for the poor can now be regarded as a possible "insurance policy" for the work ethic in the welfare state. It can allow the state to meet its egalitarian commitments to raise lower-class incomes by increasing rather than weakening the work incentives of the poor.

Considering the combined effects of these several developments, it appears that if present welfare trends continue the meaning of the earnings rate of return to lower-class education will have to be reinterpreted. In the future, as much of the economic benefits of education may be derived from the graduate's putting in more years of productive employment, working longer hours, and applying himself more diligently to his job as from the increase in his skills.

At the same time, the welfare state itself will probably become the major beneficiary of the financial gains from lower-class education. With this orientation it would be only rational for the state not only to eliminate financial barriers but to take the initiative in making education more interesting and attractive to the poor. More generally, it could endeavor to "sell" the lower class on the idea of a life of schooling and hard work. At present, welfare state trends are not so far advanced as to require the government to resort to salesmanship. And, of course, one cannot predict with certainty that such trends will continue over the lifetime of today's students. However, even if there is no further development in that direction, the arguments put forward in this chapter indicate that there is already a sound basis for a redirection of educational policy. Major benefits can follow from a more positive program to reform the educational institutions and policies that now generate inequality.

AN IMPORTANT ADDENDUM:
THE PROBLEM OF THE
TALENTED YOUTH

The arguments in this chapter all point to the conclusion that it would be economically desirable to raise public investment in the poor toward middle-class levels. However, a final word of caution is in order. The rather egalitarian conclusions reached here concern the relationship of the education of the lower class to the average citizen; they say nothing about the treatment of the exceptional student. But economic growth is also served by the subsidy of the education of the talented.[37] There are numerous individuals in each generation whose potential scientific or cultural contributions go far beyond any private financial reward they receive. Such intellectual contributions have played an important role in our past development and should not be neglected now. Outstanding talent should continue to receive special attention in a welfare state.

Whether the present *middle*-class orientation of our school system is the best way to develop this talent is open to question. Potential geniuses exist among the blacks and poor whites as well as in other groups. Perhaps the best long-run strategy for realizing their potential would be to raise the cultural level of the entire lower class so that within a generation or so conventional methods could uncover a new crop of talent among this group. This has happened again and again in countries where social revolution or evolution has extended educational opportunities to the formerly hopeless lower classes. It could also result from a more democratic education policy in the United States.

7

The political benefits of lower-class education in a welfare state democracy

While the most dramatic change in our evaluation of the social benefits of a Poverty-Reducing Education Policy has derived from the rising economic cost to society of an undereducated lower class, a second shift has resulted from the increased political costs of the traditional inegalitarian policy that have arisen from the changing role of the lower class in our democracy. This shift is perhaps as important as the first for the assessment of the social effects of educational policy.

The political costs of underinvestment in education (or, as it is usually phrased, the political benefits of investment in education) are widely regarded as one of the most significant, perhaps the most significant, effects of education on the *rest* of society. Many of the economic benefits of education are appropriated by the individual graduate as higher consumption levels (even under welfare state conditions). But the political benefits of an individual's good citizenship are dispersed throughout the entire society.[1] The individual receives virtually no personal benefit from an intelligent, well-informed decision made in the privacy of the polling booth. This lack of private incentives makes the political benefits of education of special interest to the government policy-maker.

There is little doubt about the magnitude of this class of benefits. Almost all observers agree that a political democracy must demand that its educational system help to produce adults who will participate actively and intelligently in its civic life. There is considerable empirical evidence that schooling in the United States, for all its shortcomings, does raise both the level and quality of participation of its graduates. No matter how far short of the platonic ideal the average American college man falls, he does read and know more about national and international affairs and he does play a more active role in democratic political life by voting, joining in voluntary political activities, and so forth than the average man with less education.[2] Moreover, much of this effect is observed even when other social class factors are held constant, indicating that schooling itself plays a major role in political socialization.

An index of the effect of education on political participation is afforded by voting statistics. Data for the 1970 congressional elections are summarized in table 17. The table shows that voting rates rose con-

TABLE 17. VOTING IN 1970 CONGRESSIONAL ELECTION BY FAMILY
INCOME AND EDUCATION OF HEAD (PERCENT OF VOTING AGE)

Years of School- ing	All Whites	All Blacks	Blacks by Income Class					
			Under $3,000	$3,000– $5,000	$5,000– $7,500	$7,500– $10,000	$10,000– $15,000	Over $15,000
0–7	41	36	33	33	44	47	49	*
8	54	44	30	43	51	53	52	*
9–11	50	45	33	39	46	53	60	*
12	59	49	43	39	46	50	57	66
13–15	64	58	*	52	56	58	66	70
16	69	59	*	55	50	*	70	67
17+	73	61	—	—	—	—	—	—

Source: Calculated from U.S. Bureau of the Census, Current Population Reports, Series
P-20, no. 228, "Voting and Registration in the Election of November, 1970" (Washington:
Government Printing Office, 1971).
    * Indicates less than 30,000 voting.

tinuously with educational level, so that college graduates were almost
twice as likely to vote as those with only elementary educations. This
relationship holds even when the influences of race and economic level
are held constant, as can be seen from the detailed data for blacks presented in the table.

POLITICAL IMPORTANCE OF
LOWER-CLASS EDUCATION

Despite their widely recognized importance, these political benefits are
rarely given any separate systematic treatment in the economics-of-educa-
tion literature. The omission is unfortunate in view of the present need
to reconsider the political costs of undereducating the poor and to base
a correct allocation of schooling resources on an understanding of education's political benefits, which require a different type of analysis from
that used in discussing its economic benefits.

Consideration of the political benefits of schooling virtually forces a
discussion of the problem of obtaining equality of educational *achievement*. Thus it goes far beyond the more conventional notion of equality
of educational opportunity as the basis for educational expenditures. In
this respect this analysis parallels that of the more radical critics of our
educational system who reject all definitions of schooling equality that
leave any remaining class or racial bias in scholastic achievement. Their
criticism, however, arises from their egalitarian concept of the good society
rather than a concern with education's political benefits.[3]

A possible explanation of the relative neglect of these political benefits
in the literature is the revolutionary demand a rational consideration of
this problem appears to place on our educational *institutions*. Even approximately equal attainment requires that the schools give the culturally

deprived much more than their share of educational resources. In the past, such a program would have seemed utopian to the policy-oriented economist. Even a policy of equalizing expenditures was politically unacceptable to the important "taxpayer" group (the organized resistance of taxpayer groups to educational reform is discussed in chapter 9 below). Moreover, the economist would have regarded such a policy as very possibly counterproductive to the goal of maximum economic growth (which, as we saw in chapter 6, might give higher priority to investment in machinery or middle-class education) and hence not acceptable even to many of those voters who were more concerned with this national interest than with their own pocketbooks.

This democratic approach to education policy, however, is now less utopian than it once seemed. There are three reasons. First, the educational disparities among different sectors of the American population have been reduced over the past several decades, making further equalization—or even reverse inequality—a less impractical proposition (historical trends are discussed in chapter 10). Second, the economic rationale of the welfare state requires, as we saw in the preceding chapter, a further increase in lower-class educational levels to reduce poverty costs and to stimulate economic growth. Finally, the increased political power of the poor not only removes the question of their improvement through education from the utopian category but makes the continued neglect of their schooling an impractical policy.

Lower-Class Political Power

This last point requires special clarification because of a possible confusion between the optimal policy for raising the level and quality of participation in the formal democratic process of a group that already has some political power, and that for dealing with a truly powerless group. If a group is utterly without power, educating it may enable it to obtain some power and to exercise it intelligently (although it would be a mistake to overestimate the capacity of education policy, acting in isolation, to bring about a major change in the balance of class power). But neglecting to educate such a group would not threaten the political stability of the status quo. The black minority in the United States fitted this description of a powerless group fairly well until quite recently (although it did exercise some power in the Reconstruction period and immediately afterward). Under those circumstances the neglect of their education imposed few political costs.

But underinvestment in the schooling of those with *some* power is quite a different matter. Levin summarizes the effect of poorly educating a lower-class group in the following terms. The low level of their education leads to a lower level of their voting and other participation in the democratic process. But this gap leads to domination of the political process by the better-educated and to the adoption of policies that favor these social groups at the expense of the poorly educated. This fact, together with the feeling of alienation inspired by their nonparticipation in political life, leads the poorly educated to reject the legitimacy of normal democratic processes and to react violently and rebelliously. If the group is not fully repressed politically, this reaction obviously imposes costs on the rest of society.[4]

One might add to Levin's account that, insofar as the poorly educated *do* participate in the formal democratic process, their probable ignorance of complex questions of national and international affairs pulls down the quality of collective decision-making. This result gives the larger society a definite interest in raising both the level and quality of participation of the lower class once the latter has some de facto political power.

Returning to our example, the black minority in the United States today consists not of politically suppressed sharecroppers but of urban dwellers. In fact, blacks are more likely to live in metropolitan areas, especially the important center-city districts, than are whites. It should not be necessary to labor the point that blacks acting outside the normal political channels from this position have imposed rather considerable political and social costs on the rest of society in recent years. Blacks are also far more likely to register, vote, and join political organizations than they were in the rural South, where they were effectively barred from the franchise. In the South itself the social changes of the past decade have greatly increased the level of black political participation. As a consequence of these changes, the voting rate of blacks is now only about 13 percentage points below that of whites. Thus both the de facto political power of blacks and their level of formal political participation have increased immeasurably in the recent past.

But the blacks are not the only lower-class group in this country that has moved up from a position of relative powerlessness in the past several decades. So have the southern poor whites, who now participate much more fully in political affairs. The interrelationship between the race issue and class politics in the South in the early decades of this century is complex (and has been told elsewhere[5]). But it is obvious that the breakdown of the traditional system with its poll taxes, single-party rule, and often demagogic politics, coincident with the entrance of the southern black into political life, has contributed to an important increase in poor white as well as in black participation.

A quantitative measure of this increase is provided by voting statistics. Table 18 shows the trend in the proportion of voting age adults participating in presidential elections in South Carolina, a state with a 58 percent black population in 1900. That rate was under 9 percent in the elections of 1900 and 1920 and was still only 10 percent in 1940. But it has since risen rapidly to almost one-half of the adult population. South Carolina's

TABLE 18.   VOTING IN PRESIDENTIAL ELECTIONS, SOUTH CAROLINA

Election Year	Proportion of Adults in South Carolina	Proportion in S.C./ Proportion in U.S.
1940	.10	.17
1948	.13	.25
1960	.29	.46
1968	.46	.77

Sources: U.S. Bureau of the Census, *1970 Census of the Population* (Washington: Government Printing Office, 1972); U.S. Department of Commerce, *Statistical Abstract of the United States*, 1972 ed. (Washington: Government Printing Office).

participation is still only about three-quarters of the national average (which, at 60 percent in 1968, was itself far below the level achieved in many European nations). Nevertheless the rapid increase does indicate the social change that has occurred in even the least developed areas of this country as national political standards have been imposed. Moreover, the increase in voting rates shown in table 18 probably underestimates the gain in the voting participation of the poor residing in that state in 1900, or in 1940, since both blacks and lower-class whites have left the state in large numbers for more highly urbanized areas where they have been more directly exposed to national standards of political participation.

There have also been important improvements in the political position of other lower-class groups. For example, the "company town" was replaced by the "union town" in hundreds of industrial centers in the thirties and forties, symbolizing the growing political power of industrial workers. And the urban black civil rights movement has sparked a parallel movement among the northern white urban "ethnic" groups, further challenging the traditional distribution of power.

The effect of this cumulative increase in the relative political power of the poor is that—apart from any more idealistic motives—the American republic can no longer count on the exclusion of much of its lower class from political influence. Both the potential disruption these groups can cause in our highly organized urban society and the recent increases in their political participation provide an obvious argument for a more democratic educational policy.

FAILURE OF PRIVATE DEMAND
FOR EDUCATION

But this need is not well served by present government subsidy programs. The empirical evidence in chapters 2 to 5 shows that the prevailing principle of governmental subsidy policy toward education has been, with some important exceptions, the underwriting of the private demand for education. But the private market demand encourages both a type of socialization and a distribution of educational inputs that are ill suited for generating the maximum political benefits.

Essentially, the private demand under American conditions produces graduates who can meet the needs of the labor market rather than those of the political democracy (partly because there are no material rewards to individuals for good citizenship). In practice, the labor market is dominated by corporations and other large employers with very specialized labor requirements. The private demand thus is essentially a demand for a labor force that is highly stratified in terms of skills and that is socialized to accept the conditions of corporate employment. Our labor market requires both minimally educated factory workers trained in habits of obedience and somewhat better-educated owners and executives trained to command or supervise. It also demands salesmen dedicated to the sacrifice of truth in the interest of profits, scientific researchers disciplined to the furtherance of knowledge, and so forth. The resulting distribution of skills and attitudes, whatever merit it may have in producing goods and services, does not correspond in any obvious way to the needs of collective decision-making in a democracy.

Even with the best educational system the experience of employment in this labor market would not be the optimal background for participation in political affairs. It should be equally clear that the democratic process is further impeded if the higher goals of the educational system itself are subordinated to the expected future corporate roles of its students. But there is considerable empirical evidence that the schools do train children for their expected class roles.[6] The lower-class child is typically trained to be able to carry out tasks that require obedience and regularity rather than initiative, enterprise, and abstract intelligence. There is even evidence that this differential socialization spills over into the teaching of courses designed specifically to prepare youths for their roles as citizens. In a study of schools in the Boston metropolitan area, E. H. Litt found that civics courses offered to working-class children taught a passive acceptance of the "American way of life" while those offered middle-class youth taught methods of active participation in and control of community and civic organizations.[7]

These characteristics of the private demand for education would persist and be counterproductive in a political democracy even if resources per student were equalized. Reform of the content of the education is also required.[8] But of course, as we have already seen, the private demand does generate an unequal distribution of educational resources. Where private demands dominated, blacks and poor whites typically received much less than their share of schooling resources.

As a result of the influence of private demands in the American school system, the effects of differential socialization and class differences in the distribution of educational resources *interact* in a number of ways that hamper rather than advance the political integration of the lower class. Thus, youths in working-class districts today are trained to accept an authoritarian discipline from an early age and are given an inferior education, especially if they are blacks or lower-class whites. In most cases they will leave the system after having completed fewer years of schooling than other students. As graduates they will score lower on reading and verbal reasoning tests, and will tend to have more "authoritarian" and less tolerant (or manipulative) attitudes than more advantaged youths.[9]

ECONOMIC ANALYSIS OF THE POLITICAL BENEFITS OF EDUCATION

Economic analysis has not been very helpfully applied to the problems raised by the political benefits of education. It has done little to develop policies for school reform that would deal with the increased political power of the lower class or the influence of private demand in offering poor children an undemocratic socialization and their schooling a lower level of financial support. The failure to develop a model for a suitable distribution of educational resources is the more surprising omission, since this problem is more susceptible to the tools of economic analysis. It is also, of course, the problem most relevant to the central concerns of this study.

Economists have long been aware of the argument that schooling confers political benefits that are not captured as a material gain by the individual graduate. They have often made use of this point when advocating state subsidies for education. However, the distribution implications of these benefits for education have not been worked out very carefully. Thus the knowledge that education has political value has been used most often simply to argue for an across-the-board subsidy to education—say, by lowering tuition levels. But as we have seen, this type of subsidy will simply underwrite the private demand for education and so will extend rather than resolve the problems of the present distribution of schooling resources. At a somewhat higher level of sophistication, it is argued that, since there is equality of suffrage, that portion of the education budget which is included because of expected political benefits should be distributed equally among students. Carrying this point a step further, the libertarian economist Milton Friedman, in his *Capitalism and Freedom*, argues that each student should be afforded a minimum of ten years of required schooling to enable him to discharge his duties as a citizen. All education beyond the tenth year would be provided by the student at his own expense, so that the system of state-supported senior high schools and colleges could be dismantled.[10]

These proposals, however, represent a less-than-satisfactory use of political theory. The empirical evidence indicates that ten years of schooling will generally *not* be sufficient to permit the typical slum dweller to discharge his duties as a citizen regularly and with the requisite knowledge of complex political issues.[11] In fact, if one considers only the political benefits of education in a one-man–one-vote democracy, it would seem much more plausible to conclude that expenditures on the education of the less able and of those disadvantaged by home, neighborhood, and occupation would have to be much greater than those of the middle class simply to increase the quality of their participation to a standard level.

Education for Majority Voting?

This argument can be made somewhat less intuitively by the introduction of an explicit theory—the use of a model of political democracy in which decisions are reached by the vote of a majority (directly, or indirectly through representatives). This model has been in widespread use among economists in recent years and can be employed for our purposes.[12] By assuming that political power actually follows the principle of equal suffrage, it abstracts from the problems of inequalities of political power and participation and focuses simply on the question of raising the quality of this participation. But despite this abstraction, it can serve as a starting point for a less simplistic understanding of the demands of a political democracy on educational policy.[13]

Fundamentally, the logic of majority voting dictates that the knowledge of one citizen is not much more important than that of another. This is in contrast with a discussion of economic benefits, where one can argue for higher subsidies to the education of the more productive on the grounds that it will increase economic growth. A common rationale for emphasizing total output is that, in theory at least, it is always possible to tax the wealth of a highly successful individual so that it can be shared with others. But even if his wealth is *not* to be taxed, at least the rich man himself has the enjoyment of his riches, or rather of the consumer goods and services his wealth commands.

In a majority voting model, however, a "millionaire" of political knowledge is outvoted by two ignoramuses. Not only is this extra knowledge not taxed but, since it does not significantly affect the collective outcome, it is simply wasted. The man who has trained himself to vote brilliantly has the satisfaction of knowing that he has acted correctly but also the disappointment of knowing that it has been to no avail. Most important from the point of view of society, the increase in political "output" as a result of his surplus knowledge is negligible or nonexistent. Hence a much more egalitarian distribution of educational resources must be deduced from democratic political theory than from economic considerations.

Applying the Model

In its most simplistic interpretation, the logic of majority voting would call for educating 51 percent of the voters to the point where they were competent. A more realistic variant demands a much higher proportion of qualified voters, perhaps close to 100 percent if possible. This point can be seen most clearly if we think of political decisions being reached on a number of issues, each of which is decided by the majority rule (the most commonly used model of voting).[14] But it is obvious that it is not enough to educate just 51 percent of the voters. The voting population will not line up neatly into informed and noninformed citizens on each issue. People vote on the basis of group or self-interest as well as on the basis of their political knowledge. On some issues interest group considerations will split the informed majority, permitting a know-nothing minority to determine the outcome. Since interest alignments shift from issue to issue it will be necessary to educate many more than a majority of voters to ensure that results will be dominated by trained voters in a reasonable proportion of issues.

If full knowledge of each voter on each issue is posited as the goal of education, an optimal distribution of schooling resources can then be readily deduced. Investment should be in strict inverse proportion to intellectual capacity and cultural background, with very large sums necessarily expended on the education of the disadvantaged.

Achievement of this goal, however, would in practice be absurdly expensive or perhaps even impossible to attain. The difficulties it offers can be seen once one admits that there is not a simple informed-non-informed dichotomy but rather a continuum of knowledge on each issue and that some issues are very complex indeed—so complex that even the most highly trained experts will disagree on the best policy.

But once the goal of full information for each voter is recognized as unattainable, some recession from the target of complete equality of educational attainment also becomes desirable. It can be shown that, in a majority voting model, it is better to have some variation among voters than to have all on the same but much lower level of attainment.

Reasons for Variation

There are three important cases where this variation might be encouraged. First, a small minority of the *least* able might be neglected. It would be extremely difficult or impossible to raise all members of this group up to the standard level. Some hedging on the commitment to this group might be a necessity in the development of a realistic policy; in any event, it would clearly be an option that would save the state a considerable expenditure. Moreover, insofar as the neglected "least able" were not concentrated in a particular interest group, this modification would not have a very deleterious effect on the quality of collective decision-making, since their interests could then be advanced by the activity of their more able fellows. Of course, since the lower class does have a disproportionately large number of those classified as weak students, it would be important to make a special effort with this group to guarantee that the average educational attainment of the lower class was sufficient to ensure that it had its share of influence and representation in the political process.

A second reason for permitting some variation in educational attainment arises from the positive role a well-informed minority can play even in a majority voting system. The distribution of informed voters will in practice vary from issue to issue. For example, city dwellers are likely to know more about urban problems but less about, say, agricultural productivity. An intelligent minority that can vote in an informed way on many issues will serve a useful function by joining with others who, because of their occupation or residence, are well informed on a particular issue. In this way the training of a generally informed minority of voters can help to generate informed electoral majorities.

The third reason derives from the great uncertainty of the effect of education, no matter how well designed, on adult political performance. For many youths schooling may just not "take," at least as measured by the quality of their political performance; for others the effect may be only marginal. Hence, even if one is trying to raise graduates only to some minimal standard, the additional *proportion* of those who will achieve this standard for a specified outlay of educational funds will vary from group to group. This variation may have moderately inegalitarian results, even for this democratic policy. For example, if x dollars of educational expenditure raised the proportion meeting the standard from 70 to 75 percent in one group and from 80 to 90 percent in another group of equal size, the expenditure would yield a larger addition in the number of qualified voters if it were applied to the second group.

For these three reasons, the logic of majority voting need not prescribe a goal of complete equality of citizenship quality or educational attainment among electors. These qualifications, however, should not permit us to lose sight of the principal result of this analysis: that majority voting does imply a far more egalitarian policy than we now have or than would be realized by equal investment in each child. Even to approximate equality of attainment requires that the major portion of educational resources be allocated to the education of the lower class, a reversal of present priorities. Since the poor are unable to make as large a financial contribution to their own further education, this equality also requires an even more remarkable reversal of the government policy toward educational subsidy.

This conclusion goes beyond that reached in the discussion of the economic benefits of education in a welfare state. The optimal policy for lower-class education that can be justified on the basis of benefits to the rest of society therefore is probably intermediate between the results of the economic and political analyses.

Departures from the Model

Of course, the majority voting model does not accurately depict the distribution of political power in the United States. Two departures from this model raise especially difficult political problems for educational policy. First, the children of the poor are somewhat more likely not to participate at all in the conventional democratic process. A tentative answer to this problem was provided earlier. Since the poor now have considerable de facto political power, education that channels their participation into legal political activity as well as improving its quality is clearly in the interest of the rest of society.

Second, upper-class and upper-middle-class children are more likely as adults to become members of the political and economic elites, participation in either of which will convey a disproportionate level of political power. We must consider whether such children should receive special training for their future political roles. This problem raises questions that go far beyond the scope of this study. If the role of elites is accepted as legitimate, schooling policy clearly should endeavor to provide well-educated leaders. If not, it is more difficult to say whether superior education should be continued to be offered to the children of the well-to-do through a system of private and (in the case of some upper-middle-class suburbs) public schools.

But whatever policy is adopted on *elite* schooling,[15] the conclusion of this chapter that the increased political power of the lower class supports a policy of spending more on the lower-class than on the average student would not be affected.

8

Educational reform as a redistributive tool

The argument offered so far indicates that the present unequal distribution of educational resources very likely does not favor either economic growth or political democracy and that it serves neither the long-run fiscal interests of the taxpayers nor the middle-class interest in political stability. It is worthwhile at this point to consider the inherent attractiveness of educational reform as a way of helping the poor (especially vis-à-vis the popular alternative of income maintenance) *apart* from the objective economic and political benefits it generates.

Some economists would be hostile to this line of argument. They would insist that a government policy of tying assistance to the poor to their consumption of education services is justified only insofar as it contributes to specific economic and political benefits for the rest of society. Education should not, they would argue, be subsidized beyond that level. If an effort is to be made to help the poor for their own sakes, this should be done through cash grants, which the recipients could spend either on schooling or on other needs as they saw fit.

The economists' position here is grounded in the libertarian tradition of their profession in the United States. In this view, no-strings-attached cash grants are preferable since they give the poor family complete freedom to use its subsidy as it sees fit. The poor can also see their own interest more clearly than their benefactors, and so this method is more efficient in satisfying their wants.

This argument against educational subsidies, however, does not stand up under close scrutiny. Cash grants or other income maintenance programs for the poor constrain choice in an important way. The poor man is given a stipend on the condition that he does not earn a decent living by his own efforts. His choice is therefore biased against both work and study, which prepares him to earn a better living. But (as we argued in chapter 6) education subsidies bias choice toward work after graduation as well as toward study. The individual is provided with skills that have an economic value to him only insofar as he is willing to offer his time and effort in the labor market. Hence a combination of income maintenance and education, but not the former by itself, would be expected to provide the poor with a choice that is biased neither for nor against work.

The "free choice" attributed to income transfers does not in any event extend to the children of the poor. Cash grants are normally distributed to the family head for use according to his or her judgment. In contrast, education is given directly to the child, thus providing some protection to those whose parents might choose to spend most of their benefits on their own consumption.

But altogether another reason favoring educational reform is simply that both the recipients and the taxpayers prefer it to an ordinary "dole." There is considerable evidence that the poor typically prefer work-related assistance that improves their ability to earn a living to cash handouts. In a recent paper, "The Political Feasibility of Income by Right," Bill Cavala and Aaron Wildavsky analyze the lack of support found among the American poor for either the present welfare system or the negative income tax or other welfare reform schemes. They argue that while an NIT "promises . . . to remove the stigma associated with poverty, one must seriously question whether guaranteed income would achieve this crucial goal. In America, the stigma of poverty, after all, lies less in the fact of being poor than in the implication that one is lacking in those abilities which are being rewarded." They conclude that a mere dole will never eliminate the social and psychological effects of poverty since "to say that the losers in ['our race for gain'] will not starve is very different from saying that the race itself is not a worthy one."[1]

In contrast to a welfare dole, subsidized on-the-job training, vocational training in schools, and of course general education all are intended to help the individual to acquire the capacity to rise out of poverty by his own efforts and hence can eliminate the social stigma as well as the physical deprivation of being poor.

The preference of taxpayers for educational subsidies over cash handouts is even more obvious and well-known.[2] This group has traditionally been attracted by the arguments that educational reform benefits children and that it promotes both work and study. Thus, middle-class Americans are undecided as to the extent to which the poor are poor because of their own mismanagement or laziness. But the children of the poor are often exempt from this onus, and programs to help them are considered more positively.[3]

Moreover, taxpayers are more willing to give money that is expected to relieve the squalid effects of poverty and to encourage the recipient to find his way out of his condition than they are to distribute cash grants. Some of the poor family heads may indeed get more happiness or utility by using an increment to their welfare check to buy a color TV set, alcohol, or even narcotics than by purchasing a balanced diet for their families or in planning for a less destitute future. Similarly, they may prefer less work to more. But these preferences, however important and legitimate they may appear to the libertarian economist, typically carry very little weight with the citizen who is providing the additional subsidy.

But education subsidies are looked on with more favor by the taxpayers. Study is itself generally regarded as meritorious as well as often leading to a second meritorious activity, hard work. Hence it is typically easier to obtain support for the financial succor of the poor in the form of educational subsidies than in the form of simple handouts.[4]

IMPLICATIONS FOR EDUCATION POLICY

These positive qualities of educational reform as a redistributive tool are important for two reasons. First, while one can make a reasonably good case that, under present-day welfare state conditions, a Poverty-Reducing Education Program could obtain economic and political gains, it is difficult to say on the basis of our knowledge of these benefits just how far we should go toward full equality of educational opportunity. For example, calculations of the earnings rate of return to lower-class education provide estimates that vary quite widely (see chapter 5 above), making it difficult to use a precise criterion or cutoff point for investing in the poor. Or again, if the present welfare system were replaced by a much more generous income maintenance scheme, even rather low-yield investments in lower-class education could result in a positive tax reduction (see chapter 6). Given such inevitable margins of error in the quantitative calculations, minimum and maximum estimates of the "optimum" extent of a PREP must differ considerably. A favorable view of educational reform on its own merits presumably could lead to a maximum employment of this tool, while the traditional libertarian preference for income subsidy (obviously a misplaced emphasis in the author's view) would lead us toward a minimal use of the educational strategy.

But the relative attractiveness of educational reform is of interest for an even more important reason. To this point, the analysis of the effect of welfare state changes on the valuation of a PREP has been a rather abstract discussion of its effect on broad social interests. The argument has been made that expansion of lower-class educational opportunities, by reducing the degree to which productivities vary among men, can reduce the need to divert economic resources to a "bread and circuses" economy; can help integrate lower-class blacks and whites into the work-oriented culture; and, one may hope, can also serve to channel the new power of these groups constructively in the political arena. But any realistic hope or expectation of less unequal policies must also take into account public attitudes. The fact that increased spending on lower-class education is much more popular than income maintenance with the majority of voters is a most important reason for hope that further commitments to the poor will include some democratic reforms of the educational system.

At present the distribution of educational resources is not congruent with our social needs. It continues to reflect to a considerable extent a state policy of across-the-board subsidy of the private demand for education despite reform's political and economic advantages *and* appeal to the public. Any sober assessment of the prospects for changes in this structure therefore must consider why it has continued till now. It is necessary to study the traditional obstacles to educational reform in the United States, especially the persistent efforts of organized interest groups to prevent an increase in expenditures on lower-class education. This opposition —and its diminution in the developing welfare state society—will be discussed in the next chapter.

PART III

Assessing the
prospects for change

9

Organized group opposition: the political economy of educational reform

THE DYNAMICS OF DEMOCRATIC EDUCATIONAL REFORM

The principal conclusion of the last three chapters was that a Poverty-Reducing Education Policy to raise lower-class schooling levels would now be in the interest of society as a whole. It would probably be beneficial even if considered strictly from the point of view of the taxpayers; thus, it would provide net economic and other gains to the rest of society apart from those obtained by the lower class itself, repaying the initial investment of taxes. Yet the first several chapters of this work presented detailed evidence of systematic inequality in the disribution of educational resources that has persisted in the United States. An analysis of the dynamics of reform in our system of educational finance is now of obvious interest for the light it may shed on the prospects for a policy that accords better with present social requirements.

The present unequal distribution of resources was seen in chapters 1–5 to result largely from the relative dominance of private demands for education. This dominance was in turn explained by the decentralization of school finances, which constrains the expenditures of the poorer districts and leads to an undervaluation of the social need for educating the poor in all districts. The prospects for equalization appear dim without a system of federal school finances not because federalization will necessarily lead to equality but because inequality is almost certain to persist without it.

But the political economy of schooling reform is actually a good deal more complicated than this analysis might indicate. The traditional American educational system was developed under pre–welfare state conditions when the social argument for equality was less convincing and when an egalitarian policy would probably have imposed net economic costs on the taxpayer group. As the social and economic situation shifted in the 1960s, very important steps were in fact taken to alter the traditional federal laissez-faire policy toward the schooling of the poor. The Elementary and Secondary Education Act was passed in 1965 and was followed by a number of other federal programs to assist the education of the poor.

If one were willing to give a cause-and-effect interpretation to this association between an increase in poverty costs and progress toward school reform, one could adopt a simple theory of the dynamics of educational reform in response to social needs. The steadily expanding commitment to the poor that has occurred since the passage of the ESEA, according to such a theory, must continue to yield movement toward a more democratic policy in response to the new, increasing interest of the taxpayers.

There is some basis in fact for this optimistic assessment. However, we shall endeavor to explore these points somewhat further before adopting that conclusion. It will be useful first to examine the history of the struggle for reform so as to identify better the politically important forces that have supported and opposed change and the objective or ideological basis for their position.

Under pre–welfare state conditions, one might expect political conflict over reform of our system of school finances to yield a division along the taxpayer–poor people dichotomy. If so, the division would weaken as welfare state pressures eroded taxpayer resistance to change. There are, however, other issues and interests in educational reform than those based simply on a concern with expenditure and taxes. It is essential to see how important the taxpayer point of view actually has been in blocking or advancing changes in the system of school finances.

In this regard the history of egalitarian school reform in the United States is most informative. The key feature of this history is the long and effective resistance to federal aid to education.

THE CAMPAIGN TO ENACT
FEDERAL AID LEGISLATION

General aid to education by the federal government is not a new idea, and the success of conservatives in blocking it before 1965 does not mean that there has been a national consensus against it. There is evidence that public opinion strongly supported it, at least in the decades immediately preceding passage of legislation. A political struggle was waged for almost a century before the advocates of federal support for the education of the poor obtained a partial success with the passage of the Elementary and Secondary Education Act. In the course of this struggle at least three successive crises in educational finance exposed the inadequacy of a decentralized system and appeared to require federal intervention. The long delay in enactment resulted, according to the chroniclers of that struggle, from the organized political opposition of a coalition of groups.

There is, of course, a myth that a hands-off policy by the federal government is a long and hallowed tradition deeply rooted in the history of our educational system. The facts do not support this interpretation. The Survey Ordinance of 1785 and the Morrill Act of 1862 granted federal lands to the states for educational purposes; the Smith-Hughes Act of 1917 supported vocational education; the impacted areas legislation of

1950 provided assistance to local areas whose school systems were burdened by the enrollment of children of military personnel; the G.I. Bill of Rights scholarships for war veterans and the National Defense Education Act of 1958 afforded scholarships and loans to talented university students. All established precedents for a federal role at least for special purposes, if not for general aid to education.

Early Efforts

The struggle to obtain general aid dates from 1870. The emancipation of the black slaves and the ensuing social problems of the Reconstruction South led President Ulysses S. Grant to urge Congress that year to provide federal aid to education to meet this regional crisis. In response to his request, the Hoar Bill was introduced into Congress later that year.[1] This bill would have forced the South to provide education for all children, poor whites and blacks alike, aged six to eighteen. Federal standards would have been set, and if they were not met in any state, North *or* South, the federal government itself would have administered the schools, collecting the necessary taxes from the delinquent state. The bill was not passed.[2]

A more moderate proposal, the Blair Bill, "provided for Federal funds to the States in proportion to the illiteracy therein on a matching basis." This did pass the U.S. Senate (although not the House) in 1884, 1886, and 1888.[3]

World War I and the immediate postwar period produced another upsurge of interest in federal aid to education. This interest was really continuous until the passage of the ESEA in 1965. Nevertheless, there were several distinguishable periods during which the decentralized system of finance was subject to particularly sharp challenge. The first was raised by the war and the dislocation of the immediate postwar period. Written examinations administered to all recruits during the war revealed that 25 percent were illiterate and that many others had but limited literacy skills. This was a shocking disclosure to the public, which had grossly underestimated the extent of the illiteracy problem because census statistics, based on the respondents' evaluation of their own literacy, had been misleadingly optimistic. Further support for educational reform came from the finding that

35% of the men were physically unfit for military service. Medical authorities stated to a Committee of Congress that 80% of those physically incapacitated could have been relieved of their defects if they had been taken in charge at school age for treatment. The inadequacies within the public school system prompted many Congressmen to turn their attention to securing federal aid to education.[4]

Some additional support for federal aid to education was gained as a result of the Red Scare during and after World War I. Many conservatives believed that the opposition of some "subversives" to the war and support for the communist movements in Europe was caused in part by a high level of illiteracy among immigrants and native American workers. Hence some conservatives came to advocate federal aid to education as a way of coping with this supposed threat to the nation.

It was maintained that illiteracy in any state is a problem of all the states, and, therefore, a national problem. Education was considered the foundation stone of the Republic, an insurance policy against Bolshevism, sedition and any attempt to tear down the government.[5]

To meet these needs, the Smith-Townsend Federal Aid to Education Bill was put forward. Smith-Townsend and variants of it were before Congress from 1918 to 1925. They were supported by President Woodrow Wilson (though not by Warren G. Harding) and by a number of groups with large memberships: the National Education Association, the American Federation of Teachers, the American Federation of Labor, the National Committee of Women, the National Congress of Parents and Teachers, the General Federation of Women's Clubs, the National League of Women Voters, the Free and Accepted Masons, the Women's Christian Temperance Union, and many others. The legislation was opposed primarily by various organized business groups, principally the U.S. Chamber of Commerce, with the assistance of some Roman Catholic and southern representatives.[6] Despite its popular support the bill was never reported out of committee for consideration on the floor of Congress. Popular pressure for federal aid to education nevertheless continued throughout the twenties.[7]

The Depression of the thirties produced a true crisis in education and thus afforded a second major challenge to the decentralized system.

[By 1934] there were 60,000 fewer teachers than in 1932 (although pupil enrollment was increasing), with resulting larger classes. One-fourth of the teachers were receiving less than $750 per year, the *minimum* paid factory workers under the NRA, and two-fifths of these were receiving $550 a year; the states were in debt to the teachers for over $40 million (some estimates ran as high as $100 million); 40,000 were on relief rolls and 60,000 were expected to be on relief before the end of the year. . . . [T]he public school system was near collapse. Thousands of schools were closed and others were open only because of the "faith, hope and charity" of the teachers. Every state and local unit was hard hit and the Congressmen returned with bills in hand. There were 25 or 30 bills introduced providing for federal aid in some form to public education.[8]

In the following year thirty to forty such bills were put forward in Congress. But all were successfully blocked by conservative opposition and remained in committee. The small assistance that public education did receive was as a result of other programs—work relief for teachers (under the Federal Relief Administration) and for students (under the National

Youth Administration and the Civilian Conservation Corps), some school building by other relief programs, and so on.[9]

World War II and After

A third challenge was provided by the teacher shortage during World War II. Wages of factory and other workers had risen much more rapidly than those of teachers, and the schools had extreme difficulty in obtaining and holding personnel. This time public opinion was too strong to ignore, and the Thomas-Lister Bill reached the floor of the Senate for debate and vote. The U.S. Chamber of Commerce refrained from testifying against the bill, confining itself instead to a statement exhorting local communities to increase their tax efforts. But despite widespread support in Congress, the bill was defeated by a racist parliamentary tactic. An amendment was introduced by its conservative northern opponents restricting federal aid to those states that treated its pupils in a nondiscriminatory fashion. Opponents of the bill joined northern liberals in support of the amendment, then joined with southerners (many of whom had favored the original legislation) in voting down the bill.[10]

The wartime teacher crisis passed, but segments of public opinion continued to call for federal aid to education. The issue became known as a "perennial" in the postwar period. The NEA and its allies inside and outside the "educational establishment" continued their efforts. As a representative of the U.S. Chamber of Commerce—which had resumed its leadership of the opposition to federal aid—testified to Congress in 1955:

> In good times and bad, in war and in peace, whether Treasury surplus or deficit, the NEA has pursued the notion of Federal aid to education with a single-mindedness of purpose that perhaps has never been equaled by any organization in any field over such a long period of time. It has sought to frighten the wits out of the citizenry with its dire predictions of educational catastrophe if our schools are left to the devices of State and local governments. It has sought to woo and win this same citizenry with persuasive pictures of an educational millenium to be achieved under the panacea of Federal aid.[11]

All this effort apparently was not without some effect on public opinion. Surveys (see table 19) showed that the general public favored federal aid

TABLE 19. POPULATION SUPPORTING GENERAL FEDERAL AID TO EDUCATION (PERCENT OF THOSE EXPRESSING AN OPINION)

Year	Percent
1943	80
1949	73
1955	74
1959	83

Source: Philip Meranto, *The Politics of Federal Aid to Education in 1965* (Syracuse: Syracuse University Press, 1967), p. 43.

to education by a three-to-one margin—hardly a "consensus" in favor of the traditional system.[12] But this popular opinion did not result in legislative action. The economy bloc in Congress, exhorted by the U.S. Chamber of Commerce, continued to be successful in its opposition.

As late as the early 1960s, American political scientists remained pessimistic about the prospects for federal aid to education largely because of the stability and strength of the organized opposition. Thus Munger and Fenno could conclude in 1962:

> For a believer in progress the record of government action concerning federal aid to education is a discouraging thing to follow. Even without a personal commitment to the approval of federal aid, it is disheartening to read of a dispute that has continued for almost a full century with so little change. Whether the time be the 1880's, the 1920's, or the 1960's, the arguments are much the same, the controversial issues identical, and the positions taken by the affected interest groups relatively inflexible.
>
> A comparison, for example, between the alignment of interest groups for and against federal aid to education in the 1920's with the line of battle in the 1950's, shows an almost total identity. On one side are ranged educators, women's groups, and labor. On the other side are arrayed businessmen and Catholics. Indeed the only substantial change that appears in such a comparison —and it is hardly to be described as of major consequence—is that the DAR has switched from support to opposition.[13]

In fact, the principal federal action to challenge the traditional inegalitarian practices in American education in this period came not from these attempts to obtain federal financial aid to schools but from federal court rulings that racial discrimination and segregation in education were illegal. Despite efforts to reduce discrimination and segregation, however, the southern system of racially segregated schools remained largely intact in 1965. Much of the de facto progress in desegregation, especially in the South, took place subsequent to passage of ESEA.[14] And, of course, the decentralized school system still permitted economic forces to influence the distribution of resources among schools.

INTEREST GROUPS IN THE CAMPAIGN

The political scientists who have chronicled the tortuous record of this struggle for federal aid tend to explain its persistent failure as an outcome of a struggle between two unevenly matched coalitions of organized groups. The principal groups in the coalition supporting federal legislation were, as we have seen, the educational establishment itself, parents and women's groups, and organized labor.

These accounts generally agree that the dominant party in the much stronger opposing coalition was organized business. The U.S. Chamber of Commerce is given the major role here; it is credited with conducting the necessary research, with customarily "leading a parade of witnesses" before congressional hearings on education legislation, and with providing leadership in other ways. It obtained support from other business organizations, including the Council of State Chambers of Commerce, the National Association of Manufacturers, the Southern States Industrial Council, and the Investment Bankers Association of America.[15]

This conservative force formed shifting alliances with other groups. Some of these coalitions were based only on "logrolling," or bargaining by the business groups in exchange for support on other issues. But other alliances reflected real concerns about the effects of particular provisions in the various federal aid-to-education bills. Thus many southern representatives opposed such legislation when it contained provisions that appeared likely to undercut their traditional system of racial separation. They held this stance despite the obvious economic interest of their local school systems, which were well below the national average in wealth or income, in obtaining federal funds. Similarly, many Catholics opposed federal aid as long as it contained no provision for their system of parochial schools.[16]

In some respects this lineup of opposing forces is easily understood in terms of objective interests or strong ideological positions (although it does require some modification of our original, simple taxpayers–poor people dichotomy). The support of professional educators, parents' organizations, and liberal reformers for federal aid is readily explained, as are the reservations of traditional Catholics and southerners. The weak role of the poor in this campaign simply points up their comparative powerlessness, especially in this pre–welfare state period. The division among the poor states on this issue was somewhat more complex, but the race issue does offer a basis for understanding the mixed role played by the largest bloc of poor states, those in the South.[17]

THE BUSINESS INTEREST IN BLOCKING REFORM

The crucially important opposition offered by the business community itself, however, requires a deeper analysis. There is little doubt that employers saw higher school taxes as a threat to their profits and that many opposed federal aid to education largely on those grounds. The importance of the tax issue to business was observable both here and in its opposition to the extension of other social welfare services (in contrast to their willingness to see expanded federal power in areas where it appeared likely to bolster profits). On such welfare issues the U.S. Chamber of Commerce became "the bellwether of the economy bloc in Congress."[18] Its publications and spokesmen stressed the tax costs of such legislation, it formed alliances with other groups interested in keeping down federal taxes for social programs, and in other ways it clearly led a *taxpayer* opposition to federal social welfare measures.[19]

Other indications of the importance of the tax issue in stimulating business opposition to federal spending for general education come from studies of business intervention in *local* school finances. In these the local business community has also most often been characterized as supporting and sometimes guiding the taxpayer interest in local school economy, sometimes under the leadership of national business organizations (at least at certain critical moments).[20]

Is Opposition Irrational?

This opposition seems perverse to a number of other writers on the federal aid-to-education issue. They contend that since business necessarily benefits from higher educational levels, its historic resistance to the concept must be entirely due to noneconomic or economically unsound attitudes. They have pointed to an emotional conservatism, a suspicion of any "big government" welfare program, or an unduly high rate of discounting future benefits leading to an unwillingness to make a long-term investment in the nation's labor force. These writers conclude that business must either be persuaded of its interest in education or else induced by a strong government to go along with a reform that is in its own interest. This last argument was put forward by Anne Gibson Buis in the 1950s. At the end of her detailed (and very helpful) history of the politics of education at the federal level, she concluded that:

The business group will . . . probably continue to oppose federal aid to education since they often adopt and practice policies which are based on profits from quick turnovers rather than greater profits from long-time investments. . . . If greater profits ever accrue to the business groups through an educational investment in the people by the Federal Government it will probably be against strenuous opposition from any business groups.[21]

The position taken in these pages is quite different.[22] In the author's view the political action taken by organized business to oppose federal aid to education during the pre–welfare state period accorded well with its long-term as well as short-term economic interests. This is so at least if this interest is defined in terms of maximizing the flow of profits available either for the further accumulation of private physical capital or for the employers' own consumption.[23] Similarly, the softening of business attitudes toward greater efforts to educate the poor in the past few years can better be understood as an intelligent adaptation to a new political and economic situation—the emerging welfare state—than as evidence of greater rationality or charity.

The more widely held view that the historic employer opposition to federal aid to education was irrational is based on the observation that employers, unlike other taxpayers, hire labor, and hence have an interest in having a better-qualified pool upon which to draw. A government policy that raised the quality of the labor force by rescuing lower-class youths from a lifetime of marginal employment and the dole and by integrating them into primary labor markets through better education would therefore appear to be in the interest of business.

It is true that investment in education will typically increase the supply of labor effectively available to private employers. A program for increasing schooling levels will reduce the numbers in the private labor force, since teachers and students are not available for profit-making employment; but it will also raise the quality of labor of the graduates. The net result will be a long-run increase in the effective labor supply to employers as long as the gain in quality of the labor force exceeds the current resource costs of keeping students, teachers, and other educational personnel out of the profit-making sector. The condition for this outcome is simply that the earnings rate of return to education must equal or exceed the economic growth rate—about 3 or 4 percent.[24] Since most serious proposals for investing in lower-class education are expected to meet this generous criterion (see the discussion in chapters 5 and 6), a Poverty-Reducing Education Policy could in fact be regarded as likely to increase the effective supply of labor.

This result need *not* increase the employers' net profits. An increase in the labor supply can be expected, *other things being equal*, to increase the level of business profits. In the short run, conventional economic theory leads us to expect that an increase in the quality of labor available will raise the profitability of physical capital by effectively increasing the ratio of labor to capital. The longer-run effects require a more complex analysis, but the proportion of income from physical capital in national output has changed little over the past fifty years or so, remaining within a range of about 20 to 25 percent despite a geometric increase in the level of national income. This fact can plausibly be used to infer (again with an assist from conventional economic theory) that the further increase in output resulting from an improved labor supply will yield additional profits.[25] This is the economic core of the belief Buis and others have adopted.

The argument is false, however, since its *ceteris paribus* assumption overlooks the economic effects of higher education taxes. If a long-term increase in schooling levels were paid for by a permanently increased tax rate on employer profits—which in turn curtails investment in physical capital—an increase in the effective labor supply might not increase either national income or profits. A positive effect on total output would result *only* if the net increase in the effective labor supply available to employers yielded by the education policy were large enough to compensate for the decline in the amount of machinery and other physical capital available owing to the long-term effect of the tax. This condition would require that the return to schooling be about as large as that earned by physical capital, say, 10 to 20 percent (recall the discussion of this point in chapter 6). If the investment in education met this fairly stiff criterion, pretax profits would also be likely to increase. Again invoking the constant-share-of-income theory, one could guess plausibly—though not very accurately—that about a fifth of the additional income would go to owners of physical capital.

But even if pretax profits were increased, *after-tax* profits might be reduced—even in the long run, if the policy continued to be paid for by a profits tax. And, after all, only after-tax profits are available to the employer either for his consumption or for adding to his stock of capital. For the education policy to benefit the employer it must yield an increase in pretax profits high enough to compensate for the lower *portion* retained after taxes. This requirement demands a very high rate of return from the investment in human capital financed by this policy. This point can be illustrated with a simple example, which uses some plausible values for the relevant economic variables (see appendix 5 for the economic model underlying these results).

Let the pretax rate of return to physical capital equal 12 percent, with one-half of this profit, if it is not taxed for education, to be reinvested, and, introduce some reasonable numerical values for the other parameters.[26] It follows that total consumption of goods and services will increase only if the rate of return to a proposed investment in human capital, financed entirely by a cutback in physical capital investments, is at least about 12 percent (the hypothetical rate of return to investment in physical capital). If the source of funds is a tax on employers, their after-tax profits will increase only if the human capital investment yields more than twice that rate—over 32 percent (see part A of table 20).[27] Very few investments in education can be expected to yield that much. Hence the employers' interest would *not* have been advanced if a portion of their profits

TABLE 20. HYPOTHETICAL RATE-OF-RETURN CRITERIA FOR EMPLOYER INVESTMENTS IN LOWER-CLASS EDUCATION

A. TAX ONLY ON EMPLOYERS		
To maximize:	Welfare State Criteria	Pre–Welfare State Criteria
Consumption	4%	12.4%
After-tax profits	4	32
B. TAX ON ALL TAXPAYERS		
	Percent of Cost Paid by Employers	Pre–Welfare State Criteria for Maximum Aggregate After-Tax Profits
	0%	4%
	10	7
	30	12
	50	18
	80	26

Source: See appendix 5.

had provided the sole source of expenditure for increasing the educational opportunities of the poor.

The federal legislation actually proposed, however, did not call for a tax solely on employer profits or investment in physical capital but for a tax on the entire nation, including middle-class and working-class taxpayers as well. Part B of table 20 shows the minimum rates of return to an investment in human capital required to advance the employers' interest on the assumption that they provide lesser shares of the cost. This method naturally yields markedly lower criteria. For example, if the employers' share were only 30 percent, the investment in schooling would have to yield only 12 percent to advance after-tax profits. This is a high but not improbable rate of return for some forms of investment in lower-class education. But this hypothetical example does not indicate that the employer opposition to federal aid was irrational.

Fear of Increasing Federal Taxes

Reformers often tried to win acceptance for federal aid to education by stressing that the funds could be limited to providing adequate education for the poor. But the employer organizations never accepted the idea that federal aid to education would be restricted to this purpose. Contemporary publications of the U.S. Chamber of Commerce and other business organizations forecast that if federal legislation won acceptance on such grounds there would soon be a cutback in local efforts to provide education for the poor and, somewhat later, demands that the federal government assume responsibility for middle-class education as well.[28]

Such extensive federalization was clearly *not* in the employers' interest. At that time the state and local system provided a quite adequately schooled labor force, more schooled than that of any other nation in the world, at a truly minimal tax cost.[29] A contemporary statement by the National Education Association described the problem of taxing employers in a decentralized system of school finance in these words:

[Of] the taxes paid by the organized corporations, those business organizations deriving profit from goods sold and services rendered on a regional or nationwide basis, [the] lion's share flows into the federal treasury. Corporations doing business across state lines pay taxes on their real property in the various school districts in which they happen to be located, of course, and thus some local districts receive a part of their support from this source. But the many thousands of other districts profit not at all from this tax.[30]

Others pointed out that where the corporation was taxed locally, the regressive property tax used to finance schools typically had a quite low incidence on corporate property. But under a federalized system, employers would have to support schools even when they were outside the district in which their places of business were situated. They would also lose the threat of moving to another district if the school tax rate on their property was too high. For these reasons, federalization enables the government (at least in theory) to force employers to pay a much larger share of schooling costs than is feasible under the traditional system.

In summary, while consideration of the political realities required a modification of the abstract assumption that each dollar of profits tax generates one dollar of additional educational outlay (the assumption which underlies the 32 percent rate of return to the human capital investment criterion in Part A, table 20), it was not clear in which direction that assumption erred. While others would have shared the tax cost of the proposed federal subsidy, such an expenditure might well have been made at the expense of ongoing state and local efforts where the employer contribution was quite small. Hence, a dollar of profits tax could have generated either much more or much less than a dollar of additional educational outlay. But federal aid to education would only have been of net benefit to the business community if each of its tax dollars had yielded several dollars of additional school funds. Under the circumstances, it is not difficult to understand the employers' reluctance to accept such a change in the basic rules of the game of American educational finance.

This entire rationale was shattered by the recent development of welfare state conditions in this country. Welfare costs fall on employers as well as others, giving them a powerful reason for supporting educational reform. Obviously, the bargaining problem of allocating the costs of a PREP among the different groups of taxpayers remains. But the obvious failure of the state and local system to meet this social need means that if employers try to minimize their tax burden by opposing federal assistance they will pay higher federal taxes for welfare and other costs. Thus, a reconsideration of the traditional opposition of business to reform of the state and local system of educational finance can advance the long-term economic interests of the employer class.[31]

TRADE UNION SUPPORT FOR A
MORE DEMOCRATIC EDUCATION
POLICY

The trade union movement's traditional support for federal programs to advance the schooling of the poor also has special importance in the political economy of educational inequality. The historical record is clearly one of union support's being overmatched by business opposition. But the political strength of unions has grown over the years and will probably continue to grow in the years and decades ahead. Hence an understanding of the union position is important.

The steadfast union support to lower-class education in pre–welfare state conditions appears paradoxical at first. In most of this period the unions largely represented a small "aristocracy of labor," craftsmen whose taxes would have had to go to provide schools for their less fortunate brothers (such as the blacks in the South) and whose labor market interests, it would appear, would have been hurt by the education of potential competitors.

The explanation of their support lies largely in two factors. One is the identification of the craft and other unions with the larger interests of the working class. Though weak in comparison with some European countries, working-class solidarity was strong enough in this country to produce positive trade union support for this policy as for most other welfare state reforms. The other is a craft union structure and wage theory that saw a better-educated lower class as helping to strengthen rather than weaken the position of skilled labor. While often opposing larger apprenticeship programs for the skilled trades, the unions and their leaders typically supported widespread general education, partly on the grounds that it raised the wage expectations of the young workers and helped them to work intelligently and with greater sophistication to advance trade union goals. After all, many lower-class youths did become skilled laborers despite exclusionist practices.[32]

The economic base of the trade unions in this country is not nearly so elitist today as it was thirty or forty years ago. Moreover, the welfare state now gives the upper-working-class member a positive taxpayer interest in a PREP. At the same time the older reasons for trade union support still stand. This interest of a politically stronger union movement now affords another source of optimism for the future of schooling reform.

THE ESEA OF 1965: A MAJOR
BREAKTHROUGH

The struggle for federal legislation to assist the education of the poor finally succeeded with the enactment of the Elementary and Secondary Education Act of 1965. Passage of ESEA can be attributed to a national concern with poverty costs. This significant change in the rules of the game came more from an interest in the social than in the fiscal costs of poverty. The fiscal costs began to increase more rapidly *after* passage as welfare and other efforts to alleviate poverty expanded. In fact, it is more reasonable to regard both welfare liberalization and the education act as part of the mid-sixties War on Poverty than to infer a cause-and-effect relationship between them.

The origins of the War on Poverty are complex, and interpretations vary. But if there is a consensus, it is that the program can best be understood as a response to the social turmoil of the period, especially the civil rights revolution in the South and the growing unrest in the urban ghettos of the North. (But certainly other factors, including a humanitarian concern for the plight of the poor—as described, for example, by Michael Harrington in *The Other America* in 1961—were also significant.)

There is little doubt of the importance of this social unrest and the fears it engendered in contemporary thinking about educational reform. Thus in 1961 James B. Conant interrupted a more general study of American education for the Carnegie Foundation to publish his famous *Slums and Suburbs*. In an oft-quoted passage, Conant warned that "social dynamite is building up in our large cities in the form of unemployed out-of-school youths, especially in the Negro slums"—a problem he related to systematic underinvestment in inner-city schools.[33]

This last point was made even more strongly by the then U.S. Secretary of Health, Education, and Welfare, Anthony J. Celebrezze:

> The cause of these dropouts, and the despair and disillusionment that characterize them, is not so much that students have failed education as that education, as they have found it, has far too often failed them.
>
> Education's deficiencies, we have come to recognize, are nowhere more marked than in the poverty of the schools that serve the children of the poor—in the heart of our great cities and in many rural communities. In the case of these cities and communities, poverty reduces local resources to the peril point. Because the tax base is low, funds for education are inadequate and the schools and the children suffer.[34]

Thus this crisis differed from earlier episodes in the struggle to obtain federal aid for education. Better schools, obtainable with federal financing, could be seen as providing an *immediate* relief from an urgent social problem by keeping black youths in school and hence off the streets. Hence it offered a more pressing argument for reform than the usual one of the long-term benefits of more socially useful graduates.

President Lyndon B. Johnson made federal aid to education a key plank in his 1964 campaign and had comparatively little difficulty in obtaining congressional support. During the debate in Congress organized business suspended its historic opposition to the plan. Interestingly enough, ways were now found to deal with the traditional religious and segregationist opposition. Some aid was given to the Catholic schools (under Title II of ESEA), while the issue of segregation in southern schools had been made much less important by the passage of the Civil Rights Act of 1964, which required the federal government to act to desegregate the schools. A number of Catholic and southern representatives accordingly switched to support for the bill, which was then passed by large margins in both the House and the Senate.[35]

OBSTACLES TO FURTHER
EDUCATIONAL REFORM

But passage of ESEA was only a first step toward egalitarian educational reform. Title I of the act provided that funds (approximately a billion dollars per year) be appropriated to assist schools attended by children from low-income families. In principle, the bill provided for a near-maximum use of these funds for the poor. For example, within a large city, *only* schools in the poorest neighborhoods were to obtain funds.[36]

This was, of course, a significant step forward in reducing an important dimension of schooling inequality. At present, however, the law's provisions are far too limited in scope and funding to do away with schooling inequalities in the United States. Thus, Title I appropriations in 1971 had run to only one and a half billion dollars—indeed, federal aid to education from *all* programs amounted to only 7 percent of public expenditure on elementary and secondary education. A great increase in this effort will be required for the national government to be able to bring about equality of educational opportunity.

Harold M. Baron's study of Chicago does describe how even these limited funds can be used to eliminate financial differences among schools *within* a big city school system (see the discussion of these inequalities in chapter 2 above) when the original discrimination is not too large and when the federal funds are used as compensatory education for the poor. The Chicago school system had been troubled by turbulent demonstrations and other manifestations of discontent with the traditional allocation of funds in the early sixties. As a result, when funds were made available by ESEA in 1965, they were in fact used with impressive success to correct expenditure inequalities.[37]

But this experience is not typical. City school administrators have been widely reported as using Title I funds for the general budget needs of the city school system or as otherwise diverting them from the poor. Jerome T. Murphy assigns the blame for this to a lack of sustained political pressure by the poor for a legal distribution of funds. He also cites powerful efforts by other urban groups, working through their congressmen, for a hands-off policy by the U.S. Office of Education on the distribution of Title I funds by local school boards.[38] The accounts of Murphy and others make it clear that the passage of the ESEA was only the beginning of a new phase in the struggle to obtain a federal commitment to a democratic education policy even in the limited area of reducing expenditure differences among schools.

Nevertheless, the discussion of group interests and behavior in this chapter, together with the description of the social, political, and economic requirements of the emerging welfare state presented in the preceding chapters, supports the view that the longer-term prospects for further educational reform are good. On the one hand, there is nothing in this analysis to suggest that liberals, educators, and the trade unions will cease their efforts in support of reform. On the other hand, there are reasonably sound grounds to expect a weakening of the traditional opposition to an expanded federal role in school reform. The objective basis for southern opposition to an increased federal role has been undercut, for the level of racial integration in the schools there has now actually surpassed that in the rest of the nation. At the same time there has been some progress toward resolving the church-state conflict in education that has been at the root of the anti–federal aid position of many Catholics.

The most important change here, however, may be the erosion of the *taxpayer interest* of organized business in opposing reform as the tax *advantage* of a PREP in our developing welfare state becomes increasingly clear. Some further reason for optimism on this point comes from an examination of specific manpower needs presently facing employers. Employers now have a diminishing demand for low-grade manpower both because of technological and organizational changes in their own enterprises and because of the upward trends in the minimum wages imposed by unions and government, which raise the cost of hiring the low-skilled (see the discussion in chapter 6). As a result, businessmen now have an especially strong interest as employers in an educational policy that endeavors to raise the productivity of the less able members of the labor force.

Furthermore, a more equal education policy could help alleviate two problems that are presently very troubling to business management—racial division among their workers, and absenteeism and other symptoms of reduced work involvement, especially among younger employees. Of course, educational policy alone is not going to resolve these problems. Even if it raises the skills of blacks relative to whites, managements must still introduce employment and promotion policies that will utilize their better-qualified blacks and so help to meet the black demands for workplace equality. Similarly, despite the efforts of educators to inculcate good work habits in their students, rising levels of schooling need not lead to an increase in work input, and could even be counterproductive, if managements fail to make an effort to design work so as to take advantage of the different skills and attitudes of those with better education. It is likely that the resolution of the deep social problems that contribute to such workplace ills lies beyond the powers of either personnel administrators or educators. Nevertheless, a more democratic education policy would at least provide management with the potential for making some progress.

In this new environment it appears that the rational basis for employer opposition to a PREP has been severely undercut. Moreover, there have already been some signs of change in business attitudes, of a recognition of the new business needs.[39] Thus the major political organizations of business now take a much more favorable (though still conservative) position toward government policies to help educate the poor. Looking to the future, one would not wish to predict a complete about-face by conservative employer organizations in their historical position on this issue. It is always dangerous to predict that groups will act collectively to advance their interests even when, as in the present instance, their previous behavior does appear to have supported their objective needs. But their shifting interests should at least be regarded as heralding a continued diminution of organized group resistance to a restructuring of the traditional decentralized education system. For this reason there is cause for optimism over the long-term prospects for reform.

10

Has schooling inequality been increasing?

THE CURRENT IMPASSE

The growing social need for a more democratic educational system, together with the decline of organized group resistance to the use of federal spending to achieve that result, would seem to forecast at least some progress toward this goal in the relatively near future. Yet the current impasse over educational policy appears to point to a different conclusion. Resistance to educational equality remains strong among ideological conservatives, while liberal support appears to have grown weaker and less effective.

Part of the difficulty arises from a confusion among supporters of reform over the present status of educational inequality and over the effect of past efforts to reduce or eliminate it. Some liberal writers have evaluated recent progress so positively that they have turned to discussing the problems that face American education now that this older issue has been all but resolved. Of course, the evidence offered in part I of this book of deep-seated and persistent inequality in our school system easily rebuts those who see the battle for educational reform as essentially won. It is small wonder, given their false premise, that many of these liberals are in despair over the supposed failure of equality of educational opportunity to produce its expected benefits.

On the other hand, other liberals, focusing on certain retrogressive trends in the distribution of educational resources, have concluded that, despite past governmental measures to advance equality and the untiring efforts, largely by liberals, to further this goal, inequality has actually worsened in the United States. For example, one of the most astute analysts of our educational institutions, James S. Coleman, impressed by the continuing flight of the middle class to suburban and private schools, concluded that class segregation is now introducing a new dimension into educational inequality.

Years ago the question [of class segregation in education] would never have troubled us since the possibility did not exist of persons from different social classes segregating themselves by residence and forming, in effect, homogeneous communities that could have, in a sense, private schools supported by public funds. . . . It is only in recent times that class segregation has been a problem in schools.[1]

Such pessimistic appraisals of the trends contribute to a demoralization among the liberal supporters of educational reform. But these assessments can also be shown to be in error. Even a brief description of the changes in the level of schooling inequalities over the past several decades demonstrates that these resources have become much less unequally distributed, partly as a result of reform efforts.

The analysis of these changes is of interest to us, not simply because it corrects the overly pessimistic views of some liberals, however valuable this may be in the context of the present political impasse. Even more important is the further insight it can offer into the forces affecting the distribution of schooling resources in this country over time. This discussion will complement the analysis of legislative efforts to change the basic rules of the game in educational finance offered in the previous chapter with a description of the alternative strategies, largely judicial, employed (often with much greater success) by reformers to obtain federal intervention in education. It will also consider other factors that have operated quite independently of the federal government's activity to yield a less unequal distribution of schooling resources. This fuller treatment can then help us to provide a better answer to the question posed at the end of chapter 8: Is American society in fact likely to respond to the new social need for a less inegalitarian education policy?

CHANGES IN SCHOOLING
INEQUALITIES

Only a simple, approximate analysis of the changes over time in the distribution of schooling resources can be attempted here. The empirical description in part I in effect sought to piece together a cross-sectional "snapshot" of several dimensions of schooling inequality. This was not an easy task. But attempting to determine accurately how this overall inequality has changed over time is far more difficult. Yet despite the limitations of rough data and of necessarily simple statistical analyses a clear picture emerges.

In a sense, those who argue that inequality is at a historical peak demonstrate their susceptibility to what Colin Greer calls the great school legend—that the American public school system, whatever its present failures, has had a past history of providing equal opportunity to all. This assessment does not stand up to a comprehensive examination. Coleman thus errs by basing his judgment on just one aspect of educational inequality, the population movement from central cities to suburbs segregated by class and race. Obviously this has been a significant factor; the proportion of the metropolitan population living in suburbs has risen from 43 percent in 1950 to 53 percent in 1970,[2] increasing the possibilities for schooling inequalities. When changes in other dimensions are considered, however, it appears that, on balance, educational opportunities are much less unequally distributed than they once were.

Inequality in Years of Schooling

The interpretation of the evidence on one dimension of schooling inequality, years of education, is rather straightforward. In the last fifty years, inequality within age groups in years of schooling has declined by about a third. Those educated fifty years ago have about half again as much variation in their years in school as have those trained more recently.[3]

The education gap *between* age groups has grown, especially in the past thirty years, as a result of the rapid increase in schooling levels. In fact, as a result of this gap, the overall dispersion in years of schooling has not declined.[4] This generation gap in schooling, however, generally tends to reduce earnings inequality rather than to increase it, since the less educated middle-aged worker has compensating advantages in the form of on-the-job experience and job seniority.

Declines in Interstate Inequalities

There is also abundant evidence that differences in educational quality at each level of schooling (as measured by resources allocated per student) have declined quite sharply in this century. Chapter 3 describes in some detail the large differences in educational quality that exist among states and among districts within a state. Although it is not feasible to reproduce the detailed cross-sectional analysis of that chapter for earlier decades, even the simplest analysis shows that interdistrict differences were much greater in the early years of this century.

This is understandable, since differences among the states in wealth and hence in the ability to finance education were larger at the beginning of this century. So was the progress of industrialization and thus the demand for education. Moreover, in the southern region a large class of tenant farmers then lived and worked under conditions that were still semiservile.

These regional discrepancies had inevitable results for the school systems of the various states, producing quite important differences among them. The state data show that in 1899 the proportion of children five to eighteen years of age enrolled in school at all was 85 percent or better in five states. But the proportion was less than half of this, 42 percent, in Louisiana, and well below the national average in most southern states. For those who were enrolled, the average term of attendance averaged almost twice as much in the northeastern states as in the southern states. It ranged from 146 days in Massachusetts and more than 130 days in Rhode Island, Connecticut, the District of Columbia, and New York to less than 60 days in Mississippi and Arkansas and 37 days in North Carolina. As for resources allotted per student, average expenditure for each child in average daily attendance varied from $3 in Alabama, $4 in the Carolinas, and $7 or less in six states to over $35 in six more developed states.[5]

But these serious discrepancies decreased over the next seventy years as regional differences slowly declined in importance. In 1929 Louisiana still had the lowest proportion enrolled of any state, but now 72 percent of the children five to seventeen years old were in school. The better-off states had also progressed—eight states had at least eleven out of twelve children in school—but the gap between the lowest and highest states had narrowed. Similarly, interstate discrepancies in the duration of school term were still quite large but were less than at the turn of the century. In 1929 the average duration of the term was less than 120 days in six states and more than 160 in five states. Resources allocated per child in average daily attendance reveal the same pattern: in 1929, six states spent less than $47, the top six states over $136.[6] Thus while interstate inequality was still quite severe in 1929, it was somewhat less than it had been in 1899.

The trend continues in more recent data. Comparatively little variation is now found in enrollment and attendance; the extreme range of average number of days attended is from 150 in Missouri to 170 in Washington. Significant expenditure differences do persist among states, and indeed are large enough to be inconsistent with any useful definition of equality of educational opportunity. Six states spent less than $725 per pupil in 1971 while six others spent over $1,200.[7] But the differences are much less than before. Using the same measure of inequality in each period, the ratio of the average expenditure per pupil in the top quarter of states to that in the bottom quarter,[8] a consistent decline is observed over time, from over 5 to 1 in 1899 to less than 3 to 1 in 1929 to about 5 to 3 in 1971.

Declines in Discrimination against Black Students

Discrimination within school districts has also declined sharply in the past seventy years. Considerable discrimination along class, racial, and ethnic lines has characterized the urban public school system in this entire period, and of course the wealthy have always been able to use the more expensive private schools.

Colin Greer's The Great School Legend provides vivid examples of how the children of European immigrants—a large portion of the urban proletariat in the United States in the early years of this century—were neglected, or miseducated, in the city schools of the period. He describes "the high degree of school failure and 'unspeakable' school conditions which progressives found in major cities at the turn of the twentieth century" and challenges the view that there has been a secular decline in urban lower-class education. Rather, the earlier conditions "have continued to be the experience of the majority of urban school children. Somehow the fact that this majority has been increasingly nonwhite since World War II has diverted attention from the constancy of urban school and urban slum environments."[9]

But of course the most glaring example of discrimination within school districts (and one for which abundant quantitative data are available) was provided by the southern system of segregated education. This school discrimination was quite open—part of a conscious racist policy for managing a black underclass of sharecroppers. As the state supervisor for elementary education, W. K. Tate, wrote in his official reports for South Carolina in 1910–11:

> The negro is now and will be for years to come, the tenant farmer of South Carolina. His welfare and the prosperity of the white race depend largely on his efficiency as a farmer. . . . The objections to negro education arise chiefly from the feeling that it unfits the negro for the place he must fill in the life of the State, and that the so-called educated negro too often becomes a loafer or a political agitator. If the objection be well-founded, it is not a condemnation of education in general, but of the particular kind of negro education we have been supporting. . . . I believe that the time has now come for us to attack the negro school problem with the serious intention of adapting the school to the special needs of the negro farmer in an endeavor to teach him agriculture.[10]

With this orientation, southern school administrators could confront unequal conditions in black education with a clear conscience. Thus Tate argues that while the amount spent per black child enrolled in school in his state

> is not large when reckoned on a per capita basis, it is large enough to demand better supervision in its expenditure than has been customary in South Carolina. . . . Since the negro county school is without supervision of any kind, it has in most cases reverted to the most primitive type and is *wholly without adaptation to the practical needs of the negro race.* . . . I never visit one of these schools without feeling that we are wasting a large part of this money [allocated to black education]. The negro schools are miserable beyond all description. They are usually without comfort, equipment, proper lighting, or sanitation. . . . [T]he negroes . . . are crowded into these miserable structures during the short term which the term runs. Most of the teachers are absolutely untrained and have been given certificates by the County Board not because they have passed the examination, but because it is necessary to have some kind of negro teacher. Among the negro schools I have visited, I have found only one in which the highest class knew the multiplication table. [Emphasis added.][11]

Tate's solution to these ills was not to upgrade the academic quality of black education in this state but to give it a more practical direction.

He concluded by asking: "Can we not devise a movement similar to the Boys' Corn Club as a means of producing a more intelligent cultivation of the soil on the part of the race which for years to come will form the principal agricultural class in South Carolina? This question should challenge the wisdom and patriotism of the educational leaders of the state."[12]

This mentality was the outcome of a complex of factors: the influence of the heritage of slavery on the thinking of the dominant race; the prevalence of a semifeudal system of plantation agriculture; the exclusion of blacks in the post-Reconstruction South from those skilled labor positions they had held under slavery; and the gradual suppression of the political rights of southern blacks in the same period, culminating in their almost complete disenfranchisement by the end of the nineteenth century. The dominant economic system had no need for mass education of blacks, while the political system both denied the black the means to compete for scarce school funds and regarded the educated black as a threat to the established social order.

The typical result was a degree of discrimination that dwarfs present inequalities.[13] Expenditures per black pupil in South Carolina were $1.73 in 1911, less than *one-seventh* the white level in that state and *4 percent* of the Massachusetts level. The average salary of the teachers Tate describes abusively as "the most ignorant of the state" was only one-fourth as high as that of whites.[14]

Moreover, Tate was probably right when he characterized the expenditure of even these meager funds as chaotic and wasteful. The county superintendent, he said, sometimes did not even know where the black schools in his district were located; appointment to positions as teachers and principals often went to faithful servants and other "old retainers" of powerful whites, regardless of academic qualifications; and political corruption in various other forms frequently plagued the administration of these schools.

The conditions described in South Carolina were typical of much of the South and were only more extreme than those in the remainder. In Alabama, 48 percent of the white children, as compared with only 30 percent of the black, attended school in 1909, while spending was $12.81 per white child and $3.43 per black child. In Louisiana the proportion attending school was 53 percent for whites, 37 percent for blacks; and for those who did attend school, the expenditure per child was $24 for whites but less than $6 for blacks. These racial differences in expenditures arose partly from lower salaries for black teachers (in Louisiana, salaries for blacks were a little over one-half the white level) and partly from differences in the student-teacher ratio (see table 21). Further, there were impressive differences in the physical resources allocated to the education of the two races. For example, the value of schoolhouses, sites,

TABLE 21. STUDENTS PER TEACHER IN ALABAMA PUBLIC SCHOOLS, 1909

On the basis of:	White	Colored
Pupils enrolled	46	69
Pupils in average daily attendance	29	43

Source: Annual Report of the Department of Education of the State of Alabama for the Scholastic Year Ending September 30, 1910 (Montgomery, 1910), pp. 135, 143.

and equipment per enrolled student in Louisiana was over *ten* times as high for whites as for blacks.[15]

Not only was the quality of black education inferior to that of whites in every southern state. It also varied sharply from state to state (and even from district to district), so that the schooling of some blacks was much further below the national standard than that of others.

Differences in wealth among southern states and counties provided a partial explanation of this inequality within the black group. A black pupil in Maryland, for example, actually had more spent on a year of his education than did a white pupil in Alabama, Arkansas, or Georgia. But a white pupil in Maryland had half again as much spent on him.[16]

A study in the 1930s found that the type of farming that was dominant locally was an important determinant of length of school terms. In 31 percent of the rural black schools where cotton farming was dominant, school was in session less than 81 days a year, while in areas where diversified farming dominated, only 9 percent of the rural black schools offered such short sessions and 36 percent had terms in excess of 140 days.[17] This finding gives eloquent support to the contemporary criticism of the monoculture of the southern cotton plantation: it was exploitative of child labor, and it provided a very low standard of living to the sharecroppers and laborers.

The same study found that within school districts some black children were subject to de facto discrimination by reason of the distance they had to travel to school. They generally were not furnished transportation, so they had to walk to school, and travel distances were significant because there were not enough schools for such a system. Average attendance was 118 days for those living within a mile of their school but only 97 days for those walking three miles. Even more significant was the effect of distance on dropout rates. Only 6 percent of the first-graders who had to walk at least five miles to school finished fourth grade, compared with 51 percent of those who lived within a mile of school.[18] These various studies and reports document the historical discrimination practiced against blacks, especially in the traditional southern plantation belt.[19]

There is little evidence of any ameliorative trend in the *relative* position of the blacks' place in the South before World War II. Teacher salary differentials actually widened considerably in the 1900–30 period as white salaries were raised toward the national level but those of blacks did not keep up. In thirteen southern states the ratio of white to black teacher salaries dropped from 60 percent to 45 percent.[20] Some progress was made in the thirties, but the differentials remained quite large at the beginning of the war.

The quality of teachers also remained less than satisfactory, as those in the black schools generally had much less education than those in white schools. In a study of the attainment of black teachers in fifteen southern states in 1930, McCuiston found that more than one-third had not finished high school, and that only 58 percent had finished at least two years of college.[21] The data in table 22 indicate the size of the gap in attainment that still persisted ten years after the McCuiston study.

There is also evidence that the preparation of teachers in the segregated system was inadequate in other ways. In a 1931 study, Bond administered the Stanford Achievement Test to 306 black teachers in Alabama. He found that the average achievement, using national averages as a standard, of those without a high school diploma equaled that of a child of thirteen years, five months; those with a high school diploma but less than two years of college scored equal to a child of thirteen years, eleven months; and those with at least two years of college had an average equal to that of a child of fifteen years, eight months.[22]

FACTORS IN THE DECLINE
IN INEQUALITY
Reduced Regional Differences
School discrimination against southern blacks has now declined at least as dramatically as the inequality *among* school districts. But a rather different set of forces was responsible in each case.

TABLE 22. GAP IN EDUCATIONAL ATTAINMENT BETWEEN WHITE AND BLACK TEACHERS IN THE SOUTH

Southern State	Average Teacher Salary (1939–40)		Percent of Teachers with at Least 4 Years of College Training (1939–40)		Current Expenditure per Pupil in ADA (1943–44)	
	White	Negro	White	Negro	White	Negro
Alabama	$ 878	$412	52	19	$ 70	$26
Louisiana	1,197	509	58	29	121	40
Mississippi	776	232	62	9	72	12

Sources: For salaries, Horace Mann Bond, *The Education of the Negro in the American Social Order* (New York: Prentice-Hall, 1934, reprinted by Octagon Books, New York, 1966), pp. 275–77; for training, Ambrose Caliver, *Education of Negro Leaders*, U.S. Office of Education Bulletin, 1948, no. 3 (Washington, n.d.), p. 36; for expenditures, *ibid.*, p. 31.

The decline in interdistrict differences took place entirely within the dynamics of the traditional, decentralized system. Essentially it was the result of a reduction in interregional differences in economic and cultural development, which in turn came largely from the migration of capital and management, technology, and other resources into and the movement of unskilled labor out of the less developed areas. The data clearly indicate that these homogenizing influences have had a powerful effect in raising the educational levels of the poor over the past half-century or more.

It is not equally obvious, however, that trends within the traditional system will continue to be in the direction of equalization. The currently popular emphasis on the movement of the middle class to the suburbs as a cause of educational inequality does have the virtue of pointing up the possibility (or even probability) that maintaining decentralization will in the future increase rather than reduce inequality. In any case, any reliable strategy for further reducing this form of inequality must be based on expanded federal action.

Action in Federal Courts

Discrimination against blacks in education differs from the inter-district case in that there has been less evidence of historic trends toward improvement within the decentralized system. To be sure, a number of broad historical forces favored the cause of the southern black in the past thirty-five years: the social philosophy of the New Deal; the Second World War against the Nazis and the antiracist rhetoric that developed in this country as a result; the competition with the socialist bloc after the war; the collapse of direct European hegemony over nonwhites throughout almost the entire colonial world; and, at home, the urbanization of the American black and his replacement on the farm by machines.

But specific federal initiatives, in particular, federal court actions, were necessary to narrow the gap between the educational opportunities of blacks and whites. This role dates back at least to the Reconstruction period when the federal government imposed on the former Confederacy state governments that were willing to introduce mass education for the freedmen. In more recent times federal intervention also played the decisive role, especially in the South. The gains that took place were largely the result of specific federal court actions initiated by reformers rather than the impersonal working of "forces of history."

In the early 1930s the National Association for the Advancement of Colored People, with the financial support of philanthropist Charles Garland's American Fund for Public Service, mapped out a long-term plan of action to shatter the state and local system of discrimination and segregation in the southern schools. Their principal target was the federal court system, which they hoped would be more vulnerable to legal and moral arguments than either Congress (see the discussion in the preceding chapter) or the state and county courts. The NAACP's first step was a coordinated series of suits for the elimination of racial differences in teachers' salaries. The first suits were brought against the border state of Maryland in 1936, but later actions struck at discrimination throughout the entire South. The struggle took many years, but the federal courts generally found in favor of the plaintiffs. The result was a remarkable change in the distribution of schooling resources in the South.[23] One author, Henry Bullock, concludes:

[B]y midcentury, the NAACP's campaign was complete. There was hardly a state in the entire nation that was not paying its Negro teachers salaries that equalled those paid to whites of similar positions and experience. At least this phase of the Negro's drive for equal educational opportunities had been achieved.[24]

Bullock exaggerates somewhat, but there is statistical evidence of a drastic upgrading of outlays for black education by the fifties. Louisiana, for example, had virtually equalized black and white teacher salaries by 1955, thus erasing the two-to-one difference that had persisted as late as 1940 (see table 24). Discrepancies remained—instructional expenditures per pupil in black schools were three-fourths the white level, and the values of buildings and equipment were little more than one-half as high. But the progress toward equality in a very few years had been truly remarkable.[25] Similar improvements were made in several other southern states. In Virginia the average salaries paid to black elementary school teachers rose to the point where they were actually slightly higher than those of whites in 1950.[26] Although important inequalities survived into the fifties, a marked tendency toward reducing black-white differences was observed everywhere.

The second phase of the NAACP campaign, initiated in 1945, went beyond the goal of "separate but equal" schooling and challenged the segregated school system as discriminatory as such. Its success in the historic 1954 Supreme Court decision set the stage for much of the further equalization that has since occurred. But in the South, meaningful enforcement of the decree came much later, in contrast to the border states, where its impact was almost immediate. As late as 1966 southern schools typically were still quite strictly segregated.

Data collected on southern schools for the Coleman Report in the mid-sixties reveal the extent to which this segregation still imposed differences in the *resources* available to black and white children despite the efforts to equalize *dollar expenditures*. The investigation found that, in the rural and small-town South, the verbal facility of teachers assigned to white pupils far exceeded that of those teaching blacks. The average scores were, respectively, 75.0 and 58.3 percent.[27]

TABLE 23. VERBAL COMPETENCE AMONG BLACK AND WHITE
TEACHERS IN THE SOUTH

Experience of Teacher	Percent of Correct Answers on Verbal Ability Test		Percent of Teachers Scoring above the Mean for Whites	
	Black	White	Black	White
10 years or more	62.9	78.2	24	66
5–9 years	64.6	78.3	26	64
Less than 5 years	61.9	81.3	17	61

Student Level	Verbal Ability Scores of Students Intending to Become Teachers[a]		Percent of Students Scoring above the Mean for Whites[a]	
	Black	White	Black	White
College seniors	18	30	6	45
College freshmen	27	45	9	55
High school seniors	17	35	8	52
High school freshmen	13	24	6	44

Source: James S. Coleman et al., Equality of Educational Opportunity (Washington: Government Printing Office, 1966), p. 345.

[a] Different tests were administered at each grade level so that student scores are only comparable within grade levels.

More detailed data for the South as a whole are presented in table 23. They demonstrate the rather dismal prospects for the gains in teacher quality that could have been expected for blacks within a segregated system in spite of salary equalization. The racial gap in verbal competence appears to be larger for newer than for older teachers and still larger among high school and college students planning to enter teaching.[28]

Recent Results

As a result of federal enforcement efforts, another astounding change has taken place in the southern region since 1966 in the desegregation of pupils and teachers. The dramatic turnabout in policy on federal aid to education in 1965 was described (and explained in terms of important social and group interests) in the previous chapter. This change was soon followed, presumably as a result of the same factors that had permitted the passage of ESEA, by much stronger federal enforcement of the 1954 court decision in the South—a policy that has been continued, if not accelerated, under the conservative Nixon administration. By 1968, the proportion of black pupils in all-black schools in the eleven states of the Deep South was 68 percent; by 1971 it had declined to 9 percent! In fact, pupil desegregation in the South had reached the point where it was well in advance of the North. Forty-four percent of southern black children were in majority-white schools compared with only 28 percent of northern blacks.[29]

The recent data also disclose the extent to which the tendency to assign only black teachers to black pupils has been reduced in the South. In this regard the region's record is even more impressive. Table 24 gives statistical results on both pupil and teacher segregation for the 1965–66 and 1970–71 academic years in twenty-three southern cities (the quantitative measures used in the table are those employed in chapter 2 for nonsouthern cities). Since segregation was virtually complete in 1965, all measures for that year are still fairly close to their maximum value of unity. But by 1970, our quantitative measure of pupil segregation (S, the difference between the proportion of white children in the average school attended by whites and that proportion in the school attended by the average black) had fallen to 56 percent in the Deep South and to 38 percent in the rest of the region. Our measure of the tendency to assign black teachers to black pupils (b, the increase in the proportion of white teachers assigned to a school per 1 percent increase in the proportion of white students in that school) had dropped to .22 to .23 throughout the South, and our measure of pupil discrimination (D, the difference between the probabilities of a white and a black child having a white teacher) had declined most dramatically to 8 percent in the Deep South and 13 percent in the region's other states.

Federal intervention has been less successful in changing racial patterns in northern education, but court-ordered busing and some changes in teacher assignment patterns have had a significant effect in curbing the racial segregation of teachers and pupils there. In the interval from 1965–66 to 1970–71, using the same sources as table 24, the difference in the probability of a white pupil's and a black pupil's having a white teacher (our measure of pupil discrimination) fell from 57 to 46 percent in the border states, from 20 to 15 percent in the "Deep North" (along the Canadian border), and from 33 to 21 percent in the rest of the northern region.

TABLE 24. PUPIL AND TEACHER SEGREGATION IN THE SOUTH, 1965–66 AND 1970–71

	b		D		S	
Region	1965–66	1970–71	1965–66	1970–71	1965–66	1970–71
Deep South	.98	.22	.93	.08	.95	.38
Rest of South	.96	.23	.89	.13	.92	.56

Sources: 1970–71 data calculated from U.S. Office for Civil Rights, *Directory of Public Elementary and Secondary Schools in Selected Districts, Fall, 1970* (Washington: Government Printing Office), by Hilmet Elifoglu for his Ph.D. dissertation, in progress at the New School for Social Research; 1965–66 data calculated from unpublished worksheets of the U.S. Civil Rights Commission.

Note: These measures of segregation are discussed in the text, and the variables b, D, and S are fully explained in the passage on table 2 in chap. 2, pp. 23–25 above.

Federal Expenditure Policy

In evaluating trends in the distribution of educational resources in the most recent years, one must also consider the greatly expanded federal role in school expenditures made possible by the 1965 passage of the Elementary and Secondary Education Act and by subsequent legislation.

Title I of ESEA, Operation Head Start, and other programs for compensatory education now play a useful role in a number of cities insofar as they offset the local school boards' tendency to allot fewer resources to the education of the poor. Given the limited gains to be obtained from further court-ordered pupil integration in a nation divided by race or class into large residential neighborhoods within still larger metropolitan areas, this compensatory spending policy now has a special significance for future equalization efforts.

THE IMPORTANCE OF THE
FEDERAL ROLE

This survey of the trends toward less inequality in education thus brings out the importance of a positive, forceful federal policy, especially at present. In a sense, it complements the earlier, more theoretical discussions in chapters 6–8, which argue that a less than optimal level of investment in the education of the poor could be predicted in a state and local system without federal intervention. The survey here of the dynamic forces actually generating changes in the distribution of school resources affords a less abstract way of appreciating the current need for a strong federal policy. It is apparent that a significant portion of the historic decline in educational inequality has resulted from centripetal forces acting within the decentralized system. Prominent among these forces have been a regional homogenization and economic development of more backward areas. But these forces are now being challenged by centrifugal effects, especially the movement of population to the suburbs. A heavier reliance on federal action therefore seems necessary to ensure continued overall progress toward reduced inequality.

The very considerable gains in equalizing educational opportunities for the black minority appear especially dependent on federal intervention to check the racist, or at least inegalitarian, tendencies of the state and local system. Our history does not encourage the view that the gap between the levels of resources offered to blacks and whites closes linearly with time. A poignant example is offered by this excerpt from an annual report of the New Orleans school system:

The requirements of the school law have been faithfully observed by the board, and no case has come to their knowledge of the exclusion of a pupil on account of race [or] color. Nor has this strict adherence to the law been attended by any of the unfavorable results so freely predicted in advance of the honest trial of an impartial system of education. . . . In one school where under the passionate impulse of the moment the whole number of white children was withdrawn because of the admission of colored pupils, they have returned to their places [making the school two-thirds white and one-third black at the time of the report] and the school is proceeding harmoniously. . . . It is believed that the firm, yet moderate, attitude of the board on this subject has effectually quieted the agitation formerly existing, and no further trouble is apprehended from a continuance in the course hitherto pursued.[30]

Actually this report is for the year 1871, when Louisiana was still under a federally imposed Reconstruction government. Although social and economic conditions have changed in the past hundred years, the maintenance of federal control is still probably necessary not only for further progress by the blacks[31] but simply to keep the gains of the recent past. Otherwise the 1960s may enter our history books simply as the Second American Reconstruction.

But given the changing social and group interests in federal aid to lower class education and the recent judicial and legislative breakthroughs at the federal level, there appears to be little reason to fear a full-fledged retreat to the principle of state and local control of school finances. Rather these factors indicate a long-run increase in the federal role.

11

Some suggestions
for getting on with
reform

Although the analysis of group interests in chapter 9 and the description of trends in the distribution of schooling resources in chapter 10 may support a positive long-term forecast for a less unequal education policy, the short-term outlook is clouded. At the time this is being written, the president of the United States appears to be committed to at least a partial dismantling of the innovative federal education programs of the 1960s. Journalists speak of a "snarling conservative majority" that provides popular (though not congressional) support for Nixon's retrogressive policy. A similarly mixed picture emerges when one turns from the education debate to actual policy initiatives. Important measures to further educational equality have been initiated in the courts and in Congress, and if they succeed inequality could be reduced considerably. But conservative opposition to these proposals is strong.

The role of the courts in curbing within-district school segregation has already been discussed. Integration advocates now insist that the courts go further and order that public school students in suburban school districts be integrated with those in central-city systems through extensive busing. Neither the political viability nor the inherent wisdom of this busing strategy is certain: it is a rather costly method for reducing inequalities in human as well as financial terms, especially in large metropolitan areas residentially segregated by race. Yet it would greatly increase the possible scope of racial integration, and whatever its other results, this legal effort must be counted a potentially significant step toward equalizing educational opportunity.

Other court actions have called for equalization of spending. Some have demanded a ban on inequalities in educational quality among *all* districts within a state insofar as they are based on differences in school district wealth (the *Serrano* case was one of the most important here). Other cases (especially the *Hobson* decision) provide for full resource or expenditure equality within districts. If such decisions are upheld and forcefully implemented they can lay the basis for eliminating all within-state variations in resources per student.

In addition to these legal steps, recent congressional actions appear to indicate a willingness to go much beyond the Elementary and Secondary

Education Act or similar legislation in extending equality of educational opportunity. The Higher Education Act of 1972 authorized $18 billion per year to assist the education of college and university students. Although the act falls far short of providing full equality of opportunity in higher education, the principles by which a large portion of this fund are being administered, as well as the size of the appropriation itself, do show a concern with the equality issue. The act's Basic Opportunity Grants are paid to the student rather than being used to underwrite institutional expenses; are allocated on the basis of student need as determined by a means test; and are awarded independently of measured academic ability, thus removing another source of class bias.[1]

These current judicial and legislative initiatives at the federal level support the optimistic views of those who have expected a quick end to the struggle for equality of educational opportunity. But as is becoming increasingly clear, resistance to schooling equality actually is still quite strong. In point of fact, each of the legal decisions mentioned above is now being contested in the courts; appropriations for the Higher Education Act have fallen *far* short of the sum specified in that legislation; the president has endeavored to cut back funding for other programs to help poor college students; and, indeed, he appears unwilling to fund adequately much of the educational reform legislation that is already on the books. Hence it is difficult to make a short-term forecast for egalitarian school reform.

But while avoiding such a forecast I shall attempt in these closing pages to clarify the relationship of some of the material presented or suggested in this book to the debate that now holds up further progress toward reform.

Application to Current Issues

Some of these connections are clear enough. The summary of the work of economists on the effects of education on earnings in chapter 5; the data relating declines in welfare incidence among blacks to their educational attainment in chapter 6; and the more general discussion of the social benefits of lower-class education in chapters 6–8 are all obviously relevant to the arguments of those—conservative or liberal—who hold that educational policy has not been and cannot be important in helping to resolve social problems. The description of remaining education inequalities in part I and the analysis of the decline of these inequalities over time in chapter 10 should also help rebut those who either assume away the problem of school inequality or hold a fatalistic view of efforts to reform it.

But two other important sources of the current opposition to reform ought to be discussed here. One is the concern about the structural changes required in our educational goals and institutions to effectuate a more democratic policy, even when the social value of that policy is admitted. The other is the fear that, whatever the moral right of the poor to better schooling, the economy will have difficulty in absorbing a better-educated lower class. These problems are to an extent susceptible to economic analysis, and the brief discussion in the remainder of this chapter is one economist's modest attempt to suggest directions in which solutions might be sought.

THE ORGANIZATIONAL IMPASSE

Confusion over the meaning of a democratic education policy is responsible for a considerable portion of the opposition that proposals for school reform generate, especially among conservatives. The objections here arise partly from a failure of policy makers to agree on a system-wide policy of equality and partly from a lack of consensus on the appropriate institutions for a more democratic policy.

Piecemeal efforts to aid the education of the poor are one result of these failures. These programs frequently are strictly compensatory. ESEA Title I money now can go only to low-income schools, Operation Head Start is limited to the children of the poor, and so forth. These requirements are necessary if the federal programs are to act as counterweights to the inegalitarian effects of the state and local school finance system. But they often appear, or can be made to appear, to be a form of "reverse inequality" unfairly benefiting the poor.

A similar problem arises from confusion over the organizational changes needed for a more democratic policy. When the schools try to democratize without confronting this problem, say by simply urging poorer youths not to drop out of high school or college, they meet with only limited success. This result encourages the belief that efforts to extend lower-class education are a waste of time. But if the system is changed in various ways to advance this goal, the results—in the absence of an overall, widely accepted plan for reorganizing education—inevitably strike traditionalists as improper and unfair. Thus a program of stipends to encourage the poor to remain in school, courses oriented to the blue collar jobs they are likely to attain, or the relaxation of academic standards to permit them to graduate will each seem to extend special privileges to the poor and to undermine the traditional academic function of education.

Of course these types of objection are hardly unanswerable. In response to the first, a variety of definitions of equality of educational opportunity have been put forward—by economists and others—any one of which could serve as the basis for a comprehensive rather than piecemeal policy for democratic education.[2] Definitions have been offered in terms of equal access to student loans or of equal opportunity to students of the same measured academic ability and achievement. More militant definitions in terms of equality of expenditures, of resources, or, increasingly, of academic or occupational achievement have recently become more popular. These various definitions provide an ample selection for the policy maker interested in making a commitment to school equality.

Similarly, a variety of reform schemes have been offered to deal with the problem of finding the appropriate organizational forms for a more democratic policy. These proposals would in effect build egalitarian goals into the basic structure of our educational institutions, making it unnecessary to work for reform by advancing piecemeal measures to compensate the poor for an essentially inegalitarian school system. Examples include educational parks, "free" or open schools, community control of schools, and an educational voucher system. Another is a redirection at the highest level of research resources toward developing teaching machines or other new ways of teaching lower-class children that would generate more educational progress per dollar.

Thus the problem is not a lack of proposals for a comprehensive policy or of plans for the extensive organizational changes needed to accommodate such a policy. Rather it has been a failure by government to select one of the various alternatives as the basis of federal policy.

Specific Suggestions

The detailed description of desirable organizational forms is a crucial step in any attempt to achieve educational reform. So is a broad definition of policies that would be practical to implement, economically efficient, and acceptable to most Americans. Unfortunately, that detailed analysis must introduce issues whose full treatment would range far beyond the scope of this book. Even the discussion of the relatively simple questions addressed in this work, however, brings out several points that appear to be relevant to this further analysis. They are summarized here as an illustration of the possible contribution of this type of work to the question of organizational reform in education.

In the first place, the analysis of the inegalitarian tendencies of the state and local system not only argues that money to rectify underinvestment in the poor must come from federal sources. It implies that the money must be strictly *controlled* by the federal government to ensure that the funds actually reach the poor. This point provides an obvious criticism of the revenue-sharing schemes that turn federal tax money over to the states without tight controls. This analysis also supports such measures as Title I of ESEA, which gives money only to poor schools, and the educational voucher plan of the Office of Economic Opportunity, which gives money directly to the poor child to be spent only on his schooling. More generally, this discussion would insist that each proposed program to aid the schooling of the poor should be considered in terms of the federal control it embodies, not simply the stated purpose of the legislation.

A second point emerging from this work is that limitations of the resource base available to different schools—especially the quality of the available labor supply—must be explicitly considered if a more democratic policy is to reduce real differences among them. If schools in the least developed areas have to hire their teachers locally, or if children from a minority that is below the majority in educational achievement are to be taught by teachers of the same group, then a determined effort must be made to ensure that the very best from among these groups will enter the teaching profession.

The economist is strongly tempted to recommend regional and racial integration of teachers as an *alternative* way of upgrading the teaching of the poor despite the cultural prejudice and political opposition this policy often encounters. Important cultural differences persist among regions and among ethnic groups, making it easier to recruit an academic elite for teaching from some groups than from others. Moreover, the fact is often overlooked that competing occupational demands exist for the very best among all groups, so that the wisdom of diverting this elite into teaching is not always obvious. Talented, well-educated southern blacks, for example, now have alternative openings in business and government that are not only attractive to them as individuals but that can be exploited to advance the political and economic status of their group. But whatever method of raising teachers' standards were adopted, the goal of educational equality clearly would be advanced if equal teacher quality as well as equalization of financial and physical resources was promulgated as a target for each regional, ethnic, and class subgroup.

A third point that emerges from this volume, especially from the empirical results cited in chapters 5–7, is that a heavy emphasis must now be placed on designing appropriate postsecondary education for the children of the poor. The ideological objections to extending higher education to the lower class were dealt with in chapter 4, and the empirical results cited in the later chapters also tend to rebut these objections. Yet there remains the very real and challenging problem of designing curriculums for the terminal education of this group.

Courses of study are needed that will prepare graduates for occupational roles quite different from those open to previous generations. After all, if some form of postsecondary education does become universal, the graduates will be as likely to enter blue collar occupations as the traditional white collar managerial and professional positions. At the same time curriculums will still have to offer meaningful general education to provide the cognitive abilities and socialization the graduate may need later to *improve* his occupational status, as well as the conventional but still important cultural and political benefits. Despite the innovations of many institutions, especially community colleges, much remains to be done here. The resolution of this problem appears to be of critical importance for a policy that strives for equality of educational opportunity by increasing the schooling of the poor.

Finally, the discussion in chapter 7 of the political requirements of our democracy and the related need to reduce inequalities in citizenship quality indicated that the goal of equalizing schooling resources per child was far too modest. The discussion there thus provides some support for those who would reorganize American education to pursue the much more ambitious goal of equality of educational outcomes—that is, the elimination of differences among classes, perhaps even among individuals, in both socialization and cognitive learning. The conclusion reached in chapter 7, however, was that achieving such a goal faced imposing difficulties. It suggested that some compromise between political and social ideals and economic realities would in practice have to be accepted.

Each of these four proposals is developed in terms of the interests of the majority group rather than simply those of the poor. Acceptance of these points, then, would not require conservatives to concede any special or unfair privileges to the poor or, for that matter, to take any interest in their welfare as such.

DEALING WITH LABOR MARKET DIFFICULTIES

Some opponents question the economic wisdom of a policy of upgrading the educational level of the lower class. They doubt the capacity of the American economy to absorb a larger group of highly trained manpower or to make do with fewer low-skilled workers. Economic analysis suggests that while this objection has some validity, these problems are probably not as great as the critics believe.

To take the second point first, it is easy to exaggerate the role of educational policy in determining the market supply of low-skilled workers. Economic analysis would argue that certain low-skilled labor services, such as domestic work or most repairs, will continue to be increasingly difficult to procure, higher in price, and lower in quality whether or not educational inequalities are reduced. In the first place, economic growth in the United States has typically raised the cost of labor services relative to the price of goods. Otherwise workers could not purchase more goods per hour of their work. This trend has been compounded at the lower end of the earnings scale by the welfare state changes discussed in chapter 6—minimum wages, income maintenance, and, probably, diminished work incentives for the poor, which help dry up the supply of low-cost workers. For these reasons alone still fewer maids, elevator operators, and so forth, are likely to be available in the coming decade.

It is probably true, however, that full equality of educational opportunity would exacerbate these problems by further reducing the supply of the poorly educated who could be attracted to such work. Any compensation to the consumer for this expected deterioration in services would have to derive from an easing of labor shortages in the middle and upper skill ranges, which could be hoped for from an upgrading of the workforce.

The more serious problem is whether the economy can actually absorb the graduates of a Poverty-Reducing Education Policy. This brings into question whether such a policy can actually achieve the goals of increasing national output or reducing poverty costs. This problem should in turn be broken down into two parts: Is there a market demand for additional well-educated manpower? And, will additional education permit lower-class youths (or other disadvantaged graduates) to compete with more able youths in this high-quality labor market?

Market Demand

It is difficult to give a categorical answer to the first point. Over the decades, very large increases in the supply of highly trained labor have been absorbed in an economy that was undergoing rapid technological and organizational progress, and there is little reason to forecast an end to this long-term progress. But in the short or medium run both shortages and surpluses have occurred. In the late 1950s, for example, a labor market "twist" was observed as demand for better-educated people rose relative to that for less well-educated workers. This feature led to much higher unemployment rates among the latter, relative to those with more schooling, in the sixties. The trend was stabilized in the late sixties and early seventies as an increased supply of college graduates entered the labor market, although their unemployment rates continued to be much lower than those of the poorly educated.[3] It is possible that a further rapid increase of college graduates could create at least a temporary problem in their finding jobs of the traditional sort.

But this is not a valid argument against equality of educational opportunity. Even if the threat of market oversupply were real, the social morality of rationing educational resources to those with financial and cultural advantages would still be unacceptable to those seeking egalitarian reform.

Personal Factors

There is very little reason to fear, however, that a PREP (at least on the scale usually considered to be practicable) would in fact be so successful that it could eliminate differences in schooling outcomes among individuals. Differences in genetic endowment, cultural background, and personality characteristics would still yield large differences both in academic achievement and in subsequent occupational status under almost any conceivable schooling policy. Indeed, this conclusion has been a source of considerable disillusionment among those who look to educational policy for a full resolution of the problem of earnings inequality.[4] Hence the threat of a PREP's creating an oversupply of the highly able should not be overstated.

The practical effects of equal education for all combined with fairly unequal achievement and occupational outcomes is likely to raise popular objections all the same. The sight of people with perhaps two to four years of college in office and factory jobs that were formerly handled by high school graduates is certain to lead many to feel that the schooling investment has been wasted. They are likely to charge that society is becoming overcertified, "degree crazy"; that employers are apparently no longer interested in making money but are irrationally selecting overeducated job candidates; that jobs are being pointlessly upgraded; and so forth. The possibility that, in the absence of extended educational opportunities, many graduates from culturally disadvantaged backgrounds would either be unemployed, on welfare, "hustling" in illegal and often dangerous activities, or working at truly menial jobs is, unfortunately, likely to be disdainfully rejected by such critics.

As a PREP is introduced, empirical economic analysis can continue to be used to determine whether this objection has merit. Analysis can show whether investment in improved, occupationally relevant education for the poor in fact continues to make a significant contribution both to individual earnings gains and to reductions in poverty costs. But even if strong gains continued to be measured it is unlikely that this unconventional result of a PREP would win immediate popular acceptance.

IDEOLOGICAL RESISTANCE TO REFORM

While economic analysis is relevant to many aspects of the present controversy over educational reform, it does have its limits. The economic and social disadvantages of schooling inequality can be described and the interest of the taxpayer in reform carefully delineated. Workable and fair definitions of equality of education opportunity can be promulgated, practical organizational reforms for implementing these goals devised, and the danger of an oversupply of the very qualified discounted. But resistance to change need not yield to rational argumentation. The conflicting initiatives today from the executive, judicial, and legislative branches of government appear to point to irresolution or stalemate on the issue of school inequality in the months ahead rather than to progress toward a more democratic policy.

It is not very difficult to understand this resistance. Reform means change, and some people always oppose it. Educational reform requires a federalization of education finance, considerable organizational change in the schools themselves, and adaptation by business management to a better-educated labor force. These are not insignificant adjustments to make, and each of them evokes important opposition from some groups in the population.

In addition, there is the old-fashioned conservatism that has always rejected the idea of equality of educational opportunity itself. This resistance reveals itself most clearly when real progress toward equality appears to be imminent. For example, the usually moderate *Baltimore Sun* reacted to congressional passage of the Higher Education Act of 1972 by criticizing it as "the big new Nixon program for broad financial aid in college" and concluding:

Several years ago William Powell did a feature movie kidding the American presidential campaign. His election-eve oration climaxed with the promise that when elected, he would see that every man, woman and child in the United States went through Harvard College free. In those simpler times people used to laugh and laugh, and maybe there ought to be more laughter now at the idea, quite solemnly advanced by many, that the only fruitful preparation for adult life is college for almost all.[5]

The editorial writer's equation of "Harvard College" (that is, an institution reserved for an elite) with any form of extended schooling for the poor appears to reflect the still widely held view that postsecondary education must necessarily be a privilege for the few.

On the left side of the political spectrum there is little reason to believe that American liberals, long-term advocates of educational reform, will cease to support a more democratic policy. There is, however, some hesitation among this group on the reform issue at this time. One reason is the confusion over the issues of school reorganization and labor force absorption discussed above. But another is a shift in emphasis, as the more glaring school inequalities are removed, to other issues that some now think promise more effective action against poverty—for example, income maintenance and public service employment. (Recall the argument in chapter 1 that such new, untried programs have a political advantage over education policy in that their advocates can put them forward as full solutions to the poverty problem—a claim that experience shows would not be justified for equality of educational opportunity.)

ECONOMIC ANALYSIS AND
THE LONG-RUN PROSPECTS

The long-run prospects for an extensive Poverty-Reducing Education Policy are much better than are the short-run chances for reform. Because of ideological resistance or footdragging, adoption of a PREP requires a strong commitment to change. However, a principal spur to reform, the social unrest of the 1960s, has been considerably reduced in force.

Another reason why the short-term outlook is so bleak is the current mood of our taxpayers. As everyone knows, they are not inclined to "invest" their money in *any* government policy—especially if its justification relies on an analysis by the "experts." This mood is a result partly of the higher taxes now being paid to support the military and social programs begun or expanded in the sixties, partly of the unsatisfactory or at least uncertain outcomes of so many of these adventures.

A PREP admittedly does require an initial increase in taxes, while its benefits are long-term and depend on complex economic, social, and political factors. Ironically, a PREP very likely would now advance the goals of the conservative taxpayer precisely because of the sixties' buildup in poverty costs, an important reason for the taxpayer's present negative mood. A PREP would be likely to reduce total taxes by curbing welfare and other fiscal expenditures imposed by the low-skilled in a welfare state. But to see this requires a rather complex calculation. The taxpayers and their representatives must be convinced that an increase in their current taxes will result in larger gains in the future—a difficult task of persuasion for any group of "experts" at the present time.

Given this mood, it is difficult to predict the direction of federal policy in the short run. And so—taking into account the increased importance of federal action in maintaining or expanding the nation's commitment to educational equality—it is hard to forceast whether there will be any progress soon toward reducing schooling inequality.

But the discussion in these chapters does indicate that the long-run prospects for a more egalitarian schooling policy are brighter. Unless the present conservatism actually sweeps away our commitment to income maintenance—especially the present welfare system—and eliminates legal and union minimum wages, the taxpayers' objective interest in a Poverty-Reducing Education Policy can be expected to be permanent. High tax rates for poverty costs, continued over a long period, could provide an effective "learning experience" that would eventually compel a rethinking of the true taxpayer interest in a more democratic education policy. This reappraisal, to conclude with an optimistic forecast, could finally succeed in overwhelming the ideological and institutional resistance to democratic reform in American education.

Appendixes

APPENDIX 1

Derivation of teacher and pupil segregation measures for Table 2

For a given city, let

B_i = Number of black students in the ith school
W_i = Number of white students in the ith school
N_i = Total number of students in the ith school
B = Number of black students in the city school system
W = Number of white students in the city school system
N = Total number of students in the city school system
X_i = Number of black teachers in the ith school
Y_i = Number of white teachers in the ith school
T_i = Total number of teachers in the ith school
X = Number of black teachers in the city school system

DERIVATION OF S (PUPIL SEGREGATION MEASURE)

The proportion of black students in the ith school is B_i/N_i. The proportion of black students in the school attended by the average black student is

$$\sum_i (B_i/N_i)(B_i/B).$$

The proportion of black students in the school attended by the average white student is

$$\sum_i (B_i/N_i)(W_i/W)$$

and the difference between them is

$$S = \sum_i (B_i/N_i)[B_i/B - W_i/W].$$

This is arithmetically equivalent to

$$\sum_i (W_i/N_i)[W_i/W - B_i/B],$$

the difference in the proportion of white students in classes attended by the average white and the average black pupil.

DERIVATION OF D (PUPIL DISCRIMINATION MEASURE)

The probability of a black student's having a black teacher is

$$\sum_i (X_i/T_i)(B_i/B)$$

The probability of a white student's having a black teacher is

$$\sum_i (X_i/T_i)(W_i/W)$$

and the difference between them,

$$D = \sum_i (X_i/T_i)[B_i/B - W_i/W].$$

This is equivalent, arithmetically, to

$$D = \sum_i (Y_i/T_i)[W_i/W - B_i/B],$$

the difference in the probabilities of a white and of a black child's having a white teacher.

DERIVATION OF b (TEACHER SEGREGATION MEASURE)

If teachers are assigned to classes by means of a linear discrimination rule $X_i/T_i = a + b(B_i/B)$ (so that the proportion of black teachers in a school increases linearly with the proportion of black students in attendance), then substituting for X_i/T_i in the first equation for D above, we have:

$$D = \sum_i [a + b(B_i/B)][B_i/B - W_i/W] = bS.$$

Hence, $b = D/S$, to a linear approximation.

DERIVATION OF E (ADJUSTED TEACHER SEGREGATION MEASURE)

In order to standardize for differences among cities in their black teacher–black student ratios, $E = bX/B$ was calculated. E estimates (to a linear approximation) the percentage increase in the proportion of black teachers in a school per 1 percent increase in the proportion of black students there.

These measures were then calculated from unpublished data from the 1966 study of school segregation by the U.S. Civil Rights Commission.

The statistical estimation of teacher salary and quality

THE COST-OF-LIVING HYPOTHESIS OF SALARY DETERMINATION

Table A.1 presents the results of an attempt to relate teacher salary differences to variations in local living costs and levels of per capita income. Teachers' salaries in thirty-three metropolitan areas in which it was possible to estimate a local cost-of-living index were regressed on money income [see equation (1)] and on both money income and the local cost-of-living index [see equation (2)]. Teachers' salaries deflated by the cost-of-living index were then regressed on deflated money income [see equation (3)].

These results clearly support the income but not the cost-of-living theory. (a) The simple coefficient of determination between teachers' salaries and income is .59 [see equation (1)], more than four times the simple coefficient of determination between salary and the cost-of-living index, .14;[1] (b) when

TABLE A.1. RELATIVE IMPORTANCE OF INCOME AND COST-OF-LIVING LEVELS IN DETERMINING TEACHER SALARIES (33 METROPOLITAN AREAS)

Estimating equation	R^2
(1) $S = 16.74\ Y^{.645}$ t ratio (3.32) (6.6)	.59
(2) $S = 6.49\ Y^{.75}\ P^{-.34}$ t ratio (1.72) (6.07) (1.37)	.61
(3) $S/P = 11.59\ (Y/P)^{.687}$ t ratio (2.04) (5.0)	.45

Y = weighted median family income.
Note: State and local income weighted by percentage of educational support from state and local sources.
Source: Income for 1959 from *U.S. Census of Population: 1960*, vol. 1, *Characteristics of the Population*, pts. 2–52 (Washington: Government Printing Office, 1963), table 76.
S = SMSA median teacher salaries.
Source: Ibid., table 124.
P = cost-of-living index.
Note: Cost of living in several cities is available only since 1966. Living costs for 1959 were estimated for these cities by extrapolation of the average city family budget.
Source: Cost-of-living index for 1959 from Helen H. Lamale and Margaret S. Stotz, "The Interim City Worker's Family Budget," *Monthly Labor Review* 83, no. 8 (Aug. 1960): 785–808.

salary is regressed on income and the cost-of-living index [equation (2)], income is statistically insignificant and the cost-of-living index is not; (c) when real salary is regressed on real income [equation (3)], a much lower level of correlation is obtained. These results imply that once community income per capita is taken into account, local cost-of-living effects add little to the explanation of teacher salary determination.

DETERMINATION OF TEACHER
SALARY AND QUALITY

A simple statistical model can be used to test the model described on p. 38 of chapter 3.

If the level of teacher salary (s) a school board is willing to offer is a function of the per capita income of the area it serves (Y) and of the quality of teachers (q) that can be obtained at that salary, then equation (4) below would be appropriate for statistical estimation (the u term in equation (4) and following equations is a stochastic error term). If the salary required by teachers (s) is a function of their quality relative to the quality of the labor supply (Q) in the area where they are employed (the modified Carlsson-Robinson hypothesis of quality determination), equation (5) would be appropriate for estimation.

$$s = s_4(q, Y, u_4) \tag{4}$$

$$s = s_5(q, Q, u_5) \tag{5}$$

If the role of salaries in competing occupations (S) in determining teacher salaries is also to be tested (the second hypothesis), this variable can be added to the regression, as in equation (7) (the equation set (6) and (7) will be referred to as the alternative model):

$$s = s_4(q, Y, u_4) \tag{6}$$

$$s = s_7(q, Q, S, u_5) \tag{7}$$

The estimating equation sets (4) and (5) or (6) and (7) each contain two dependent or endogenous variables (s and q), so that estimation by the ordinary least-squares method will yield biased, inconsistent results. However, consistent estimates can be obtained by the two-stage least-squares method, in which the parameters of the two equations are estimated simultaneously.[2] In this estimation, q is first regressed on the independent or exogenous variables Y and Q (Y Q and S in the alternative model) by the ordinary least-squares method. The estimates of q obtained in this fashion are then used as proxies for the values of q in equations (4) and (5) [(6) and (7)], and these equations estimated by ordinary least squares.

The results of these estimations are given in table A.2, along with estimates obtained by ordinary least squares for comparison. For further comparison table A.2 presents estimates obtained by regressing the jointly determined variables—teacher salary and teacher verbal ability—directly on the inde-

TABLE A.2. SIMULTANEOUS DETERMINATION OF TEACHER SALARY
AND TEACHER QUALITY

Two-stage least-squares estimates	R^2
(4) $s = 19.7\ \hat{q}^{.12}\ Y^{.70}$	.86
t $\quad$ (9.06) $\quad$ (.61) $\quad$ (8.29)	
(5) $s = 0.1\ \hat{q}^{3.92}\ Q^{-1.32}$	.88
t $\quad$ (4.85) $\quad$ (14.13) $\quad$ (9.18)	
(6) $s = 19.9\ \hat{q}^{.07}\ Y^{.72}$	.86
t $\quad$ (4.08) $\quad$ (.38) $\quad$ (8.48)	
(7) $s = .03\ \hat{q}^{1.97}\ Q^{-.60}\ S^{.62}$	.87
t $\quad$ (3.39) $\quad$ (3.50) $\quad$ (2.58) $\quad$ (3.46)	
Ordinary least-squares estimates	
(4) $s = 19.7\ q^{.11}\ Y^{.71}$	.86
t $\quad$ (9.14) $\quad$ (.74) $\quad$ (10.32)	
(5) $s = 65.1\ q^{1.40}\ Q^{-.09}$	.56
t $\quad$ (3.75) $\quad$ (4.56) $\quad$ (.54)	
(6) $s = 19.7\ q^{.11}\ Y^{.71}$	.86
t $\quad$ (9.14) $\quad$ (.74) $\quad$ (10.32)	
(7) $s = .16\ q^{.43}\ Q^{-.012}\ S^{1.06}$	.85
t $\quad$ (2.01) $\quad$ (2.05) $\quad$ (.13) $\quad$ (9.61)	
Reduced form estimates	
$\hat{s} = 22.6\ Y^{.73}\ Q^{.03}$	.86
t $\quad$ (6.59) $\quad$ (13.01) $\quad$ (.31)	
$\hat{q} = 7.8\ Y^{.18}\ Q^{.36}$	.82
t $\quad$ (6.44) $\quad$ (4.89) $\quad$ (7.56)	
$\hat{s} = 3.94\ Y^{.50}\ Q^{.06}\ S^{.40}$	.87
t $\quad$ (1.24) $\quad$ (3.50) $\quad$ (.84) $\quad$ (1.74)	
$\hat{q} = 14.4\ Y^{.27}\ Q^{.33}\ S^{-.14}$	.82
t $\quad$ (3.52) $\quad$ (2.71) $\quad$ (6.97) $\quad$ (.90)	

q = teacher verbal ability; s — teacher salary. Y – state per capita income; see table A.1. Q = proportion in state passing the Armed Forces Qualification Test, mental section; source: U.S. Department of Health, Education, and Welfare, *State Data and State Rankings* (Washington: Government Printing Office, 1968), p. S-28. S = median income of managers, officials, and proprietors; source: *U.S. Census of Population: 1960*, vol. 1, *Characteristics of the Population*, pts. 2–52 (Washington: Government Printing Office, 1963), table 124.

pendent exogenous variables: per capita income, quality of the local labor force, and salaries in competing occupations.

The results shown in table A.2 give little support to the view that salaries offered are determined by quality considerations. In both of the two-stage, least-squares estimates (as well as in the ordinary least-squares estimates) of the school boards' willingness to pay higher salaries [equations (4) and (6)], teacher quality is statistically insignificant. Moreover, when teacher salary is estimated directly as a function of the independent exogenous variables, the quality of the local supply of labor is not statistically significant.

Hence these results do not reject the hypothesis that local teacher quality considerations have no effect on teacher salaries.

THE CAUSAL CHAIN MODEL

If salaries are determined by local school systems as a function of local per capita income and possibly of salaries in competing occupations but are not responsive to local quality conditions, equation (8) would be suitable for the statistical estimation of teacher salary. If the quality of teachers the school system can hire is responsive to the level of salary offered as well as to the quality of the local labor supply—the modified Carlsson-Robinson hypothesis of quality determination—then equation (9) would be appropriate for the statistical determination of teacher quality.

$$s = s_8(Y, S, u_8) \tag{8}$$

$$q = q_9(s, Q, u_9) \tag{9}$$

In this framework q does not appear in the first equation, so that teacher salary and quality are not jointly determined. Rather, equations (8) and (9) might be regarded as a recursive system or "causal chain" in that a line of causation runs from salary to quality, as shown in figure 1 in chapter 3.

A recursive or causal chain system may be estimated by the ordinary least-squares method. See the text of chapter 3 for the statistical results obtained by using the causal chain model here.[3]

Optimum college scholarships policy under a fixed college student subsidy constraint

It is argued in chapter 4 that there are at least three reasons why an organization of colleges such as the College Scholarship Service should not be expected to allocate subsidies in a way that would yield a socially optimal distribution of college resources: (1) the inability of a voluntary association to obtain major policy changes from all of its members, (2) the association's use of academic rather than social values in making decisions, and (3) inadequate subsidy funds. The first two problems are discussed in the text, but the third requires further exposition.[1]

This problem is in a sense the most serious, since unlike the first two it cannot be rectified by a simple reorganization of the agencies distributing student aid. For example, if scholarship funds were federalized,[2] the government would not have a compliance problem and could easily adopt social values in allocating funds. But it would still have the task of allocating a socially suboptimal level of funds for student support unless Congress increased the allocation for this purpose. Hence it is especially worthwhile to consider the effect of underfunding on the allocation of college resources, especially the resulting bias in favor of those students whose economic circumstances permit them to attend college on a relatively small subsidy.

MODEL FOR AN OPTIMUM COLLEGE SCHOLARSHIPS POLICY UNDER A FIXED CONSTRAINT

Let V_i = Social value of the college education of the ith student (i.e., the net social gain of educating the ith student *minus* the net social cost)

S_i = Subsidy cost of the college education of the ith student

Then it can be shown that the maximum social value can be obtained from a limited subsidy fund if all students are ranked in terms of the ratio of the social value of their proposed college education to the cost ($R_1 = V_i/S_i$) and are admitted in descending order until subsidy funds are exhausted. To see this, consider a violation of the rule in which part of the subsidy—say, $X million—is spent on a group of students for whom the value-subsidy ratio is less than it is for another group that has been rejected for aid. Then an increase in total value can always be obtained by reversing this decision, rejecting the first group and using the $X million to accept the second group.

The allocation decision is complicated by the fact that variations in the amount of resources allotted to an individual's college education will affect its quality and hence its social value. Although such variation may increase the amount that the student and his family are willing to pay for schooling, it will still generally be true that more expensive education for a given student will required a greater subsidy for him.

Defining k_i as the social cost of the college education of the ith student, it follows that the social gain from allocating an additional subsidy dollar to improving his schooling will be equal to:

$$dV_i/dS_i = \frac{dV_i/dk_i}{dS_i/dk_i} \tag{1}$$

The subsidizing agency must compare the gain from using funds to increase the quality of students' education with the gain to be had by using funds to permit more poor but socially valuable students to attend.

In general, an optimal allocation will occur only if the social gain from spending an extra subsidy dollar on improving the quality of schooling for each student attending college is just equal to the social gain per subsidy dollar from admitting one more student to college.

Denoting the lowest ranked student admitted to college as m, it follows that the optimal marginal decision rule will be:

$$\frac{V_m}{S_m} = \frac{dV_i}{dS_i}(\text{all } i) = \lambda \tag{2}$$

where λ is the cutoff value-subsidy ratio, determined by the size of the total subsidy budget and the number and size of competing student subsidy needs.

INEGALITARIAN EFFECTS OF A
SUBSIDY LIMIT

A subsidy limit can have an important negative effect on the probability of admission and on the quality of school attended by the poor. This effect can be seen more clearly (and related better to the discussion in chapter 5 of the causes of educational inequality) by pursuing the above analysis a bit further.

Let $v\,(P.B.)_i$ = The dollar value the ith student and his family place on his college education (i.e., the amount they are willing to pay for it)

$P.C._i$ = The dollar cost to them of this education, in the absence of subsidy

and $\hat{V}_i$ = The net private value of the college education of the ith student to himself and his family

That is,

$$\hat{V}_i = v(P.B.)_i - P.C. \tag{3}$$

and the required subsidy to ensure the ith student's attendance can then be written

$$S_i = -\hat{V}_i \tag{4}$$

Substituting $-\hat{V}_i$ for S_i in equation (2) above, the marginal conditions for a decision rule to maximize social welfare, given a subsidy constraint, become:

$$\frac{V_m}{-\hat{V}_m} = \frac{dV_i}{-d\hat{V}_i} (\text{all } i) = \lambda \tag{5}$$

Hence the larger the dollar amount the individual is willing to sacrifice for education, the more likely (given the social value of his schooling) he is to get a place in college. Chapter 5 offers several reasons why this private demand for education will be higher for the middle class than for the poor. Because of this tendency, it follows that, even if the government is free of any bias against the poor in evaluating the social value of schooling them—in fact, even if it has a mild preference for allocating resources equally among socioeconomic groups and races—it may still be moved by a subsidy limit to support an allocation that favors the middle class.

The importance of this inegalitarian effect declines with the size of the education subsidy budget. As the subsidy increases, λ, the cutoff value-subsidy ratio, falls, so that subsidy costs and hence poverty become relatively less important as determinants of schooling. If funds are adequate, λ falls to zero, so that no student for whom the social benefit of higher education is believed to exceed its social cost is denied admission, even to the highest quality college, because of his lack of financial resources.

AN EXAMPLE OF THE COLLEGE
ADMISSIONS DECISIONS RULE

The subsidy limit problem can be illustrated with a very simple example[3] (which abstracts from differences in college quality). Tony Ascoli, Jim Smith, Pete Stein, and Mike Shea are four high school seniors in the town of Mudvale who have applied for college scholarships. The net dollar value to society of educating each of them at the Mudvale extension of the state university is estimated on the basis of nonacademic as well as academic values. Their SAT scores and high school grades would suggest an ordering "Ascoli, Smith, Stein, Shea." But Jim Smith is a black youth who has been elected president of his integrated high school class and Mike Shea is a polio victim whose blue collar options are thus sharply limited. Applying these nonacademic values yields the ordering "Smith, Ascoli, Shea, Stein." However, the four youths also vary in their economic circumstances, and the resulting differences in the subsidy cost of their education yield still a different ranking.

The full cost of educating a student at Mudvale State is $40,000 (i.e., if tuition were charged at full cost and if each student were paid a competitive wage for attending college). However, each of the four youths requires only the subsidy given opposite his name in column 2 below. The resulting ratio of social value to subsidy cost (λ) is given in column 3. Here, the four are ranked "Shea, Smith, Stein, Ascoli." Since the net value to society of their education is positive for all four youths (see column 1), *all* will be admitted if scholarship subsidies are adequate. However, if a scholarship budget constraint sets a cutoff social value–subsidy ratio (λ) of say, 1.5, so that each dollar paid out in subsidy must, in the estimation of policy makers, yield a return of at least one and a half dollars in net educational value, then Smith and Shea will be accepted but Stein and Ascoli rejected as scholarship candidates.

	(1) Net Social Value of Student's Education	(2) Scholarship Required by Student	(3) Value Obtained per Dollar of Subsidy Required (1)/(2)
Pete Stein	$15,000	$12,000	1.25
Mike Shea	$20,000	$10,000	2.00
Jim Smith	$32,000	$20,000	1.60
Tony Ascoli	$24,000	$30,000	0.80

The most important result of a subsidy limit here is that Tony Ascoli is rejected because of his poverty despite the academic and social value of his education. At a higher level of subsidy λ will decline and, when it drops below .80, Ascoli will be admitted. Social welfare is maximized, of course, if funding rises to the point where λ = 0 and any student for whom the *net* social value of college education is positive is admitted regardless of his lack of financial resources.

Economic growth criteria for a PREP

CRITIQUE OF THE CONVENTIONAL METHOD

The analysis of the economic and fiscal effects of a long-run commitment to a Poverty-Reducing Educational Policy (e.g., a commitment to increase the level of schooling of lower-class youths by two years and to maintain this higher level indefinitely or, alternatively, a commitment to a permanent reduction in class size) is not well served by the method conventionally used to evaluate the private and the fiscal and other social benefits and costs of schooling. The conventional method calculates several separate rates of return on a proposed investment in human capital: a *private* rate of return, which compares a graduate's earnings gains with his expenditures on education; a *fiscal* rate of return to the state, based on a comparison of government expenditures on an individual's education with the stream of tax benefits from it; and a *social* rate of return, obtained by examining the flow of benefits to society at large from an individual's education and comparing them with the social costs of his schooling. These internal rates of return are then assessed for policy purposes by comparing them with the rates of return available on alternative investments in government or corporate securities.[1]

There are several reasons why this conventional technique must be modified if it is to be used to evaluate the long-run economic and fiscal effects of a PREP.

1. A simple, static comparison of earnings and tax returns does not provide an analysis of the economic contribution of repayments to the state, the "fiscal feedbacks" of lower-class education. It simply regards them as a return to the state to be used for a variety of purposes. But a long-term policy of investment in the poor requires that much, perhaps all, of the fiscal feedback from the schooling of one generation—the reduction in welfare and other poverty costs during their adult lives—in effect be used to provide subsidies for the education of the next. This reinvestment is an integral and inevitable component of the program. Only if the fiscal stream of these cost reductions in the long run exceeds current educational costs is there a flow of funds to the state that can be used freely—i.e., either for investment or consumption. Apart from this surplus, if one is generated, the fiscal feedback is committed to investment in lower-class human capital, and hence its economic interpretation has to be more definite.

2. Simple comparisons of rates of return typically do not make use of any theory of the determination of poverty or education costs and hence do not accurately forecast either the fiscal benefits or the reinvestment costs of a PREP. Yet it is argued in chapter 6 that changes over time in these benefits and costs could have an important effect on our expectation of the likely impact of this policy. A simple forecast of future changes of these benefits and costs can be made that will very likely be much less inaccurate than the conventional usage, which implicitly assumes constant costs.[2]

3. In a long-term evaluation, the assumption that the economic effect of a government policy to subsidize human rather than physical capital investment can be measured simply by comparing the rates of return to the two types of investment is not valid. An increase in the quality of labor due to education would probably raise the productivity and earnings of the capital stock and hence stimulate rather than discourage the accumulation of physical capital. Public investments that were perfect substitutes for private investment in physical capital would not be expected to have this positive effect.[3]

4. The conventional analysis ignores the effects of educational investment on sectoral unemployment and wage rates. But, as we saw in chapter 6, changes in these rates may constitute a significant portion of the gain from a PREP.

THE ECONOMIC GROWTH CRITERION
UNDER WELFARE STATE CONDITIONS

The long-run growth effects of a PREP can be interpreted in terms of the changes it yields in the effective labor supply available for economic production and in the rate of investment in physical capital—the conventional savings ratio. It can be shown that under welfare state conditions both these effects will be positive (ensuring a positive effect on growth) if the investment in a PREP meets the "golden rule" criterion of yielding a rate of return at least equal to the economic growth rate. In this long-run evaluation, the conventional analysis must be modified in several significant ways. Assume:

1. Subsidies to the education of the poor will be obtained at the expense of investment in physical capital and not of consumption. Any fiscal feedback from this investment will be used to help meet the reinvestment needs of the education program—in effect, to reduce the tax on physical capital. To simplify the analysis, the ratio of investment in physical capital to output is assumed to be constant, apart from this tax on investment and its repayment.[4]

2. Both welfare and education costs will rise at the same rate as the wage bill or, in the long run, at the same rate as the national economy (cf. the discussion of this point in chapter 6).[5] The growth in welfare costs can, however, be diminished by a PREP.

3. Capital stock in the long run adjusts to changes in the labor supply and in the savings or investment ratio, while output in turn is a function of labor and capital stock. Labor input is a function of the size of the work force and

of the latter's educational distribution. Educational levels are a function of student time and of teacher and other resources allocated to schooling.

Output is defined net of investment in human capital. This definition is preferable to regarding a conversion of investment streams from physical to human capital as a simple reallocation within the capital goods sector of the economy since it makes allowance for two special characteristics of the education sector (at least as it is organized in the United States): that it does not earn a profit and that it is extremely labor intensive. But it does yield a measure that is biased against a positive interpretation of human capital investment. For example, in the initial investment period the education investment policy, according to assumption 1, simply exchanges investment in physical capital for investment in human capital. But while consumption is stable, the "output" measure will always record a decline, since it includes investment in physical but not in human capital. Hence an unbiased index, production of consumption goods and services, will be used here as a social criterion for judging education investments.

Assumption 3 can be expressed in the following four-equation model. Let

C = Aggregate consumption in a given year
Y = Aggregate output in a given year
K = Stock of capital goods in a given year
$I = \Delta K$ = Gross investment in physical capital in a given year
L^* = Effective labor supply available for the production of output

$s = \dfrac{I}{Y} = $ The savings ratio, i.e., the ratio of physical capital investment to output

e = Proportion of output allocated to the PREP

Then

$$C = (1 - s)Y \tag{1}$$

$$Y = f(K, L^*) \tag{2}$$

$$(a)\ K = g(I, K_0) \qquad (b)\ K = h(I) \tag{3}$$

$$I = sY \tag{4}$$

(3a will apply in the short run and 3b in the long run.)

One can now consider the effect of an educational policy instrument on this system. Assume initially no effect of the policy on sectoral unemployment or wage rates. Then define a Poverty-Reducing Education Policy as one in which government education subsidies are permanently increased so that a given additional proportion of output (e) is henceforth allocated to the schooling of the poor. By assumption 3, this policy will yield a permanent increase in the schooling level—e.g., an additional year of schooling—for a given fraction of the poverty group (cf. the definition of a PREP on p. 77).

This PREP will determine two intermediate variables, the savings ratio, s, and the effective labor supply, L^*, which in turn will determine the other variables in the system. Thus in these first four equations of the model, s and L^* are control or exogenous variables, while the social criterion variable, C, as well as Y, K, and I, are dependent or endogenous variables.

This can be seen more clearly when the endogenous variables are written in their reduced forms. In the long run,[6] from equations (2), (3b) and (4), it follows that

$$Y = f[h(sY),L^*] \tag{5}$$

This yields the reduced form equation,

$$Y = i(s,L^*) \tag{6}$$

When this value of Y is substituted in equation (1), one obtains

$$C = (1 - s)i(s,L^*) \tag{7}$$

Aggregate consumption is a positive function here (equation 7) of both the effective labor supply, L^* and the investment ratio, s.[7] The remaining endogenous variables, K and I, can also be written in terms of the exogenous variables. Moreover, K and I are also positive functions of both s and L^*. Thus

$$I = si(s,L^*) \tag{8}$$

$$K = h[si(s,L^*)] \tag{9}$$

It is clear from the reduced-form equations (6)–(9) that not only the social interest in aggregate consumption, equation (7), but also the taxpayers' interest in higher after-tax income is advanced if an educational policy increases s and L^* in the long run. By assumption 1, the tax rate is reduced when s is increased. Moreover, the output base (Y) from which the taxpayers' income is obtained is seen to be a positive function of L^* and s.

Hence, if a criterion can be established for a positive effect on *both* s and L^*, the major economic effects of the PREP can be valuated without recourse to a more complicated macroeconomic model.

The long-run impact of a PREP on the first of these intermediate variables, the effective labor supply (L^*), will be positive if, after the policy is fully effective, the continuing reduction in labor supply required in each period for teaching the additional group of students is offset by a sufficient improvement in the productivity of the program's previous graduates in the labor force in the current period. Its effect on the second variable, the investment ratio (s), will be positive if the annual educational subsidy required from the government for the continuance of the program is exceeded by the annual flow of fiscal feedbacks in the form of reductions in welfare and other poverty costs resulting from the long-term effects of the program.

The Labor Supply Criterion

Hence the labor supply effect will simply be a function of the productivity of the education program in increasing the economic effectiveness of its graduates. Note 24 in chapter 9 presented a heuristic demonstration that the effective labor supply will be increased if the economic rate of return to the education subsidized by a PREP is larger than the economic growth rate. This point can now be made more directly. Let:

n = Number of students in the PREP in a given year (assuming, for convenience, a one-year educational program)

N = Total number of graduates of the PREP in the labor force at a given time

l_0 = Effective labor input per year of a poverty-group youth without the proposed additional education

j = Ratio of direct to opportunity costs of schooling in this program

Δl = Individual labor quality gain: difference between the effective labor input per year of a graduate and that of a nongraduate of the program

r_e = Earnings rate of return to investment in the educational program (conventional measurement)

r_e' = Earnings rate of return to investment in the educational program (conventional cross-sectional measurement)

d_e = Rate of depreciation of individual (assumed constant here to simplify exposition)[8]

p = Rate of growth of population

w = Rate of growth of real wage rate

g = Rate of growth of the real wage bill, assumed to be equal in the long run to the rate of growth of the economy

W = Efficiency wage of labor (i.e., price of labor standardized for differences in educational quality)

The gross labor supply gain per year from an improvement in the quality of labor supplied by the program's graduates can then be written as:

$$N\Delta l \tag{10}$$

and the resource costs in a given year as

$$n(1 + j)l_0 \tag{11}$$

The net gain of the effective labor supply L^* will then be equal to (10) − (11), or

$$\Delta L^* = nl_0 \left[\frac{N\Delta l}{nl_0} - (1 + j) \right] \tag{12}$$

If earnings improvements due to education are accepted as a measure of the

resulting quality gain in labor input, it follows from the conventional definition of the cross-sectional rate of return that[9]

$$\frac{\Delta l}{l_0} = (r_e' + d_e)(1 + j) \tag{13}$$

Then, taking into account the fact that the actual earnings return will here
exceed the cross-sectional rate by the growth rate of the price of labor
$(r_e' = r_e - w)$; making use of the assumption that the economic growth rate
equals the sum of the wage and population growth rates $(g = w + p)$, and
substituting equation (13) into equation (12), one obtains:

$$\Delta L^* = n l_0 (1 + j) \left[\frac{N}{n} (r_e - g + p + d_e) - 1 \right] \tag{14}$$

Since the ratio of graduates effectively in the labor force to students enrolled
in the program here will be $N/n = 1/p + d_e$, equation (14) can be rewritten,

$$\Delta L^* = n l_0 (1 + j) \left[\frac{r_e - g}{p + d_e} \right] \tag{15}$$

Thus there will be a net increase in the labor supply if the conventional earnings rate of return to the investment in education exceeds the economic
growth rate $(r_e > g)$.

The reader is again referred to note 24, chapter 9, for a discussion of the
intuitive plausibility of this result.

The Savings Rate Criteria

The criterion for the success of a PREP in increasing the second intermediate variable, the investment ratio (s), by reducing the tax rate depends on the
share of the educational investment the government subsidy must provide and
the extent to which education-based earnings gains feedback in the form of
fiscal poverty cost reductions, as well as on the productivity of the education
investment itself. It can be shown that if the share of earnings gains from a
PREP received by the government exceeds the share of the education costs of
the program paid by the government, *and* if the rate of return to the education
sponsored by this program equals or exceeds the economic growth rate
$(r_e \geq g)$, then the tax rate is reduced and the savings rate may be increased.

If a = share of poverty-reducing education investment that must be paid
        by the government
$a + b$ = share of graduate's earnings gain, due to PREP, received by the
        government in the form of a reduction in poverty costs (the "fiscal
        feedback")
it follows that the government's current educational subsidy cost will be

$$a W n l_0 (1 + j) \tag{16}$$

and that its annual fiscal feedback or return after the program is effective will be

$$(a + b)WN\Delta l \tag{17}$$

The yearly flow of net fiscal gains will then be equal to (17) − (16) or, using equations (13)–(15),

$$aWnl_0(1 + j)\left[\left(1 + \frac{b}{a}\right)\left(\frac{r_e - g}{p + d_e}\right) + \frac{b}{a}\right] \tag{18}$$

Thus, there will be a net gain in s as long as (1) $r_e > g$ and (2) $b \geq 0$.

Conclusions

Since the first of the two conditions for an improvement in the savings ratio is also the condition for a positive labor supply effect, it follows that if the two conditions are met, *both* intermediate variables, s and L^*, will be increased.

Applying these results to the model in equations (6)–(9), it further follows that, given the welfare state condition $b \geq 0$ (cf. the discussion in chapter 6), if the conventionally measured rate of return to investments in a PREP exceeds the economic growth rate ($r_e > g$), aggregate consumption (C) will be increased, the tax rate reduced (since s is increased), and the level of physical capital stock (K) augmented, thus advancing the interest of society and of the taxpayers (and, as I argue in appendix 5, that of the employers). Moreover, the interest of the poverty-group student will also be advanced in that he is enabled by the program to obtain a profitable return on the investment of his time as a student.

EFFECTS OF CHANGES IN SECTORAL WAGE RATES

The effects of sectoral wage changes can easily be incorporated into this analysis. Let the workforce be composed of two groups of workers, a majority group (1), and a minority poverty group (2) consisting of those below average in educational attainment.[10] Let the aggregate labor supply then be a function of the two types of labor inputs:

$$L^* = L^*(N_1, N_2) \tag{19}$$

where N_1 and N_2 are the number of workers in each group.

Then, if the additional assumptions are made that wage differences are proportional to differences in marginal labor inputs and that poverty payments are used to meet a fixed proportion of the gap between the earnings of the lower class and those of the majority, it follows that:

$$T = t(L_1 - L_2)N_2W \tag{20}$$

where L_1 and L_2 are the labor inputs of individuals in the majority and minority groups respectively (i.e., are equal to the partial derivatives of the effective labor supply with respect to an additional member of one group or the other); t is the proportion of the poverty gap bridged by subsidy; and T is the total subsidy or transfer payment.[11]

Then, if a poverty-reducing education subsidy is thought of as raising a worker from the second to the first group, the reduction in poverty subsidy per worker educated will be equal to:

$$tW \cdot [L_1 - L_2 - N_2(L_{11} + L_{22} - 2L_{12})] \tag{21}$$

where L_{11} and L_{22} are the second derivatives and L_{12} is the cross-derivative of L with respect to its arguments.

If L is a linear homogeneous function of N_1 and N_2, equation (21) can be rewritten as:

$$tWL_2 \left[\frac{L_1 - L_2}{L_2} + E_1(N/N_1)^2 \cdot 1/\sigma \right] \tag{22}$$

where E_1 is the share of labor earnings going to the majority group and σ is the elasticity of substitution between the two types of labor.

The first term inside the brackets represents the direct gain attributable to the positive return to education itself (i.e., that obtained by reducing the numbers in the poverty group), while the second term represents the indirect saving obtained by reducing the rate of return to education through narrowing the earnings gap between the two groups. The relative importance of these direct and indirect effects will depend, negatively, on the elasticity of substitution between the two types of labor and on the proportion of the labor force in the minority group.[12]

As an illustration, a plausible division of the labor force into groups (1) and (2) would be between the upper four-fifths and the bottom fifth. In the 1960 census, employees in the bottom fifth of the educational distribution reported earnings per worker of less than three-fifths the average level of the upper group. Entering these values in equation (22), a ratio of direct to indirect subsidy gains of $\sigma/1.8$ is obtained. Hence only if $\sigma \geq 1.8$ would the direct effect have been as large as the indirect effect, and even if σ had been quite high, say 3 or 4, the indirect effect would still have been of considerable relative importance.

This indirect effect will raise the tax savings from investing in the education of the poor, giving the taxpayers an interest in investments in the poor even when the conventional rate of return is quite low. When indirect effects are taken into account, the criterion for a tax savings will be (if $b \geq 0$, so that the conditions for a welfare state are just met):

$$\frac{r_e - g}{p + d_e} + \frac{1}{1 + D/I} > 0 \tag{23}$$

where D/I is the ratio of direct to indirect effects.

In our example, $D/I = \sigma/1.8$ and inequality (23) can be written:

$$\frac{r_e - g}{p + d_e} + \frac{1}{1 + \sigma/1.8} > 0 \tag{24}$$

implying a significantly more generous criterion for investment in lower-class education unless σ is quite large.[13]

EFFECTS OF CHANGES IN SECTORAL
UNEMPLOYMENT RATES

This model can also be readily modified to incorporate the case in which youth employment is constant or at least declines less than proportionately as youths are withdrawn into education from the teenage labor market.[14]

Let the rate at which youth employment is diminished as school enrollment increases be:

$$-h(1 - u) \qquad (0 \le h \le 1)$$

If a youth's annual earnings are accepted without modification as a measure of the social cost of his time, then $h = 1$, while if aggregate youth employment is constant, $h = 0$.

Equation (15) may then be rewritten in a more general form:

$$\Delta L^* \cong n l_0 \left[\frac{r_e - g}{p + d_e}(1 + j) + 1 - h \right] \tag{25}$$

where r_e is calculated in the conventional way, by using the sum of direct costs and the expected value of annual forgone earnings to measure education costs, and j continues to be the ratio of direct to opportunity costs.

If another welfare state institution is taken into account and unemployed youths are assumed to receive a subsidy from the state, a more positive estimate of the fiscal return from education to the taxpayer also emerges. Now, when an increase in the number of students reduces unemployment, it saves the government unemployment or welfare benefits, thus minimizing the actual subsidy cost of education.

It can be shown that if $b = 0$ (so that the student pays the same fraction of his education costs as he obtains of its earnings benefits)[15] the net gain in subsidy reduction to the taxpayer continues to be:[16]

$$Wa\Delta L^* \tag{26}$$

but now ΔL^* is defined as in equation (25).

The use of a zero value for b is probably too conservative here. Under the present system, unemployment among young people not only imposes on the state the burden of unemployment payments, but since it contributes to family breakups, can also impose welfare burdens for years afterwards. Moreover, high unemployment among lower-class teenagers, and the resulting idleness and poverty, are widely believed to contribute to delinquency and other social ills that impose further costs on the state.

But even with this restrictive assumption, equations (25) and (26) imply a much more generous investment criterion if h is significantly less than unity. If $h = 0$, these equations actually argue that a rate of return to poverty youth education of zero or less, conventionally measured, could be consistent with a gain both in the savings ratio, s, and in the effective supply of labor, L^*.

THE ECONOMIC GROWTH CRITERION FOR A
PREP UNDER PRE–WELFARE STATE CONDITIONS

In the absence of welfare state conditions—i.e., with no fiscal feedback from lower-class education—it can be shown that this model affords a rate-of-return criterion for economic growth from a PREP approximately equal to the marginal product of physical capital or, as the latter is conventionally measured, the pretax rate of profit.

Without fiscal feedbacks, it follows that, even in the long run:

$$ds/de = -1 \tag{27}$$

Hence any positive labor supply effect of the policy would have to be balanced against the negative effect on growth of this reduction in the savings ratio (unlike the welfare state case, where both the labor supply and the savings rate could be increased by a PREP in the long run). The problem of weighing these offsetting factors complicates the analysis somewhat and also makes the result more sensitive to macroeconomic assumptions.

Since aggregate consumption (C) is a function, in the long run, of the effective labor supply (L^*) and the savings ratio (s), it follows that

$$dC/de = \frac{dC}{dL^*}\frac{dL^*}{de} + \frac{dC}{ds}\frac{ds}{de} \tag{28}$$

using the definition of e,

$$e = \frac{anl_0(1+j)W}{Y} \tag{29}$$

and the expression for ΔL^* in equation (15), one obtains, approximately:

$$dL^*/de = \frac{Y}{aW}\left[\frac{r_e - g}{p + d_e}\right] \tag{30}$$

Then, letting

$c =$ Elasticity of output with respect to stock of capital goods
$Y_K =$ Gross marginal product of physical capital
$\Pi =$ Net marginal product of physical capital
$d_k =$ Rate of depreciation of physical capital
$v =$ Long-run elasticity of capital goods stock with respect to investment
$Y_l =$ Marginal product of labor

One obtains from equations (5)–(7),

$$dC/dL^* = \frac{(1-s)Y_l}{1-cv} \quad \text{and} \tag{31}$$

$$dC/ds = \frac{Y}{s}\frac{cv-s}{1-cv} \tag{32}$$

Hence, from equations (27), (28), (30), (31), and (32), it follows approximately, that:

$$dC/de = \frac{Y}{1-cv}\left[\frac{(r_e-g)}{p+d_e}(Y_l/Wa)(1-s) - \frac{1}{s}(cv-s)\right] \tag{33}$$

This expression can be simplified if the physical capital stock is assumed to be proportionate to investment in the long run (i.e., $K = I/d_K + g$). Then,

$$dC/de = Y\left[\frac{\frac{(r_e-g)}{p+d_e}(Y_l/Wa)(1-s) - \frac{(\Pi-g)}{d_K+g}}{1-c}\right] \tag{34}$$

Using equation (34), the rate-of-return criterion for a PREP for maximum long-run consumption can now be written as a weighted average of Π and g.

$$r^* = \Pi am + g(1-am) \tag{35}$$

where $m = \dfrac{p+d_e}{g+d_K} \times \dfrac{W}{Y_l(1-s)}$.

m is plausibly near unity, so that if a youth is completely penniless ($a = 1$), the criterion for investment in human capital is similar to that obtained in the conventional analysis—the net marginal product of capital (Π) or, as it is usually measured in practice, the pretax rate of return to investment in private capital.

The employers' objective interest in a PREP

AN ECONOMIC ANALYSIS

The effect of a PREP on after-tax profits or, in the long run, on the accumulation of physical capital (assumed here to be privately owned) can be deduced from equations (8) or (9) of appendix 4.

The long-run effect on physical capital accumulation was given by:

$$K = h[si(s,L^*)] \tag{1}$$

Under welfare state conditions, it was argued that s and L^* will both be increased, as long as $dL^*/de > 0$. Hence the long-run accumulation of physical capital, as well as income, consumption, and the after-tax income of taxpayers, are all advanced if a fairly generous criterion is met.

Under pre–welfare state conditions, the accumulation of physical capital can still be advanced, but only if the increase in the effective labor supply (L^*) is large enough to offset the expected decline in the savings ratio (s). Moreover, since $K = sY$, a decline in s has a much more deleterious effect on physical capital accumulation than on income itself. Hence a much larger gain in the labor supply is necessary to maintain the rate of capital accumulation in spite of a lower investment ratio than is needed to provide for maintenance of the growth rate of income.

It follows from equation (1) and other elements of the model developed in appendix 4 that the criterion for a positive (or at least nonnegative) effect of an employer-financed PREP[1] on the accumulation of the employers' physical capital stock is, if pretax factor shares are constant,[2]

$$\frac{r_g^* - g}{p + d_e} = \frac{(Wa)}{Y_1}\left(\frac{\Pi - g}{d_k + g} + \frac{1}{c}\right) \tag{2}$$

Clearly, this is a much stricter criterion than that developed for aggregate consumption growth under pre–welfare state conditions [see equation (34) in appendix 4] since the principal source of the difference between the two criteria, $+1/c$, the reciprocal of the share of capital in income, is a rather large number. The simple numerical example discussed on pp. 128–30 of chapter 9 illustrates this point.

A COMPARISON WITH EMPLOYER INTERESTS IN OTHER INVESTMENTS IN PEOPLE

Individual and Class Interests in Specific and General Training

The financial interest of an individual employer in underwriting the costs of education when education takes the form of specific training (training that provides employees with skills useful only to this employer) is familiar. Here the condition for profitability is only that the payoff equal that available from other potential investments by the firm. But it is equally well known that the individual employer has but little interest in providing formal education or other general training for which a wide market exists among employers, since the subsidizing employer cannot expect to capture its economic benefits. Unless he raises the employee's wages to the full extent of the increase in the latter's productivity, the employee-graduate may exercise his option of obtaining a higher wage from a competitive employer.

Employers as a class do have an interest, however, in providing formal education or other general training if it increases the effective labor supply available in the economy and as a result increases output. But this interest is weakened, as we have seen, by the fact that most of the gain (perhaps three-fourths or more) is distributed to labor in the form of higher wage income.

The Analogy with Productive Consumption in Developing Nations

The employer interest in subsidizing formal education in advanced nations such as the United States also has some similarities with the employer interest in raising the general level of consumption of the workforce in a developing nation. The individual employer in the developing nation (in the absence of contract or servile labor) typically does not have an interest in raising wages in order to achieve a long-run improvement in the health of his workforce. But employers as a group do, at least if wages are so low that, when they are raised, a more than proportionate increase in effective labor inputs is assured. Then, after an initial period in which a subsidy is paid (e.g., a wage in excess of that required by the market), the productivity of the worker is enhanced to the point where he is able to earn enough by the sale of his labor at the market rate to maintain the health of his family without further special assistance. In this case the employers obtain a permanently enhanced labor force without the necessity of long-term subsidy.

From the viewpoint of the employers, however, there is a crucial difference between the subsidy of total worker consumption in a developing nation and the subsidy of education in the United States. Educational investment will (in the absence of fiscal feedbacks) require a continuing financial subsidy. Unlike total consumption, educational outlay is a quite specific use of wages. When education expenditures lead to a higher level of wages for graduates, these individuals are likely to allocate freely only a small portion of the wage gain to the educational needs of the next generation. Most of the increment will be spent on less "productive" consumption goods and services. Hence, in order to maintain educational investment at a higher level permanently, a continuing subsidy is necessary. Moreover, this need for subsidy may continue to quite a high level of economic development. Because it is very labor intensive, the cost of education rises with the wage rate, and so many parents continue to find education expensive despite the increase over time in their own wage income.

When the welfare state provides fiscal feedbacks, the repayment to the state (i.e., the reduced poverty costs) affords a social mechanism for ensuring that a large portion of the wage gain can in effect be channeled into meeting the educational needs of the next generation. Hence it is similar to the case of a general consumption subsidy in requiring only a temporary subsidy. But since employer-financed investment under pre–welfare state conditions may require a permanent subsidy, to advance the employers' interests it must meet a stricter criterion than would be necessary either in productive consumption investment in the developing nation or in the modern welfare state.

Notes

NOTES FOR CHAPTER 1

1. For a general treatment of the American faith in education, see, for example, Henry J. Parkinson, *The Imperfect Panacea: American Faith in Education, 1865–1965* (New York: Random House, 1968).
2. See the discussion of this point in chapter 9 below.
3. For recent discussions of this argument, see Stephan Thernstrom, *Poverty and Progress: Social Mobility in a Nineteenth Century City* (Cambridge: Harvard University Press, 1964); Michael Katz, *The Irony of Early School Reform* (Cambridge: Harvard University Press, 1968); or Michael Katz, *Class, Bureaucracy and Schools: The Illusion of Educational Change in America* (New York: Praeger, 1971).
4. See Bernard Bailyn, *Education in the Forming of American Society* (Chapel Hill: University of North Carolina Press, 1960), for a presentation of this argument, as well as a critical evaluation of it. A useful long-run perspective on the development of the modern school as a social institution is afforded in Philippe Ariès, *Centuries of Childhood* (New York: Vantage, 1965).
5. See, for example, Rush Welter, *Popular Education and Democratic Thought in America* (New York: Columbia University Press, 1962).
6. Not all socialists have taken this positive view. See Zalman Slesinger, *Education and the Class Struggle: A Critical Examination of the Liberal Educator's Program for Social Reconstruction* (New York: Covici-Friede, 1937), for the critical analysis of a radical socialist.
7. For negative evaluations of the effects of variations in schooling on a child's learning, see, for example, Harvey A. Averch *et al., How Effective Is Schooling? A Critical Review and Synthesis of Research Findings* (Santa Monica, Calif.: RAND Corp., 1972) and the work cited in Christopher Jencks *et al., Inequality: A Reassessment of the Effect of Family and Schooling in America* (New York: Basic Books, 1972).
8. Jensen, *Educability and Group Differences* (New York: Harper & Row, 1973).
9. Eric A. Hanushek, *Education and Race* (Lexington, Mass.: D. C. Heath, 1972). See also the discussion in U.S. Department of Health, Education, and Welfare, *Do Teachers Make a Difference?* (Washington: Government Printing Office, 1970).
10. James S. Coleman *et al., Equality of Educational Opportunity* (Washington: Government Printing Office, 1966). See also the evaluations of the Coleman results in Samuel S. Bowles and Henry M. Levin, "The Determinants of Scholastic Achievement—an Appraisal of Some Recent Evidence," *Journal of Human Resources* 3 (Winter 1968): 3–24; *idem*, "More on Multicollinearity and the Effectiveness of Schools," *ibid.* (Summer 1968): 393–400; and James S. Coleman, "Equality of Educational Opportunity: Reply to Bowles and Levin," *ibid.* (Fall 1968): 422–34.
11. Henry M. Levin, "A Cost-Effectiveness Analysis of Teacher Selection," *Journal of Human Resources* 5 (Winter 1970): 24–33. See also his "Recruiting Teachers for Large City Schools," mimeographed (Washington: Brookings Institution, 1968).
12. Historical trends in black educational opportunities are discussed in chapter 10 below.
13. U.S. Department of Health, Education, and Welfare, *Digest of Educational Statistics*, 1971 ed. (Washington: Government Printing Office, 1972), p. 3.
14. While school finance has remained decentralized, national influences have been quite strong on the organization of the schools, on the curriculum offered, and

on most of their educational practice. See James Koerner, *Who Controls American Education?* (Boston: Beacon Press, 1968), for a strong statement of this apparent paradox. See chapter 9 below for an attempt to explain it. Traditionally, nationalization has stopped short of a federal system of finance.

15. Charles M. Tiebout, "A Pure Theory of Local Expenditure," *Journal of Political Economy* 64 (October 1956): 416–24.

16. Cited in Elizabeth Durbin, "Family Instability, Labor Supply and the Incidence of Aid to Families with Dependent Children" (Ph.D. diss., Columbia University, 1971), pp. 72–73. Five percent had fathers born in New York City; 7 percent had mothers born there.

17. See the discussion of the College Scholarship Service in chapter 4 below.

18. See chapter 9 below for a discussion of the employer interest in this issue.

NOTES FOR CHAPTER 2

1. For school composition, see the discussion of the 1970 data in chapter 10 below. Racial composition of voting-age population for major cities is given in U.S. Bureau of the Census, *The Social and Economic Status of the Black Population in the United States, 1971,* Current Population Reports, Series P-23, no. 42 (Washington: Government Printing Office, 1972), p. 133. Racial participation data are also given there as well as in periodic reports in the series U.S. Bureau of the Census, Current Population Reports, Series P-20 (Washington: Government Printing Office).

2. This is not the end of the center-city schools' problems. Because of the concentration of lower-class children there, the school system generally has a higher proportion of educationally disadvantaged children and others requiring special schooling, increasing its relative need for resources. Moreover, school resources are often much more expensive in the center city. Teachers sometimes require a salary premium to commute into difficult areas from their suburban homes. Higher land costs also increase the price of building new plant. James W. Guthrie *et al., Schools and Inequality* (Cambridge: MIT Press, 1971), reports that the city of Detroit paid over $100,000 an acre for school sites in 1967, while surrounding suburban districts paid an average of $6,000.

3. Some useful discussions by economists of these school financing problems are found in Milton Friedman, "The Role of Government in Education," in *Capitalism and Freedom,* ed. Milton Friedman (Chicago: University of Chicago Press, 1962), pp. 85–107; W. C. Stubblebine, "Institutional Elements in the Financing of Education," *Southern Economic Journal* 32 (July 1965): 15–35; Bertram A. Weisbrod, *External Benefits of Public Education,* Princeton University Report Series 105, Industrial Relations Section (Princeton, N.J.: Princeton University, 1964); Mark V. Pauly, "Mixed Public and Private Financing of Education," *American Economic Review* 57 (March 1967): 120–30; Walter Hettich, "Mixed Public and Private Financing of Education: Comment," and Pauly's "Reply," *American Economic Review* 59 (March 1969): 210–13.

4. See Henry M. Levin, "Decentralization and the Finance of Inner-City Schools," Research and Development Memorandum no. 50 (Stanford, Calif.: Stanford Center for Research and Development in Teaching), for an interesting discussion of these problems.

5. For example, see David Rogers, *110 Livingston Street* (New York: Random House, 1968).

6. Gerald Kahn, "Current Expenditures per Pupil in Public School Systems 1958–59," Circular no. 645 (Washington: U.S. Department of Health, Education, and Welfare, 1961), tables 2 & 3, pp. 15 & 36.

7. The assignment of teachers can, of course, be controlled by administrators, including school principals. But there is little evidence that the net effect of administrative influence is to encourage experienced teachers to seek transfers to slum schools.

8. This teacher career pattern is described in Howard S. Becker, "The Career of

the Chicago Public School Teacher," *American Journal of Sociology* 57 (March 1952): 471–72. See also Albert P. Blaustein, "Philadelphia," in U.S. Commission on Civil Rights, *Civil Rights U.S.A./Public Schools North and West, 1962* (Washington: Government Printing Office, 1962), and Kenneth B. Clark, *Dark Ghetto: An Analysis of the Dilemma of Social Power* (New York: Harper & Row, 1965), p. 134.

9. Most cities do not have an effective merit system of payment for their teachers. See Henry M. Levin, "Recruiting Teachers for Large City Schools," mimeographed (Washington: Brookings Institution, 1968), for a discussion of this problem and for proposals for reform. See also the discussion in chapter 3 below.

10. See Martin Theodore Katzman, "Distribution and Production in a Big City Elementary School System" (Ph.D. diss., Yale University, 1967).

11. This finding was based on a test of verbal facility designed especially for the Coleman survey by the Educational Testing Service of Princeton, N.J.; James S. Coleman *et al., Equality of Educational Opportunity* (Washington: Government Printing Office, 1966).

12. *Education and Race* (Lexington, Mass.: D. C. Heath, 1972).

13. See H. Becker, "Career of the Chicago Teacher," for an analysis of the reasons why the more able teachers leave and the less able teachers remain in slum schools.

14. See, for example, Coleman *et al., Equality of Educational Opportunity*. Henry M. Levin, "Recruiting Teachers for Large City Schools," mimeographed (Washington: Brookings Institution, 1968), presents further evidence of the difference between the racial preferences of black and white teachers in ghetto schools. David Gottlieb, "Teaching and Students. The Views of Negro and White Teachers," *Sociology of Education* 37 (Summer 1964): 352–53, found that while white teachers regarded their black pupils as "talkative, lazy, high-strung, and rebellious," black teachers found them to be "happy, cooperative, energetic and ambitious."

15. See A. Harry Passow, *Toward Creating a Model Urban School System: A Study of the Washington, D.C., Public Schools* (New York: Teachers College, Columbia University, 1968), p. 64; *Supplemental Studies for the National Advisory Commission on Civil Disorders* (Washington: Government Printing Office, 1968), pp. 16, 36; and Richard E. Day, *Civil Rights U.S.A./Public Schools Southern States, 1963/North Carolina*, U.S. Commission on Civil Rights (Washington: Government Printing Office, 1964), pp. 33, 53–59.

16. See Albert P. Blaustein, "Discrimination against Teachers," in his "Philadelphia," pp. 154–70. See also H. Becker, "Career of the Chicago Teacher." The informal pressures on black teachers are varied. Both Becker and Blaustein agree, however, than an important factor is the black teacher's fear that if he does succeed in transferring to a white school against the advice of its principal, the latter will interfere with his career by giving him low ratings, difficult classes, or the like.

17. Patricia Cayo Sexton, *Education and Income* (New York: Viking, 1961); Jesse Burkhead, Thomas G. Fox, and John W. Holland, *Input and Output in Large-City High Schools* (Syracuse, N.Y.: Syracuse University Press, 1967); and Katzman, "Distribution and Production." See also James W. Guthrie *et al., Schools and Inequality* (Cambridge: MIT Press, 1971), including the review of literature on intracity studies presented there, pp. 34–35.

18. Coleman *et al., Equality of Educational Opportunity*.

19. The quality of the data themselves has also been criticized. See Samuel S. Bowles and Henry M. Levin, "The Determinants of Scholastic Achievement—an Appraisal of Some Recent Evidence," *Journal of Human Resources* 3 (Winter 1968): 3–24, and *idem*, "Equality of Educational Opportunity—More on Multicollinearity and the Effectiveness of Schools," *ibid.* (Summer 1968): 237–46. To use these data for the present study it was necessary to make a number of corrections on the data tapes. Within the Coleman sample, all elementary schools

in the chosen cities were studied. Center cities were defined by their political boundaries.

20. Estimated from census tract data by using transparent overlays. Since neighborhood income levels were changing in the period from 1959, the census year, to 1964, when the Coleman study was made, the estimates of family incomes based on the Coleman Report questions on consumer durables in respondents' homes were used to correct the census data for recent changes in income level.

21. Cf. the discussion in Gary S. Becker, *The Economics of Discrimination* (Chicago: University of Chicago Press, 1957). Becker found that this hypothesis was not supported in his study of earnings data.

22. Algebraically, if the total racial discrimination is (1) bW_s, where W_s is the proportion of whites in the school, and if there is a positive interaction with W_c, the proportion of whites in the city, so that (2) $b = c + dW_c$, then (1) can be rewritten (3) $cW_s + dW_sW_c$. If there is no interaction, $d = 0$, $b = c$, and (3) reduces to (1).

23. Both the school income and the city income variables were deflated by the U.S. Bureau of Labor Statistics city cost-of-living index. The deflated income data afford a more accurate measure of intercity variations in real income.

24. In regression equation (1) to (3), citywide values for the dependent variables were first regressed against average family income in the city. The regression coefficients thus obtained were used to obtain values of the dependent variables net of the influence of city income. These values were then used as dependent variables in regressions (1) to (3). This method permitted the use of citywide rather than sample values for the dependent variable in estimating the city income relationship, hence obtaining a more reliable result. It also served its conventional function of coping with any multicollinearity between city income and either neighborhood income or the racial composition variables.

25. An adequate explanation of these racial differentials is beyond the scope of this study. The lower average experience level of black teachers is probably due to a more rapid increase in the hiring of black than of white teachers. It has been suggested that the lower verbal ability scores are accounted for by the recruitment of many black teachers who were trained in segregated schools and colleges. Further explanations might be sought in a possible cultural bias built into the test of verbal ability.

26. A partial exception was found in the case of experience level of white teachers, where a relationship with income of the school neighborhood was found that was significant at the 5 percent level.

27. Unless, of course, blacks and whites were segregated by classrooms within schools.

28. Hjardis G. Ohberg, "Does the Black Child Need a Black Teacher?" *Integrated Education* 10, no. 2 (March-April 1972): 27–28.

29. Opinions differ widely on this issue. See, for example, Clark, *Dark Ghetto*, or Robert Herriott and Nancy St. John, *Social Class and the Urban School* (New York: Wiley, 1966). In a recent study of the distribution of teacher verbal ability within three northern and one southern metropolitan areas, Henry Levin found that about one-fourth of the explained variance in the teachers' verbal competence in the northern areas and "fully three-quarters" of this variance in the southern area were due to the racial factor (the remainder was associated with such factors as social class background, urbanization, sex, years of schooling, and quality of education). He also found that black teachers tended to be assigned to black students in all four metropolitan areas. He describes this as a "perverse pattern," since the result is that "the teachers with the lowest verbal skills have been assigned to a group of students whose participation in a middle-class society has depended largely on its prowess at linking the language pattern of its culture to that of the majority." See Levin, "Recruiting Teachers," chap. 3, pp. 18, 37, 38. Edward C. Banfield takes a different view in his *The Unheavenly City* (Boston: Little, Brown, 1968), arguing that if black nationalist sentiment becomes sufficiently strong, black children may eventually resist instruc-

tion by whites to the point where teacher resegregation will be necessary to maintain educational standards in the ghetto.
30. The independent variables were those used in the first three lines of regression results in table 1.

NOTES FOR CHAPTER 3

1. Quoted in Percy E. Burrup, *The Teacher and the Public School System* (New York: Harper, 1960).
2. See, for example, Harvey E. Brazer, "City Expenditures in the United States," Occasional Paper no. 66 (New York: National Bureau of Economic Research, 1959); Jesse Burkhead, Thomas G. Fox, and John W. Holland, *Input and Output in Large-City Schools* (Syracuse, N.Y.: Syracuse University Press, 1967); Otto A. Davis, "Empirical Evidence of Political Influences Upon the Expenditure Policies of Public Schools," in *The Public Economy of Urban Communities*, ed. Julius Margolis (Baltimore: The Johns Hopkins Press, 1965); Solomon Fabricant, "The Trend of Government Activity in the United States since 1900," Occasional Paper no. 56 (New York: National Bureau of Economic Research, 1952); Werner Z. Hirsch, "Expenditure Implications of Metropolitan Growth and Consolidation," *Review of Economics and Statistics* 41, no. 3 (August 1959): 232–41; Werner Z. Hirsch, "Determinants of Public Education Expenditures," *National Tax Journal* 13, no. 1 (March 1960); Werner Z. Hirsch, "Income Elasticity of Public Education," *International Economic Review* 2, no. 3 (September 1961): 330–39; Werner Z. Hirsch, "Demand and Supply of Teachers in California," *California Management Review*, Fall 1967, pp. 27–34; Thomas H. James et al., *Determinants of Educational Expenditures in Large Cities of the United States*, Cooperative Research Project No. 2389 (Washington: U.S. Office of Education, 1966); Herbert Kiesling, "Measuring a Local Government Service: A Study of School Districts in New York State," *Review of Economics and Statistics* 48, no. 3 (August 1967); Jerry Miner, *Social and Economic Factors in Spending for Public Education* (Syracuse, N.Y.: Syracuse University Press, 1963); and Conrad Harold Potter, "Educational Expenditure in Large School Districts, 1950–1960" (Ph.D. diss., Stanford University, 1966).
3. A number of interesting studies of educational resource inequality have been made at a level intermediate between the within-central-city distribution discussed in the preceding chapter and that of the analysis of variation among states or among major American cities presented here. For example, see Henry Levin, "Recruiting Teachers for Large City Schools," mimeographed (Washington: Brookings Institution, 1968), a study of variations within four metropolitan areas; Martin Theodore Katzman, "Distribution and Production in a Big City Elementary School System" (Ph.D. diss., Yale University, 1967), which includes an analysis of variations among Massachusetts towns; a number of analyses of individual states, including J. A. Thomas, *School Finance and Educational Opportunity in Michigan* (Lansing: Michigan Department of Education, 1968), and James W. Guthrie et al., *Schools and Inequality* (Cambridge: MIT Press, 1971); and more general analyses of variations among larger numbers of states, such as John E. Coons, William H. Clune, and Stephen D. Sugarman, *Private Wealth and Public Education* (Cambridge: Harvard University Press, Belknap Press, 1970), and Stephan Michelson, "The Political Economy of School Finance," in *Schooling in a Corporate Society*, ed. Martin Carnoy (New York: David McKay, 1972).
4. Martin Lapinsky, in "A Study in Occupational Labor Supply Elasticities: The Labor Market for Teachers" (Ph.D. diss., New School for Social Research, 1966), found salaries in the occupations in the group "managers, officials, and proprietors" most useful in estimating the supply of teachers. Hence a state index of those salaries was employed here.
5. The Coleman investigation found a standard deviation among individual schools of teachers' verbal ability scores of 2 to 3 (the standard deviation was 2.15

for those teaching white students and 3.23 for those teaching the black minority). See James S. Coleman *et. al., Equality of Educational Opportunity* (Washington: Government Printing Office, 1966), pp. 353–57.

6. The test data are for males, and most elementary school teachers are females. However, male and female scores are expected to be highly correlated.

7. For a more general treatment of the problem of wages and quality determination of public employees, see John D. Owen, "Towards a Public Employment Wage Theory: Some Econometric Evidence on Teacher Quality," *Industrial and Labor Relations Review* 25, no. 2 (January 1972): 213–22, and Robert J. Carlsson and James W. Robinson, "Towards a Public Employment Wage Theory," *ibid.*, 22, no. 2 (January 1969): 243–48, and the references cited there (especially James A. Craft, "Comment," *ibid.*, 23, no. 1 [October 1969]: 89–95, and Hirschel Kasper, "The Effects of Collective Bargaining on Public School Teachers' Salaries," *ibid.*, 24, no. 1 [October 1970]: 55–72), for discussions of the effects of teacher unionism on wage determination.

8. *New York Times*, July 7, 1971.

9. See U.S. Department of Health, Education, and Welfare, *State Data and State Rankings* (Washington: Government Printing Office, 1968), p. S–28.

10. This situation could, of course, be altered if "paraprofessionals" were assigned some of the teachers' duties and class size increased. Student monitors were widely used for this purpose in working-class schools in the nineteenth century (the so-called Lancastrian system), and, of course, higher education has some experience with this technique (with graduate students teaching sections of large undergraduate classes). Both systems have been criticized, however as sacrificing quality in the interest of fiscal economy. See the discussion of the Lancastrian system in Michael B. Katz, *Class, Bureaucracy and Schools: The Illusion of Educational Change in America* (New York: Praeger, 1971), pp. 10–11, 13. The graduate teaching assistant system was, of course, a significant factor in the student unrest that swept the campuses in the late 1960s.

11. See Levin, "Recruiting Teachers," for an interesting critique of this salary system. Levin advocates that beginning teachers not only be required to demonstrate a minimum level of verbal competence but that their salary depend in part on how much their scores exceed this minimum.

12. Cf. the discussion of the problem in chapter 2 above of weighting the relative importance of teacher experience and verbal ability. See also Hazel Davis, "Evolution of Current Practices in Evaluating Teacher Competence," in *Contemporary Research on Teacher Effectiveness*, ed. Bruce J. Biddle and William J. Ellena (New York: Holt, Rinehart and Winston, 1964), for a review of the evidence on the problem of measuring teacher effectiveness. There seems to be general agreement, however, that very long-term experience has little if any additional value. In fact, since the very experienced teacher is by necessity an older teacher, long-term experience may be negatively correlated with teaching performance. Warren A. Peterson, "Age, Teacher's Role and the Institutional Setting," in *ibid.*, argues: "Teachers seem to recognize a short orientation period, a 'best teaching period' while still young and vigorous, and a decline beginning at the age of 35 or 40. . . . In the opinion of a large number of mature teachers, the students get worse every year, the teaching load becomes more burdensome, and the prospect of retirement becomes more attractive" (pp. 311, 282–83).

13. In the short run the situation is even worse because school systems will hire only graduates with the requisite courses in education. But even in the longer run, the potential supply of those preparing for teaching is limited by the total number of college graduates. See Lapinsky, "Study in Occupational Labor Supply Elasticities."

14. This would be expected to lead to the greatest inefficiency if the school system paid very high wages, hoping to attract applicants of very high quality. Such personnel are in relatively short supply, and high ability generally commands a premium in the labor market, so that most employees hired would actually

be very much overpaid. Alternatively, if the government is hiring in the middle ranges of ability, where there is a much denser concentration of potential employees in each ability rank (the more typical case in elementary school teaching), there will be less overpayment.

15. See the use of teacher verbal ability data in table 4.

16. *Annual Statistical Report of the Superintendent of Public Instruction* (Springfield: State of Illinois, 1964). Examination of beginning salaries, average salaries paid, and salary scales all yielded similar results. In the national sample, the introduction of a regressor, percentage change in population, showed that population growth was an important negative determinant of average teacher experience, but a negative partial correlation of experience and income was still obtained.

17. Alternative measures of wealth also were employed in the regressions (based on the assessed and market value of property in the state) with rather similar results.

18. The salary figures used in the demand equations are statewide averages. When sample salary data from the Coleman report were fitted to these equations, very similar results were obtained.

19. See note 3 above.

NOTES FOR CHAPTER 4

1. *A Fact Book on Higher Education*, 3d issue, 1973 (Washington: American Council on Education, 1973).

2. See Michael Katz, *The Irony of Early School Reform* (Cambridge: Harvard University Press, 1968), for a useful discussion of this controversy in nineteenth century Massachusetts politics.

3. Quoted in James B. Conant, *Slums and Suburbs* (New York: McGraw-Hill, 1961), pp. 142–43.

4. See the references cited in note 4, chapter 10, for data on the upward trend in the proportion of youths attending high school.

5. Heber Hinds Ryan and Philipine Crecillius, *Ability Grouping in the Junior High School* (New York: Harcourt, Brace, 1927), pp. 8–9.

6. Quoted in Henry J. Parkinson, *The American Faith in Education, 1865–1965* (New York: Random House, 1968), p. 150.

7. See Colin Green, *The Great School Legend* (New York: Basic Books, 1972), for a discussion of lower-class failure rates and class differences in the duration of schooling in this period.

8. See, for example, R. Clyde White, *These Will Go to College* (Cleveland: Western Reserve University Press, 1952), p. 54, for an evaluation of the effect of the G.I. Bill on the social class composition of the postwar college student body.

9. U.S. President's Commission on Higher Education, *Higher Education for American Democracy*, vol. 1: *Establishing the Goals* (New York: Harper & Bros., 1947).

10. *A Fact Book on Higher Education*, 3d issue, 1973; *The American Freshman: National Norms for Fall, 1971*, ACE Research Reports, vol. 1, no. 6 (Washington: American Council on Education, December 1971). Calculated from data on pp. 16 and 23.

11. A study of the large-scale expansion of the University of Minnesota into the cities of that state in the 1950s concluded: "The state university and other colleges are more easily accessible to metropolitan students and among the large number of metropolitan men now attending college socio-economic variables have become less important determinants of college attendance." Ralph F. Berdie and Albert B. Hood, *Trends in Post-High School Plans Over an 11-Year Period*, Cooperative Research Project 951 (Washington: U.S. Office of Education, 1963), p. 55.

12. *A Fact Book on Higher Education*, March 1972 supplement (Washington: American Council on Education).

13. *American Freshman.*
14. *New Approaches to Student Financial Analysis,* Report of the Panel on Student Financial Need Analysis (Alan W. Carter, chairman) (Princeton, N.J.: College Entrance Examination Board, 1971), table 1, pp. 16–17.
15. *Ibid.,* tables 4 and 5, pp. 22–25. Some have argued that a class bias is introduced into the CSS scholarship calculation itself. Like income tax deductions, they say, the interpretation of the family's mortgage, retirement fund, and other financial "needs" is subject to middle-class lobbying so that the actual price structure finally set by the colleges favors the middle class. Moreover, the CSS has found that college aid officers themselves further adjust its analysis of student financial need in 44 percent of the applications they receive. *Ibid.,* p. 311.
16. This point must be modified in practice since a student's scholarship need is greater at a more expensive college. See appendix 3 for a further discussion of this point.
17. See, for example, *New Approaches to Student Financial Need Analysis.*
18. J. C. Flanagan *et al., The American High School Student,* Technical Report to the U.S. Office of Education, Cooperative Research Project 635 (Pittsburgh: University of Pittsburgh, Project TALENT Office, 1965), pp. 11–12.
19. See the less informal discussion in appendix 3. A more concrete analysis of the social benefits of educating different types of students is offered in chapter 6.
20. *New Approaches to Student Financial Need Analysis,* p. 28.
21. U.S. Bureau of the Census, "Educational Attainment, March 1971," Current Population Reports, Series P-20, no. 229 (Washington: Government Printing Office, 1971).
22. Stanley H. Master, "The Effect of Family Income on Children's Education: Some Findings on Inequality of Opportunity," *Journal of Human Resources* 4, no. 2: 158–78. Of course, other factors also contribute to high school dropouts. See Solomon O. Lichter *et al., The Dropouts: A Treatment Study of Intellectually Capable Students Who Drop Out of High School* (New York: Free Press, 1962), for an interesting analysis of the emotional stresses leading to dropping out among those for whom financial factors are less important.
23. Flanagan *et al., American High School Student,* pp. 11–22.
24. Calculated from *American Freshman,* pp. 23, 24.
25. *A Fact Book on Higher Education* (Washington: American Council on Education, 1969), pp. 9050–51.
26. W. Lee Hansen and Burton A. Weisbrod, *Benefits, Costs and Finance of Public Higher Education* (Chicago: Markham, 1969), p. 71. For costs, see chapter 3, esp. pp. 42–44; for ability, pp. 72–73. The authors found that less than 11 percent of high school graduates from low income families but 40 percent of those from high income families met the academic eligibility requirements of the state university.
27. Alan L. Sorkin, "Some Factors Associated with Tuition in Public and Private Colleges and Universities." Sorkin established a relationship between the college's tuition and a vector of quality characteristics generally regarded as desirable in an institution of higher learning. An earlier study, Alexander W. Astin and John L. Holland, "The Distribution of Wealth in Higher Education," *College and University,* Winter 1962, pp. 113–25, found that endowment per student (a measure of the financial subsidy per student) was higher at those schools charging higher tuition.
28. Stephen A. Hoenack, "The Efficiency Allocation of Subsidies to College Students," *American Economic Review* 61, no. 3 (June 1971): 302–11.

NOTES FOR CHAPTER 5

1. See Stephan Michelson, "The Political Economy of Public School Finance," in *Schooling in a Corporate Society,* ed. Martin Carnoy (New York: David McKay, 1972), for a discussion of the effects of state subsidies on local school district inequalities.

2. See H. Borow, "Development of Occupational Motives and Roles," in *Review of Child Development Research*, ed. L. W. Hoffman and Martin L. Hoffman (New York: Russell Sage Foundation, 1966), vol. 2, for a review of research on these pressures.

3. This formulation is, of course, an expository simplification. It assumes a constant rate-of-time discount and a constant flow of earnings and consumption benefits, and it ignores interactions between the two types of benefits. It also omits an adjustment for the finitude of the benefit streams. See Gary S. Becker, *Human Capital* (New York: Columbia University Press, 1964), for a treatment of the measurement of earnings returns to education. Also see Jacob Mincer, *Schooling, Experience, and Earnings* (New York: National Bureau of Economic Research, 1974), and the references cited there for recent discussions of the problems of empirical measurement of the return to education.

   If the individual is considering the expenditure of an additional dollar to improve the quality of his education—for example, by considering a more expensive but better-quality college—an equation similar to that given in the text could be employed to weight the costs and benefits. However, the cost calculations would have to be modified in two ways: (1) there need not be an increase in forgone earnings when the student elects a more rather than less expensive college, and (2) the consumption value comparison would be with the less expensive school rather than with a year in the labor force.

4. Thus the resistance to large-scale investment in education by the poor may have two economic roots: a high preference for present over future benefits (what economists call positive time preference), and an unwillingness to sacrifice necessities in order to obtain luxuries (consistent with a declining marginal utility of money). This resistance is sometimes mistakenly attributed entirely to the first factor, time preference. The error of this approach can be seen by contrasting the effort of poor parents to rise in social status by putting aside a large sum to educate a child so that he can enter one of the professions, with the same parents' saving to protect themselves against destitute old age. Savings appear to be more rational in the latter case despite the effects of time preference.

5. For recent discussions by economists of the loan or income share approach to student subsidy, see Robert W. Hartman, "Equity Implications of State Tuition Policy and Student Loans," *Journal of Political Economy* 80, no. 3, part 2 (May–June 1972): S142–S171, and the references cited there, especially Karl Shell, Franklin W. Fisher, Duncan K. Foley, and Ann F. Friedlander, "The Educational Opportunity Bank: An Economic Analysis of a Contingent Repayment Loan Program for Higher Education," *National Tax Journal* 21 (March 1968): 2–45.

6. Of course there are some goods on which the poor will spend *more* than will others, such as items from pawnshops and used clothing. (Economists call such items "inferior goods.") But educational expenditures generally do not fall into this category.

7. Peter M. Blau and Otis Dudley Duncan, *The American Occupational Structure* (New York: Wiley, 1967), p. 42.

8. Census data indicate that in the past 30 years the traditionally white collar occupations (professional, technical, sales, and clerical) have risen from about one-fourth to two-fifths of the employed labor force, while the occupation groups requiring least schooling (farmers, laborers, and servants) fell from three-tenths to about one-eleventh of the work force.

9. The internal financial rate of return to education equates the present value of the earnings benefits (or other financial benefits) of education to its present financial costs—the sum of forgone earnings, tuition, and other direct costs. If the simplifying assumptions are made that the earnings gains from schooling are constant each year of working life and that the adjustment for finite working life is negligible, this rate can be approximated by the ratio of the annual financial gain from an additional year of schooling to the financial cost of that

schooling. In practice, the assumption of constant earnings gains affords the most difficulties; see the discussion in the references cited in note 3 above. However, if we think, as a first approximation, of the *average* annual gain from education as determining the rate of return, the text discussion of class biases in this rate can readily be integrated with the larger literature.

10. Moreover, the private costs may also be lower for the poor youth: his opportunity costs are often reduced by his being confined to a ghetto or slum area where youth employment prospects are slim. At the college level, he most commonly considers an inexpensive or "free" commuter college or community college. (The *social* costs of his education, including the outlays of governments and others, are certainly lower than those for the more affluent as a result of the processes described in the present work. But this fact is more relevant to the discussion in the next chapter of the social benefits of lower-class education.) See Finis Welch, "Black-White Differences in Returns to Schooling," *American Economic Review* 63 (December 1973): 893–907, for a discussion of discrimination against blacks in schooling as a factor in the calculation of the rate of return to their schooling.

11. Shane J. Hunt, "Income Determinants of College Graduates and the Return to Educational Investment," *Yale Economic Essays* 3, no. 2 (1963), found that the rate of return on increments to investments in resources per student had a strong positive relationship with student ability (although Hunt himself questioned the validity of this result). D. C. Rogers, "Private Rates of Return to Education in the United States: A Case Study," *Yale Economic Essays* 9, no. 1 (1969) found no relationship between ability and return to education; but John C. Hause, "Ability and Schooling as Determinants of Lifetime Earnings, Or, If You're So Smart, Why Aren't You Rich?" (*American Economic Review* 61 [May 1971]: 289–98), working with the same data, did find a positive relationship. A positive relationship between ability and the return to college quality is observed in B. A. Weisbrod and P. Karpoff, "Monetary Returns to College Education, Student Ability and College Quality," *Review of Economics and Statistics* 50, no. 4 (November 1968): 491–97. Data presented by Dael Wolfle and Joseph Smith, "The Occupational Value of Education for Superior High School Graduates," *The Journal of Higher Education*, April 1956, pp. 201–13, on earnings of high school and college graduates at different ability levels strongly suggest a positive relationship between ability and the private rate of return on college education.

12. G. S. Becker, *Human Capital*, p. 94; Giora Hanoch, "An Economic Analysis of Earnings and Schooling," *Journal of Human Resources* 2, no. 3 (Summer 1967): 310–20; Bennett Harrison, *Education, Training, and the Urban Ghetto* (Baltimore: The Johns Hopkins Press, 1972); R. D. Weiss, "The Effect of Education on the Earnings of Blacks and Whites," *Review of Economics and Statistics* 52 (May 1970): 150–59; Lester C. Thurow, *Poverty and Discrimination* (Washington: Brookings Institution, 1969).

13. Earnings data in table 14 are averages for individuals over the preceding five years. Rates of return were calculated from cross-sectional data, affording a measure of percentage gain in earnings per additional year of schooling. This cross-sectional method underestimates the rate of return to schooling because it omits the earnings gains individuals will obtain as a result of expected future upward trends in the wages of all workers (see the discussion in G. S. Becker, *Human Capital*) while overestimating it in that it does not make an adjustment for the finitude of individuals' working lives (see G. S. Becker and Barry R. Chiswick, "Education and the Distribution of Earnings," *American Economic Review* 56 [May 1966]: 358–69, and Jacob Mincer, *Schooling, Experience, and Earnings* [New York: National Bureau of Economic Research, 1974]). Cross-sectional estimates of the earnings return to education are also biased downward if they are not standardized for the lower level of job experience that better-educated individuals will have at a given age; that is, the observed education coefficient will then measure the education effect *minus* the lost experience effect

(see the discussion in note 15 below). The lower rate-of-return figure given for each group in the table is the one obtained without adjustment for experience. The upper estimates were adjusted by the use of an experience factor (6 percent) calculated from Mincer, *Schooling, Experience*, table 10.

The data base for the table, the Coleman-Rossi Continuous Life Histories Study, is a random national sample of approximately 1,000 white and 1,000 black males in their thirties who provided detailed job and earnings chronologies. The ability breakdown (based on a test of verbal ability given to the interviewees) uses cutoffs to obtain roughly equal numbers in each ability-race subgroup. Hence, since the average ability scores differed for the two races, different ability cutoffs were necessarily employed for each group. This work is described further in John D. Owen, "Ability, Race, and the Earnings Return to Education," mimeographed (Baltimore: Johns Hopkins University Center for the Social Organization of Schools, 1971). Further work is now being carried out with these data in a joint project by the author and Jacob Mincer. The estimates presented here should be regarded as preliminary results from this larger study.

14. Welch, "Black-White Differences." See also Leonard Weiss and Jeffrey G. Williamson, "Black Education, Earnings, and Interregional Migration: Some New Evidence," *American Economic Review* 62, no. 3 (June 1972): 372–83.
15. B. R. Chiswick, "Schooling Achievement and Earnings of Low Achievers: A Comment," *American Economic Review* 62, no. 4 (September 1972): 752–54. In a recent interchange, W. L. Hansen, B. A. Weisbrod, and W. J. Scanlon, "Schooling and Earnings of Low Achievers," *ibid.*, 60, no. 3 (June 1970): 409–18, reported an earnings rate of return of only 1 percent to the education of youths rejected by the armed forces on intellectual grounds. By introducing a variable to control for job experience (see note 3 above), Chiswick obtained an estimate of the earnings rate of return of 12 percent for the same group. In a rebuttal, Hansen, Weisbrod, and Scanlon (*ibid.*, pp. 760–62) used a different job experience measure and obtained an intermediate estimate of 4–6 percent for the education of this group.
16. See Harrison, *Education, Training*, for an extreme statement of this view. His study design affords him a minimal estimate of the earnings return to education.

NOTES FOR CHAPTER 6

1. Adam Smith, *An Inquiry into the Nature and Causes of the Wealth of Nations*, Modern Library ed. (New York: Random House, 1937).
2. Hence, if the community is regarded as composed of two homogeneous groups, taxpayers and recipients, equality of educational opportunity might now be described as "Pareto optimal"—it would make everyone better off and no one worse off. Of course, interests do vary within each group. Cf. the discussion of the interests of employers and of labor in equality of educational opportunity in chapter 9 below. See also the discussion of noneconomic benefits in chapters 7 and 8.
3. Edward F. Denison, *The Sources of Economic Growth in the United States and the Alternatives Before Us*, Supplementary Paper no. 13 (New York: Committee for Economic Development, 1962).
4. The critics are quite numerous. See, for example, Ivar Berg, *Education and Jobs: The Great Training Robbery* (New York: Praeger, 1970); Bennett Harrison, *Education, Training, and the Urban Ghetto* (Baltimore: The Johns Hopkins Press, 1972); Christopher Jencks *et al.*, *Inequality: A Reassessment of the Effect of Family and Schooling in America* (New York: Basic Books, 1972); and Herbert Gintis, "Alienation and Power: Towards a Radical Welfare Economics" (Ph.D. diss., Harvard University, 1969).
5. Cf. the discussion in Gintis, "Alienation and Power."
6. Michael Harrington, *The Other America: Poverty in the United States* (New York: Macmillan, 1962), p. 161.
7. See John M. Peterson and Charles T. Stewart, Jr., *Employment Effects of Minimum Wage Rates* (Washington: American Enterprise Institute for Public

Policy Research, 1969), p. 19. Inflation has since reduced the ratio of the minimum to the average wage, but proposals before Congress at this writing more than make up this gap.

8. U.S. Bureau of the Census, *Labor Union Membership in 1966*, Current Population Reports, Series 210, no. 216 (Washington: 1971), p. 4.

9. AFDC expenditures quadrupled from 1965 to 1972. See *Social Security Bulletin* 35, no. 12 (December 1972): 3–17; and U.S. Department of Health, Education, and Welfare, "Social Welfare Expenditures, 1971–1972," in *Public Assistance*, various issues.

10. See appendix 4 for a less informal presentation of the argument offered in the following paragraphs.

11. This growth rate would be necessary to maintain a constant ratio of physical capital stock to output. See appendix 4.

12. For discussions of the "poverty line" concept, see Lowell F. Gallaway, "The Foundations of the War on Poverty," *American Economic Review* 55, no. 1 (March 1965): 122–30; Thomas I. Ribich, *Education and Poverty* (Washington: Brookings Institution, 1968); and Lester C. Thurow, *Poverty and Discrimination* (Washington: Brookings Institution, 1969).

13. Still another line of criticism of the constant poverty line notion stresses the fact that changes in technology and in our laws would make it almost impossible to live today on the "real" income needed to sustain life in, say, 1900. One need only think of the importance of the telephone and auto in earning a living today or of the housing laws and food regulations that control consumption to see the validity of this point.

14. For AFDC program data see note 9 above. For spendable income of non-supervisory workers in private, nonagricultural employment, see *Manpower Report of the President* (Washington: Government Printing Office), various editions. For GNP and disposable income, see *Survey of Current Business*, various issues.

15. See *The Budget for the Year 1974* (Washington: Government Printing Office, 1973), p. 142.

16. U.S. Congress, Joint Economic Committee, Subcommittee on Fiscal Policy, *How Public Welfare Benefits Are Distributed in Low Income Areas*, Studies in Public Welfare, no. 6 (Washington: Government Printing Office, 1973). See table 1, pp. 4–6, for data, and the text, *passim*, for an interpretation.

17. For example, Allen L. Sorkin, "Education, Ability, and the Distribution of Wages" (Ph.D. diss., The Johns Hopkins University, 1966). See also the analysis of empirical evidence that Americans' standards of an appropriate welfare minimum have risen with the wage rate since the 1930s in Jencks *et al.*, *Inequality*, p. 4.

18. U.S. Department of Health, Education, and Welfare, *Statistics of State School Systems, 1967–1968* (Washington: Government Printing Office, 1970).

19. In a statistical estimation of welfare incidence for the group with children but no husband present, the t ratio of the effect of number of children on welfare incidence was over four; the absolute value of the t ratio of the education effect on number of children was over three. (The author is now engaged in further research on these Parnes tape data on welfare incidence.)

20. U.S. Bureau of the Census, *Educational Attainment, March, 1969*, Current Population Reports, Series P-20, no. 194 (Washington: Government Printing Office, 1970).

21. Indirect evidence of a negative relationship between training and welfare incidence is provided in Elizabeth F. Durbin, "Family Instability, Labor Supply, and the Incidence of Aid to Families with Dependent Children" (Ph.D. diss., Columbia University, 1971). In her study of differences in welfare incidence among New York City's health districts, she found a positive relationship between incidence and the proportion of unskilled females in the district even when both the poverty and unemployment rates were held constant.

22. Henry Levin, *The Costs to the Nation of Inadequate Education*, U.S. Senate,

Select Committee on Equal Educational Opportunity (Washington: Government Printing Office, 1972).

23. U.S. Department of Health, Education, and Welfare, *Digest of Educational Statistics* (Washington: Government Printing Office, 1972).

24. See Peterson and Stewart, *Employment Effects*, for a survey of empirical studies on this effect. Thomas W. Garrett, "Youth Unemployment and Minimum Wages," *Monthly Labor Review* 93, no. 3 (March 1970), presents some useful statistical data on youth unemployment and minimum wages.

25. See the discussions of the benefits of training or retraining the unemployed in Michael Borus, "A Benefit-Cost Analysis of the Economic Effectiveness of Retraining the Unemployed," *Yale Economic Essays* 4, no. 2 (Fall 1964): 371–430; and Samuel Gubins, "The Impact of Age and Education on the Effectiveness of Training: A Benefit-Cost Analysis" (Ph.D. diss., The Johns Hopkins University, 1970).

26. U.S. Bureau of Labor Statistics, *Handbook of Labor Statistics* (Washington: Government Printing Office, 1972).

27. *Regulating the Poor* (New York: Random House, 1971).

28. U.S. Bureau of the Census, *Household and Family Characteristics: March, 1970*, Current Population Reports, Series P-20, no. 218 (Washington: Government Printing Office, 1971).

29. "The Impact of Public Assistance on Labor Supply and Family Stability," mimeographed (New York: Columbia University Labor Workshop, 1972).

30. See Joseph Gastwirth, "On the Decline of Male Labor Force Participation," *Monthly Labor Review* 95, no. 10 (October 1972): 44–49, and the references there for a discussion of a decline in male labor force participation in the United States in the past decade.

31. Cf. the discussion of earnings studies in chapter 5.

32. Press release, March 26, 1973, to accompany U.S. Congress, Joint Economic Committee, *How Benefits Are Distributed*.

33. There are, of course, contrary views on the work incentives of the poor and, especially, on their susceptibility to the negative income tax. See Leonard Goodman, *Do the Poor Want to Work?* (Washington: Brookings Institution, 1972); and Harold W. Watts and Glen C. Cain, "Basic Labor Supply Response Findings from the Urban Experiment" (paper presented at the annual meeting of the American Economic Association, New York, December 1973). However, the empirical evidence cited in these works is not, in the author's opinion, adequate to provide a forecast of the long-term effects on work incentives of a national negative income tax plan.

34. Cf. the discussion "Education and the Demand for Leisure" in John D. Owen, *The Price of Leisure* (Montreal: McGill-Queens University Press, 1969).

35. See *ibid.* for a mathematical model of this effect.

36. Jacob Mincer, *Schooling, Experience, and Earnings* (New York: National Bureau of Economic Research, 1974).

37. Including special programs to seek out the unusually talented among the disadvantaged. I owe this suggestion to Julian Stanley.

NOTES FOR CHAPTER 7

1. See Mancur Olson, *The Logic of Collective Action* (Cambridge: Harvard University Press, 1965), for a discussion of the relationship between the size of a group and the problem of providing incentives for its members.

2. See, for example, the empirical work of Angus Campbell *et al.*, *The Voter Decides* (Evanston, Ill.: Row, Peterson, 1954); V. O. Key, Jr., *Public Opinion and American Democracy* (New York: Alfred A. Knopf, 1961); and Edgar Litt, "Civic Education, Community Norms, and Political Indoctrination," in *The Political Imagination*, ed. Edgar Litt (Glenview, Ill.: Scott, Foresman, 1966). For reviews of a number of such studies, see Burton A. Weisbrod, *External Benefits of Public Education,* Princeton University Research Report Series 105, Industrial Relations Section (Princeton, N.J.: Princeton University, 1964), pp. 95–99, and

Arnold Morrison and Donald McIntyre, *Schools and Socialization* (Baltimore: Penguin, 1971).

3. See the discussion of definitions of equality of educational opportunity in chapter 10 below.

4. Henry Levin, *The Costs to the Nation of Inadequate Education*, U.S. Senate, Select Committee on Equal Opportunity (Washington: Government Printing Office, 1972).

5. V. O. Key, Jr.'s *Southern Politics* (New York: Random House, 1949) is most informative in this regard. In describing South Carolina, for example, he pointed out that its "preoccupation with the Negro stifles political conflict. . . . Mill worker and plantation owner alike want to keep the Negro in his place. In part, issues are deliberately repressed, for, at least in the long-run, concern with genuine issues would bring an end to the consensus by which the Negro is kept out of politics. One crowd or another would be tempted to seek his vote. In part, the race issue provides in itself a tool for the diversion of attention from issues. When the going gets rough, when a glimmer of informed political self-interest begins to well up from the masses, the issue of white supremacy may be raised to whip them back into line." Key considered that South Carolina's majority or near-majority of disenfranchised blacks accentuated these trends in its politics but believed that, for this reason, "South Carolina's record . . . illuminates the real effects of race over the entire South" (p. 131).

6. See Morrison and McIntyre, *Schools and Socialization*, for a review of this literature.

7. Litt, "Civic Education." Litt found that these civics courses did have an effect on the development of students' attitudes. For further discussion of the effects of high school civics courses on political socialization, see Kenneth P. Langton and M. Kent Jennings, "Political Socialization and the High School Civics Curriculum in the United States," *American Journal of Political Science* 12, no. 3 (September 1968); and M. Kent Jennings and Richard G. Niemi, "Patterns of Political Learning," *Harvard Educational Review* 38, no. 3 (Summer 1968): 443–67.

8. Apart from the dysfunctional political effects of class differences in socialization, the dominance of the private demand for education imposes a broader problem. It does not provide an incentive structure that gives proper emphasis to improving the citizenship quality of either working-class or middle-class children. The private interests of the family are better served by a relative neglect of this type of training. But society has a considerable interest in encouraging schooling in civics, history, the social sciences, and the like, whether or not the study of these subjects makes the same contribution to occupational success as, say, courses in engineering. See John D. Owen, "Education for Majority Voting," *Journal of Public Choice,* Spring 1969, for a presentation of the problems of providing financial or other incentives that would ensure that the young apply themselves to the study of politically important material. See Thomas F. Green, *Work, Leisure, and the American School* (New York: Random House, 1968), p. 114, for a statement of the case that the subordination of education to vocational ends at the expense of the development of "an informed electorate" is increasingly characteristic of the American school system.

9. See Morrison and McIntyre, *Schools and Socialization*, p. 149, for a discussion of the relationship between social class and authoritarian attitudes.

10. Chicago: University of Chicago Press, 1962, pp. 85–107.

11. In the 1970 congressional elections, voting participation rose from 50 to 73 percent among whites and from 45 to 60 percent among blacks as educational attainment went from 9–11 years to the highest grade (see table 20 and the reference cited there). Similar gains are obtained in political knowledge and in other indexes of the quality of political participation (see the references in note 2 above).

12. See, for example, the use of this model in James M. Buchanan and Gordon Tullock, *The Calculus of Consent: The Logical Foundations of Constitutional*

Democracy (Ann Arbor: University of Michigan Press, 1962); and in Anthony Downs, *An Economic Theory of Democracy* (New York: Harper, 1957).

13. The following paragraphs are based on the more extended argument in Owen, "Education for Majority Voting."

14. In a variant on the simple majority voting model, decisions are made by elected representatives. This may permit vote trading or logrolling and so complicates the analysis, although it does not contradict the conclusions for educational policy derived in the simpler model. See *ibid.*

15. See the discussion of this subject in *ibid.*

NOTES FOR CHAPTER 8

1. *Public Policy* 18 (Spring 1970): 332–33.

2. For the difficulties of raising funds for income maintenance, see, for example, *ibid.*, or Frances Fox Piven and Richard Cloward, *Regulating the Poor* (New York: Random House, 1971). See also the discussion of trends in educational finance in chapters 9 and 10 below.

3. John E. Coons, William H. Clune, and Stephen D. Sugarman, *Private Wealth and Public Education* (Cambridge: Harvard University Press, Belknap Press, 1970), put the point this way in discussing school district inequalities: "When persons are distinguished from one another by their relative wealth, irrelevancy is risked, for the subject then has become not school children, but their parents. Children in a true sense are all poor. It is difficult to perceive how children residing in poor districts . . . deserve less in terms of public education. If government is to educate at all, these children should be as prepared to participate and compete in our society as their peers who live in wealthy neighborhoods" (p. 9).

4. It can be shown that, if the taxpayers are concerned with maintaining what they regard as a minimal level of consumption of necessities by the poor but not their "vices," grants of education or other in-kind gifts rather than cash payments would be one optimal means of redistributing income (in the sense that, if the present educational subsidies to the poor were replaced with cash grants of somewhat smaller amounts, both the poor and the taxpayers would probably regard themselves as worse off).

   John D. Owen, "The Political Economy of Equality of Educational Opportunity," mimeographed (New York: New School for Social Research, 1971), contains a discussion of many of the points raised in this chapter. For a further discussion of the argument for subsidizing an activity on the grounds that it is considered "meritorious," see Richard A. Musgrave, *The Theory of Public Finance* (New York: McGraw-Hill, 1959), pp. 13–14; and two papers by J. G. Head, "On Merit Goods," *Finanzarchiv*, N. F., 28, no. 7 (March 1966): 1–29, and "Merit Goods Revisited," *Finanzarchiv*, N. F., 29, no. 2 (March 1969): 214–25.

NOTES FOR CHAPTER 9

1. Frank J. Munger and Richard F. Fenno, *National Politics and Federal Aid to Education* (Syracuse, N. Y.: Syracuse University Press, 1962), p. 99.

2. Anne Gibson Buis, "An Historical Study of the Role of the Federal Government in the Financial Support of Education, with Special Reference to Legislative Proposals and Actions" (Ph.D. diss., Ohio State University, 1953), pp. 37–38.

3. *Ibid.*

4. *Ibid.*, pp. 52, 53.

5. *Ibid.*, p. 55.

6. *Ibid.*, pp. 60, 61.

7. The Brand-Nye Bill of 1929 for rural elementary education elicited the following argument by one of its authors: "Brand pointed out that the wealth was concentrated in the cities, while a preponderance of children was found in the rural areas; and that the cities continued to increase their wealth by draining the edu-

cated producers of wealth from the rural areas which were becoming less and less financially able to provide educational opportunities for future producers of wealth." *Ibid.*, pp. 116–17.

8. *Ibid.*, pp. 160, 165.

9. *Ibid.*

10. See *ibid.*, pp. 296 ff., for a fuller discussion of the fate of the Thomas-Lister Bill.

11. Munger and Fenno, *National Politics*, p. 20.

12. Interestingly, this percentage fell to a bare majority in the 1964–65 period, "precisely at the time that Congress enacted legislation." It is hard to disagree with the conclusion that "this rather surprising development raises some questions about the relationship between public attitudes and congressional policy-making" in Philip Meranto, *The Politics of Federal Aid to Education in 1965* (Syracuse, N.Y.: Syracuse University Press, 1967), p. 44. But Meranto also points out that the general public was often not aware of some of the controversy surrounding this issue. Presumably this gap was filled by conservative argumentation during the political debate over the bill.

13. *National Politics*, p. 76.

14. See the discussion of these developments in chapter 10 below.

15. For example: "By the 1949 House hearings [Thomas C. Boushall, the U.S. Chamber of Commerce representative] was serving as floor manager for a parade of witnesses opposing federal aid [to education], a role the Chamber of Commerce has maintained ever since." Munger and Fenno, *National Politics,* pp. 27–28.

16. See, for example, Buis, "Historical Study"; Munger and Fenno, *National Politics;* and Meranto, *Politics of Federal Aid.*

17. A state-by-state analysis of the interplay of class politics and the interest of local power elites in educational policy would, of course, be beyond the scope of the present study.

18. Munger and Fenno, *National Politics*, p. 26.

19. See the discussions of business opposition in Buis, "Historical Study"; Munger and Fenno, *National Politics;* and Meranto, *Politics of Federal Aid.*

20. Raymond E. Callahan, *Education and the Cult of Efficiency* (Chicago: University of Chicago Press, 1962), provides useful evidence from the first several decades of the century. But see Michael Katz, *Class, Bureaucracy, and Schools: The Illusion of Educational Change in America* (New York: Praeger, 1971), p. 124, for a criticism of Callahan's assessment. Katz holds that "the men who ran schools differed little in their attitudes and outlook from the men who ran businesses" and that Callahan exaggerates the conflict between them.

   More recent evidence is available in the now vast collection of "community power structure" studies by sociologists and political scientists. Floyd Hunter, *Community Power Structure* (Chapel Hill: University of North Carolina Press, 1953), and Robert A. Dahl, *Who Governs? Democracy and Power in an American City* (New Haven: Yale University Press, 1961), provide classic statements of, respectively, the direct and indirect models of business influence. See Laura L. Morlock, "Business Interests, Countervailing Groups and the Balance of Influence in 98 Cities," mimeographed (Baltimore: The Johns Hopkins University, 1972), for an empirical analysis that stresses the diversity of the degree of influence exerted by organized business on community education decisions.

21. "Historical Study," pp. 662–63.

22. A more rigorous treatment of this argument is given in appendix 5, which also endeavors to relate the question of employer investment in education both to the literature on human capital and to that on "productive consumption" in the developing nations.

23. Many would argue, of course, that the primary political interest of employers as a group is maintenance of the capitalist system, without which they cease to earn any profits or maintain their hegemony as employers. A number of revisionist historians have argued that employers or employer groups in the United

States have sometimes solicited the government to introduce social reforms to curb socialist or other radical tendencies that challenged the economic system. See, for example, James Weinstein, *The Corporate Ideal in the Welfare State: 1900–1918* (Boston: Beacon Press, 1968), or the readings collected in Ronald Radosh and Murray N. Rothbard, eds., *A New History of Leviathan* (New York: Dutton, 1972). However, the debate over federal aid to education in the first six decades of this century generally did not raise the issue of the survival of capitalism, despite the concern over illiterate "subversives" during the Red Scare after World War I.

24. A zero rate of return would not be sufficient for two reasons. First, the earnings rate of return, as conventionally calculated, is inflated by the fact that, in a growing economy in which the wage rate is increasing, the student will gain a benefit by withholding his labor at a time when the wage rate is low and selling it as a graduate when wages are higher. This benefit does not represent a productivity gain that would be relevant for estimating whether the effective supply of labor is increased and should be deducted for that purpose from the observed rate. Second, it is necessary that the remainder be greater than the population growth rate to take account of the fact that, when population is growing, the student age cohort is disproportionately large relative to those in the labor force as graduates, raising the current labor costs of the program in comparison to its labor benefits. But the sum of the growth rate of wage rates and population is in the long run approximately equal to the rate of growth of the economy. Hence, demanding that the rate of return to education at least equal this economic growth rate will generally ensure that it will yield an increase in the effective labor supply. See appendix 5 for a less informal discussion of this point.

25. See, for example, Jan Pen, *Income Distribution* (New York: Praeger, 1971), for a discussion of historical changes in the share of labor and capital in the national income. Appendix 5 presents an analysis of the effect of education on profit levels.

26. An economic growth of 4 percent, a population growth rate of 2 percent, a 5 percent rate of depreciation on physical capital, and a ratio of physical capital investment to output of one-sixth.

27. Introducing other plausible values for the parameters produces similarly high employer profit criteria. These mathematical calculations assume that the pretax share of capital in income is not affected by increases in educational levels. Empirical studies suggest that an increase in the labor supply might lead to a small increase in the employers' share, but the effect of increasing labor supply through education may have more complex effects. On the one hand, there is some evidence that physical capital has strong complementary relations with educated labor, indicating that an increase in the latter would increase the productivity of the former considerably. On the other hand, there may be a positive effect of better education on labor's bargaining strength and hence a negative effect on capital share. Very little indeed is known about these secondary effects of increasing the educational level of the labor force. Cf. the discussion in Zvi Griliches, "Notes on the Role of Education in Production Functions and Growth Accounting," in *Education, Income and Human Capital*, ed. W. Lee Hansen (New York: National Bureau of Economic Research, 1971).

28. The "camel's nose in the tent" theme is a leitmotiv of Chamber of Commerce material opposing and, later, criticizing federal aid to education. Examples are Chamber of Commerce of the United States, *Education: An Investment in People* (Washington, 1944 [?]); *idem, Which Way Education?* (Washington, 1948); and "Should Rich Kids Get Handouts?" in the July 1966 issue of *Nation's Business*, a publication of the Chamber of Commerce of the United States.

In 1959, the Committee for Economic Development, a relatively liberal business group, did support a limited form of federal aid to education. The proposal called for federal subsidies only to states that needed them to bring their spending up to 80 percent of the national average. Any state that responded by reducing its per student contribution below the level prevailing before the program went into effect would have its federal subsidy revoked. See Committee for Economic Development, *Paying for Better Schools* (New York, 1959).

29. Employers have on occasion suffered because of underinvestment in the education of the poor. One has only to think of the frenzied efforts during World War II to convert poorly educated rural migrants into useful factory labor or the new interest of downtown banks, department stores, and the like in ghetto education as they begin to have difficulty in attracting white clerical labor from the suburbs, to which their traditional labor supply has fled. But labor market demand is usually less tight than this at the level of educational attainment which the lower class is likely to reach, even with a PREP. Shortages are more common in certain technical specialties or in fields requiring a very high level of attainment than in the fields where the average person competes, and a PREP has been defined here as a policy that endeavors to bring the lower class up to average levels. See the discussion of labor market difficulties in the next chapter.

30. Quoted in Percy E. Burrup, *The Teacher and the Public School System* (New York: Harper, 1960), p. 151.

31. If the package of tax changes used to fund a PREP were designed to reduce investment in physical capital rather than the consumption of workers or "capitalists" (see the discussion in chapter 6), the employers would not suffer physically even in the period in which taxes were raised (i.e., in the interval between initiation of the program and the point at which it resulted in a decline in welfare and other poverty costs). The capitalists might or might not *perceive* themselves as poorer during this period. On the one hand, they would see funds channeled into the education of the poor and hence not available for investment in their companies. On the other hand, they would know that the investment would increase their profits more than one with a similar payoff period in their own enterprises because the better labor supply would increase the return per dollar of invested capital and because reduced poverty costs would leave more after-tax profit. In practice, whether employers would experience a sense of loss during this interval would undoubtedly depend largely on whether the advocates of a PREP could convince employers that the plan really would work. See the discussion of ideological conservatism in chapter 10 below.

32. For useful summaries of labor attitudes, see Frank C. Carlton, *Economic Influences upon Educational Progress in the United States, 1820–1850* (Madison: University of Wisconsin Press, 1908; reprint ed., New York: Teachers College Press, 1965); the foreword by Lawrence Cremin to the reprint edition of Carlton, reviewing criticism of the latter; Philip R. V. Curoe, *Educational Attitudes and Policies of Organized Labor* (New York: Bureau of Publications, Teachers College, Columbia University, 1926; reprint ed., New York: Arno Press and the New York Times, 1969); and Rush Welter, *Popular Education and Democratic Thought in the United States* (New York: Columbia University Press, 1962).

33. New York: McGraw-Hill, 1961, p. 2.

34. Quoted in Meranto, *Politics of Federal Aid*, p. 36.

35. See Stephen K. Bailey and Edith H. Mosher, *ESEA: The Office of Education Administers a Law* (Syracuse, N.Y.: Syracuse University Press, 1968), pp. 30–31 on the racial issue and pp. 51–53 on the religious issue. The House vote was 263–153 and the Senate vote 73–18.

36. Bailey and Mosher, *ESEA*, give a useful discussion of the contents of this act.

37. "Race and Status in School Spending: Chicago, 1961–1966," *Journal of Human Resources* 6, no. 1 (Winter 1971): 3–24.

38 "Title I ESEA: The Politics of Implementing Federal Education Reform," *Harvard Education Review* 41, no. 1 (1971): 35–63.

39. See, for example, the enthusiastic support for such programs given in CED publications, at least since the middle 1960s. Even the much more conservative Chamber of Commerce appears to have modified its attitude considerably. See "Should Rich Kids Get Handouts?" in the July 1966 issue of *Nation's Business*, which confines itself to criticizing the distribution of ESEA Title I funds on grounds that that program's critics on the left would heartily support.

NOTES FOR CHAPTER 10

1. Interview in *Saturday Review, Education*, May 1972.
2. U.S. Bureau of the Census, *Statistical Abstract of the United States, 1972* (Washington: Government Printing Office).
3. Christopher Jencks *et al., Inequality: A Reassessment of the Effect of Family and Schooling in America* (New York: Basic Books, 1972), p. 21. See also the calculations in Barry Chiswick and Jacob Mincer, "Time Series in Personal Income Inequality in the U.S. from 1939," *Journal of Political Economy* 80, no. 3, pt. 2 (May-June 1972): S34–S66.
4. Susan B. Orr, "An Estimate of the 'True' Education Distribution of the United States Population" (M.A. thesis, Florida State University, 1966); John K. Folger and Charles B. Nam, *Education of the American People: A 1960 Census Monograph* (Washington: U.S. Bureau of the Census, 1967); and *Educational Attainment of the American People, March, 1972*, Current Population Reports, Series P-20, no. 243 (Washington: U.S. Bureau of the Census, 1972).
5. See *Report of the Commissioner of Education for the Year 1899–1900* (Washington: U.S. Bureau of Education, 1901), pp. LXVI, LXIX, LXXIX.
6. U.S. Office of Education, *Biennial Survey of Education, 1928–1930*, Bulletin, 1931, no. 20 (Washington: Government Printing Office, 1932), pp. 43, 50, 79.
7. U.S. Office of Education, *Digest of Educational Statistics, 1971* (Washington: Government Printing Office, 1972), pp. 26, 59. Data are for 1967–68.
8. As measured by the median expenditure level within each group of states.
9. New York: Basic Books, 1972, p. 53. Greer also describes the special problems of the black minority in the northern city school systems in that period.
10. *Forty Third Annual Report of the State Superintendent of Education of the State of South Carolina, 1911* (Columbia, 1912), p. 116, and *Forty Second Annual Report of the State Superintendent of the State of South Carolina, 1910* (Columbia, 1911), pp. 120–21.
11. *Forty Second Annual Report of South Carolina*, p. 115.
12. *Ibid.*, p. 121.
13. Useful works on this period in black education include Horace Mann Bond, *The Education of the Negro in the American Social Order* (New York: Prentice-Hall, 1934; reprint ed., New York: Octagon Books, 1966); Henry A. Bullock, *A History of Negro Education in the South* (Cambridge: Harvard University Press, 1967); and Louis R. Harlan, *Separate and Unequal: School Campaigns and Racism in the Southern Seaboard States 1900–1915* (Chapel Hill: University of North Carolina Press, 1958). For more general views of the development of southern education, see, for example, Charles W. Dabney, *Universal Education in the South* (Chapel Hill: University of North Carolina Press, 1936), and Edward W. Knight, *Public Education in the South* (Boston: Ginn, 1922).
14. *Forty Third Annual Report of South Carolina*, pp. 678, 680. The Massachusetts datum is based on *Report of the Commissioner of Education for the Year Ended June 30, 1912* (Washington: U.S. Bureau of Education, 1913), 2:10, 18.
15. *Annual Report of the Department of Education of the State of Alabama for the Scholastic Year Ending September 30, 1910* (Montgomery, 1910), pp. 135–50, 171 (data are for public schools, which enrolled 97 percent of all pupils); *Biennial Report of the State Superintendent of Instruction: School Sessions of 1909–1910 and 1910–1911* (Baton Rouge: State of Louisiana, 1912), pp. 11, 19, 24, 56, 59 (data are for public schools, which enrolled 85 percent of all pupils).
16. David T. Blose and Ambrose Caliver, *Statistics of the Education of Negroes, 1929 and 1931–1932*, U.S. Office of Education Bulletin, 1935, no. 13 (Washington: Government Printing Office, 1936), p. 16.
17. Ambrose Caliver, *Availability of Education to Negroes in Rural Communities*, U.S. Office of Education Bulletin, 1935, no. 12 (Washington: Government Printing Office, 1936), p. 37.
18. *Ibid.*, p. 39, 61.
19. For a very instructive account of the schooling offered by the U.S. Steel Company in the "minerals belt" of Alabama to children of its black employees, see

Horace Mann Bond, *Negro Education in Alabama: A Study in Cotton and Steel* (Associated Publishers, 1939; reprint ed., New York: Atheneum, 1969). Black children in these schools were performing at national norms, far ahead of black pupils in the surrounding "black belt" counties, which were dominated by plantation agriculture.

20. Ambrose Caliver, *Education of Negro Leaders*, U.S. Office of Education Bulletin, 1948, no. 3 (Washington: Government Printing Office, n.d.), p. 37.

21. Fred McCuistion, "The South's Negro Teacher Force," *Journal of Negro Education* 1 (1932): 17–24.

22. Bond, *Education of the Negro*, p. 22.

23. For descriptions of the "plan," see Jack Greenberg, *Race Relations and American Law* (New York: Columbia University Press, 1959), pp. 34–46; Thurgood Marshall, "An Evaluation of Recent Efforts to Achieve Integration in Education through Resort to the Courts," *Journal of Negro Education* 21, no. 3 (Summer 1952), 316–27, esp. p. 318; Henry A. Bullock, *History of Negro Education*, pp. 213–19; and Robert G. Newby and David B. Tuack, "Victims without Crimes: Some Historical Perspectives on Black Education," *Journal of Negro Education* 40, no. 3 (Summer 1971): 192–206. For a description of the actual campaign, see Ada B. Coleman, "The Salary Equalization Movement," *Journal of Negro Education* 16, no. 2 (Spring 1947): 235–41, and numerous other entries in that journal's regular "Current Trends and Events of National Importance to Negro Education" section, which summarize the outcome of individual court cases. For a statistical evaluation of the success of this campaign, see Leander I. Boykin, "The Status and Trends of Differentials between White and Negro Teachers' Salaries in the Southern States, 1900–1946," *Journal of Negro Education* 18, no. 1 (Winter 1948): 40–41.

24. *History of Negro Education*, p. 219.

25. *107th Annual Report for the Session 1955–1956*, State Department of Education of Louisiana (Baton Rouge, 1956), pp. 166–67, 217, 221, 281, 283, 341, 359. As late as 1946 salaries of white teachers were almost double the black level, but this ratio fell quickly in the late 1940s.

26. *Annual Report of the Superintendent of Public Instruction of the Commonwealth of Virginia, School Year 1949–1950* (Richmond, 1950), p. 255. A considerable racial difference in teacher salaries persisted in Virginia up to World War II; see *Annual Report of the Superintendent of Public Instruction of the Commonwealth of Virginia, School Year 1941–1942* (Richmond, 1942). See also David T. Blose, "Negro Public Schools in States Maintaining Segregated School Systems, 1948–1949," U.S. Office of Education, Circular 286 (Washington: Government Printing Office, 1951), for evidence that very considerable inequalities in resources per student persisted in some Deep South states in the 1948–49 school year.

27. James S. Coleman *et al.*, *Equality of Educational Opportunity* (Washington: Government Printing Office, 1966), p. 132.

28. The racial segregation of teachers in the South thus affords an example of the "agency hiring constraint" criticized in chapter 3. In this case, the black schools were effectively barred from hiring any teachers not produced by the same inferior, segregated school system.

29. See the notes to table 24.

30. *Annual Report of the State Superintendent of Public Education for the Year 1871* (New Orleans, 1872). Even under Reconstruction relatively few southern schools were actually racially mixed. Expenditures per pupil, however, were often equalized between the races. In fact, the instruction offered blacks by northern women (the famous New England "schoolmarms" who went South with missionary zeal after the defeat of the Confederacy), as well as by southerners of both races, was said to be often as good as that available to whites, sometimes better. See the references on black education cited in note 13 above.

31. Relative to whites. Considerable gains in the absolute levels of black educational quality were claimed by the advocates of the southern segregated school system

even before the upgrading in the decade preceding the 1954 court decision. Many black families also improved their educational opportunities by moving North. But white educational levels were also increasing in the nation as a whole and especially in the South, so that the *relative* gains by blacks were more modest.

NOTES FOR CHAPTER 11

1. Cf. the discussion of egalitarian principles in the allocation of subsidies to higher education in chapter 4. There is considerable controversy concerning the effects of these Basic Opportunity Grants on the poor. The BOGs have a maximum value of $1,400 a year for families actually below the poverty line in income, and in any case a grant can never exceed one-half of college costs. Hence they obviously require some supplementation to be of use to the poor. Moreover, there is concern that monies appropriated for the BOGs will come at the expense of other federally funded programs now used to assist the college education of the poor, so that this task of financial supplementation will now become more difficult.
2. For recent discussions of the meaning of equality of educational opportunity, see John E. Coons, William H. Clune, and Stephen D. Sugarman, *Private Wealth and Public Education* (Cambridge: Harvard University Press, Belknap Press, 1970), or Thomas Ribich, "The Case for Equal Opportunity," in *Schooling in a Corporate Society*, ed. Martin Carnoy (New York: David McKay, 1972), pp. 123–29.
3. For a discussion of changes in the fifties and sixties, see Denis F. Johnston, "The Labor Market Twist 1964–1969," *Monthly Labor Review* 94, no. 7 (July 1971): 26–36. For more current data on the inverse relationship between unemployment and educational attainment, see chapter 6 above.
4. See, for example, Christopher Jencks et al., *Inequality: A Reassessment of the Effect of Family and Schooling in America* (New York: Basic Books, 1972), or Bennett Harrison, *Education, Training and the Urban Ghetto* (Baltimore: The Johns Hopkins University Press, 1972).
5. Editorial page, *Baltimore Sun*, June 24, 1972.

NOTES FOR APPENDIX 2

1. Not shown as a separate regression.
2. See C. F. Christ, *Econometric Models and Methods* (New York: Wiley, 1966), pp. 432–46.
3. See Edmund Malinvaud, *Statistical Methods in Economics* (Amsterdam: North Holland, 1966), and Herman Wold, *Econometric Model Building* (Amsterdam: North Holland, 1964), for useful discussions of the causal chain method.

NOTES FOR APPENDIX 3

1. For further discussion of this problem, see John D. Owen, *Towards a More Consistent, Socially Relevant College Scholarships Policy* (Baltimore: Johns Hopkins University Center for the Social Organization of Schools, 1970).
2. Cf. the discussion of the Higher Education Act of 1972 in chapter 10.
3. This example is developed further in John D. Owen, "The Economics of College Scholarships Policy," *Social Research* 39, no. 1 (Spring 1972): 53–69.

NOTES FOR APPENDIX 4

1. See, for example, Michael Borus, "A Benefit-Cost Analysis of the Economic Effectiveness of Retraining the Unemployed," *Yale Economic Essays*, vol. 4, no. 2 (Fall 1964), pp. 371–430, or Samuel Gubins, "The Impact of Age and Education on the Effectiveness of Training: A Benefit-Cost Analysis" (Ph.D. diss., The Johns Hopkins University, 1970).
2. The lack of a theory of poverty costs will, moreover, blur the distinction between the effects on welfare costs of investing in the education of all and of

investing in the poor and so may lead to a serious policy error. If an increase in the educational attainment of the entire labor force raises the average wage but does not change the relative distribution of income, it is likely to lead to an increase in the poverty floor set by society without reducing the proportion of the population earning below that level. The result will be an increase in welfare costs. Only an educational policy that seeks to raise the productivity or employability of the poorest group relative to the average will be likely to reduce poverty costs.

3. A policy of subsidizing lower-class education would reduce the return to education and hence could, in principle, reduce private investment in college and other education by middle-class families. But this is not a very plausible result. It is more likely that more middle-class families would try to maintain their social position by increasing the educational distance between their children and the lower class than would allow their children to be equaled or surpassed educationally. But if the middle class did reduce its educational investment, there would be a mixed effect: a reduction in the net labor supply or education gain of the policy, but also a reduction in its net tax cost, since the earnings gap between the middle class and the lower class would be further reduced, making it more likely that poverty cost taxes could be cut. See the method presented at the end of this appendix for weighing these offsetting changes.

4. A full specification would have to describe the mix of fiscal instruments to be used and, especially, the proposed method for coping with the various biases present in the policy instruments available in the United States today. Moreover, the optimal adjustment over time to long-run equilibrium might best be discussed with the help of a decision rule that made use of the technique of dynamic programming under the likely constraints. (This approach could consider, for example, the question of whether a still better economic result would follow if a PREP were financed out of consumption.) See K. J. Arrow, "The Social Discount Rate," in *Cost-Benefit Analysis of Manpower Policies*, ed. G. G. Somers and W. D. Wood (Kingston, Ont.: Industrial Relations Centre, Queens University, 1969), pp. 56–75; A. C. Harberger, "Discussion," in *ibid.*, pp. 76–88; and K. J. Arrow and M. Kurz, *Public Investment, the Rate of Return, and Optimal Fiscal Policy* (Baltimore: The Johns Hopkins Press, 1970) for a treatment of these problems.

5. In the past fifty years, the annual growth rate of labor income has at most exceeded that of national income by only a small fraction of a percent.

6. In the short run, the benefits of the policy will be deferred until the first graduates enter the labor force. The initial effect on the effective labor supply of a policy to increase the level of schooling will thus be to reduce the effective labor supply by withdrawing students, teachers, and other educational personnel from the production of "output." Only as more productive graduates enter the labor force and the quality of the effective labor supply is increased can the continuing labor withdrawal needs imposed by the education program be partly or fully offset. Similarly, the physical investment–output ratio will first decline to provide funds for the education program, but may then increase as funds become available from a reduction in poverty costs.

The time path of capital stock to equilibrium will be fairly complex, since it is influenced by a fluctuation both in labor supply and in the investment ratio, but it will eventually be determined by the long-run levels of these two intermediate variables.

Consumption need not decrease, even in the short-run. While output will decline at first as the supply of labor is reduced, this reduction will be entirely at the expense of physical capital investment.

7. In the United States, an increase in the investment ratio would probably increase consumption in the long run, since the investment ratio is rather low. In many growth models, long-run consumption is positively related to the investment ratio as long as the latter is less than the pretax share of capital in output (as it is in the United States).

8. The assumption of a constant depreciation of human capital was relaxed in variants of this model. Similar results were obtained in each case.
9. If an infinite life of labor and a constant rate of depreciation on human capital, as well as a constant rate of increase in wages, are assumed to simplify the exposition, the conventional definition of r_e would yield the following equation:

$$l_0(1 + j) = \int_0^\infty \Delta l e^{-(r_e + d_e - w)t} dt$$

Solving this expression for $\dfrac{\Delta l}{l_0}$ then yields equation (13).

10. This division could correspond to those seeking work in what some labor economists call the primary and secondary labor markets.
11. This variant of the model assumes that wages are proportionate to marginal product. An alternative theory of wage determination could be used to explore the strength of these indirect effects as long as sectoral wage rates were assumed to decline with increases in the supply of labor to a sector.
12. If there is very little substitution the indirect effect will dominate, while if the two types of labor are perfect substitutes the indirect effect vanishes. Increasing the proportion in the first group will at any positive level of the elasticity of substitution increase the relative importance of the indirect effect (as increasing numbers are raised by education from the second to the first or majority group, the earnings gap itself, the direct effect, will decline rapidly and will eventually go to zero, while the indirect effect will fall less quickly and will never reach zero).
13. This model, in which the contribution of education is seen as producing a different type of labor rather than simply more labor, helps shed light on one aspect of the controversial subject of "education discrimination." Employers in high-status occupations (what is sometimes called the primary labor market) may refuse to hire poorly educated workers not because of any lack in their productivity but simply because of the employers' prejudice. This discrimination may come from prestige associated with hiring the better educated, their "better" manners, or a mistaken belief that they are more productive. In this case an earnings gap based on education will still develop as those without schooling are crowded into the few occupations that will take them (i.e., what is sometimes called the secondary labor market) and their marginal product is driven down as a result. Because of this crowding effect, education for the lower classes would then have just as much effect in increasing the effective labor supply and in reducing subsidy cost by giving the graduates the *labeling* necessary for their movement to the high-status occupations as it would by giving them skills essential for their movement. See Barbara R. Bergman, "The Effect on White Incomes of Discrimination in Employment," *Journal of Political Economy* 79, no. 2 (March–April 1971); 294–313.
14. No attempt is made here to analyze the case where the overall level of economic activity is insufficient to yield full employment regardless of educational policy or of any other measure to improve the structure of labor markets. Under those circumstances, the assumption that the incidence of a tax to support a PREP falls entirely on investment in physical capital would probably be unrealistic, for the government would then be more likely to prefer to integrate the financing of this program into an expansionary fiscal policy that would reduce the resource cost of a PREP.
15. If the student pays the same fraction of his education costs as he obtains of its earnings benefit, it can be shown that the government will provide a subsidy equal to the income minimum plus its share of the direct costs of education. But since this minimum would have been paid if the youth had remained unemployed, the actual net subsidy cost to the government is confined to its contribution to direct costs. In this way, the subsidy costs as well as the resource costs of lower-class education are limited to direct costs when youth employment is assumed to be constant.

16. If $b \neq 0$, the tax reduction is given by:

$$a^W L^* + bnl_0(1 - u) \left[\frac{r_e - g}{p + d_e} + 1 \right] (1 + j)$$

NOTES FOR APPENDIX 5

1. The remainder of the costs are paid either directly by students and their families or indirectly through education taxes. Then, in equation (2) below, the factor a must be interpreted as the ratio of direct and indirect family subsidies to total education subsidies.

2. If pretax profit equals the stock of capital goods times its marginal product. Otherwise the profit share will not equal the elasticity of output with regard to capital stock and equation (2) must be modified. Using c' to denote the profit share and continuing to represent the elasticity of output with regard to capital stock as c,

$$\frac{r_e^* - g}{p + d_e} = \frac{(aW)}{Y_l} \left[\frac{\Pi - g}{p + d_e} + \frac{1}{c'} + \frac{c' - c}{c'} \right]$$

is then the correct expression.

Since employer-subsidized investments in human capital would be expected to increase the labor–physical capital ratio, and since the elasticity of substitution between these factors is usually measured as being somewhat less than unity, the pretax profits share might be expected to increase as a result of this type of educational subsidy policy. But experimentation with empirically plausible values of σ indicates that this will not constitute an important offset.

Index

Index

Aid to Families of Dependent Children Program, 4, 11, 76–77, 81, 84–89, 94–95
Alabama, 141, 142
Allocation of physical resources in schools, 1, 25–26, 41, 139, 140–41, 144
American Council on Education, 54
Arrow, Kenneth, 206
Assignment of teachers, 16–18, 153; by race, 21–25, 143, 144–48, 153, 161–62

Baltimore Sun, 157
Banfield, Edward C., 188–89
Baron, Harold M., 133
Becker, Gary S., 188, 193, 194
Becker, Howard S., 186–87
Bergman, Barbara R., 207
Blau, Peter M., 65–66
Blaustein, Albert P., 187
Bond, Horace Mann, 142, 203, 203–4
Bowles, Samuel, 185, 187
Brand-Nye Bill, 199–200
Buis, Ann Gibson, 126, 127, 199, 200
Bullock, Henry, 203
Bureaucratic rules as a source of inequality in urban school systems, 12–13, 14–18, 27
Burrup, Percy E., 189, 202

Cain, Glen C., 197
Caliver, Ambrose, 142, 203, 204
Callahan, Raymond E., 200
Cartter, Alan W., 192
Cavala, Bill, 114
Celebrezze, Anthony J., 132
Chiswick, Barry R., 68, 194, 195, 203
Cloward, Richard, 93
Clune, William H., 189, 199, 205
Coleman, James, 8, 17, 18, 21, 25, 26, 30, 37, 68, 135, 136, 144, 145, 185, 187, 189–90, 191
College Scholarship Service, 11, 49–53, 167, 192
Committee for Economic Development, 201–2
Conant, James B., 131–32, 191
Coons, John E., 189, 199, 205
Crecellius, Philipine, 46
Cultural sources of educational inequality, 65–66

Davis, Hazel, 190
Denison, Edward F., 71
Distance to school as a source of inequality, 141
Duncan, Otis Dudley, 65–66
Durbin, Elizabeth, 186, 196

Elementary and Secondary Education Act, 119, 120, 124, 131–33, 145, 147, 149–50, 151, 152
Elite education, 45–46, 100–101, 112
Employer class: efforts to block school reform, 10, 122, 123, 124–26; new interest in a more egalitarian policy, 130, 133–34, 184; need to adjust to a better-educated labor force, 134, 154–56; economic interest in blocking reform, 125–30, 182–84
Equality of educational achievement goal, 103–4, 110–11, 151–52, 154

Federal aid to education policy: need for, 10–11, 119, 147–48, 152; and effort to obtain federal aid to education legislation, 120–25. *See also* Elementary and Secondary Education Act; Higher education policy
Fenno, Richard F., 124, 199, 200
Financial return to education, 7, 67–69, 72, 128–29, 130; criticized as a criterion for investment in education, 72–101, 171–81
Friedman, Milton, 108, 186

Garland, Charles, 143
Gintis, Herbert, 195
Goodman, Leonard, 197
Grant, Ulysses S., 121
Green, Thomas F., 198
Greer, Colin, 136, 138–39, 191
Griliches, Zvi, 201
Guthrie, James W., 186, 187, 189

Hansen, Lee, 54–55, 61
Hanushek, Eric, 8, 17
Harding, Warren G., 122
Harrington, Michael, 75, 131
Harrison, Bennett, 195, 196, 205
Head, J. G., 199
Higher education policy, 47, 150, 157.

See also Federal aid to education policy
Honig, Marjorie F., 94

Ideological gap in education policy, 45–47, 156–57

Jencks, Christopher, 185, 196, 203, 205
Jensen, Arthur R., 7
Johnson, Lyndon B., 75, 132
Joint Economic Committee, study on multiple welfare benefits, 81, 88, 95–96

Katz, Michael, 185, 190, 191, 200
Key, V. O., Jr., 197, 198

Lapinsky, Martin, 189, 190
Levin, Henry, 8, 88, 104–5, 185, 186, 187, 188, 189, 190
Liberal support for school reform, 6, 135, 136, 143, 157
Litt, Edgar, 107, 197, 198
Louisiana, 140–41, 144, 147–48
Lower-class political power, 104–6, 112

McCuiston, Fred, 142
Majority voting model, 109–12
Maryland, 141, 144
Massachusetts, 140
Master, Stanley, 53
Meranto, Philip, 123, 200, 202
Merit as good argument for redistributing education resources, 114–16
Mincer, Jacob, 193, 194, 197, 203
Minimum wages, legal, 4, 75–77, 90–93
Mississippi, 32, 33
Mixed public-private school system, 9–10, 59–61
Morlock, Laura L., 200
Munger, Frank J., 124, 199, 200
Murphy, Jerome T., 133

National Association for the Advancement of Colored People (NAACP), 143–44
National Educational Association, 28, 122, 129
Negative Income Tax (NIT), 82–83, 93, 96–97
New Deal, 4, 75–76, 143
New Orleans, reconstruction desegregation in, 147–48
Nixon, Richard M., 145, 149

Ohberg, Hjardis, 25
Olson, Mancur, 197

Petersen, Warren A., 190
Piven, Frances Fox, 93
Political socialization in schools, 107–8, 154
Poverty line, 80–82
Poverty-Reducing Education Policy (PREP), 77–100, 102, 115, 116, 117, 119, 127, 131, 134, 154–58; rate of return criterion for, 78–79, 171–81
Powell, William, 157

Radosh, Ronald, 200–201
Ribich, Thomas, 196, 205
Rossi, Peter, 68
Rothbard, Murray N., 200–201
Ryan, Heber Hinds, 46

Segregation of pupils, 24–25, 124, 144–46, 147–48, 161–62
Sexton, Patricia Cayo, 187
Smith, O. R., 32
Sorkin, Alan L., 192, 196
South Carolina, 105–6, 139–40
Southern school systems, 137, 138–42; progress in reducing discrimination in, 143–48
Stanley, Julian, 197
Sugarman, Stephen D., 189, 199, 205

Tate, W. K., 139–40
Teacher salaries, 19, 30, 31–40, 41–42, 140, 142, 144, 163–66, 190–91
Tiebout, Charles, 11, 31

Unemployment effects of education policy, 90–93, 155–56, 179–80
Unions, 76, 106, 122, 130–31
U.S. Chamber of Commerce, 122, 123, 124, 125, 129, 201, 202

Verbal ability of teachers, 21–22, 30, 31–40, 41–42, 144–45, 153, 163–66, 190
Virginia, 144

Wage structure effects, 89–90, 154–55, 177–79
Watts, Harold M., 197
Weinstein, James, 200–201
Weisbrod, Burton, 54–55, 186, 194, 195, 197
Welch, Finis, 68, 194
Welfare Incidence: effects of education on, 83–89
Welter, Rush, 185, 202
Wildavsky, Aaron, 114
Wilson, Woodrow, 122
Work incentives, 93–99, 113–14, 197, 198

Employment and earnings inadequacy
A NEW SOCIAL INDICATOR
Sar A. Levitan and Robert Taggart III

The authors here formulate an "Employment and Earnings Index" (EEI) which considers individual and family incomes as well as employment status to determine a new set of criteria for labor market pathologies. They draw conclusions concerning the components of the index by race, sex, etc., and concerning the relationship between unemployment and cyclical fluctuations. In the series Policy Studies in Employment and Welfare. *$6.00 cloth, $2.50 paper*

Education, training, and the urban ghetto
Bennett Harrison

"A carefully researched, well-documented, and provocative monograph. . . . Economist Harrison contends that the impact of education is at best marginally efficient. . . . As outlined by Harrison, the strategy to correct the disequilibrium consists in 'remaking the economy,' in comprehensive economic planning involving direct governmental intervention in urban markets."—*Educational Studies* $10.00

Economic analysis for educational planning
RESOURCE ALLOCATION IN NONMARKET SYSTEMS
Edited by Karl A. Fox

"This book is a good contribution to the whole movement of educational planning. It is a major step in moving educational planning in the quantitative direction. . . . The approach is one of studying resource allocation in systems where there is no market pricing mechanism to provide the guidance."—*Journal of Economic Literature* $15.00

THE JOHNS HOPKINS UNIVERSITY PRESS
Baltimore, Maryland 21218

ISBN 0-8018-1596-7

THE JOHNS HOPKINS UNIVERSITY PRESS

This book was composed in Linotype Times Roman by the Monotype Composition Company from a design by Susan Bishop. It was printed on S. D. Warren's 60-lb. 1854 regular paper and bound in Columbia Mills Bayside linen cloth by Universal Lithographers, Inc.

Library of Congress Cataloging in Publication Data

Owen, John D
    School inequality and the welfare state.

    Includes bibliographical references.
    1. Education—United States—Finance. 2. Educational equalization—United States. I. Title.
LB2825.O93   379'.1'0973   74-6834
ISBN 0-8018-1596-7